West Nipissing Public Library

The Sudbury Region

Picture Research by Michael J. Mulloy
Partners in Progress by Gary Peck

Produced in cooperation with the
Sudbury and District Chamber of Commerce

Windsor Publications, (Canada) Ltd.
Burlington, Ontario, Canada

The Sudbury Region

An Illustrated History By Graeme S. Mount

To Joan, Fraser, and Andrew Mount, and to Marjory Mulloy, who provided every encouragement for this book and who tolerated our absences because of our involvement in it.

Windsor Publications, (Canada) Ltd.—History Book Division

Publisher: John M. Phillips
Editorial Director: Teri Davis Greenberg
Design Director: Alexander D'Anca

Staff for *The Sudbury Region*
Senior Editor: Gail Koffman
Text Editor: Jerry Mosher
Assistant Editor: Marilyn Horn
Editorial Development: Julie Jaskol
Director, Corporate Biographies: Karen Story
Assistant Director, Corporate Biographies: Phyllis Gray
Editor, Corporate Biographies: Judith Hunter
Layout Artist, Corporate Biographies: Mari Catherine Preimesberger
Editorial Assistants: Kathy M. Brown, Laura Cordova, Marcie Goldstein, Pat Pittman, Sharon L. Volz
Design and layout: Christina McKibbin
Sales Representatives, Corporate Biographies: Don Foster, Hughes Winfield

Library of Congress Cataloging-in-Publication Data

Mount, Graeme S. (Graeme Stewart), 1939-
  The Sudbury region.

  Bibliography: p. 156
  Includes index.
  1. Sudbury (Ont.)—History. 2. Sudbury (Ont.)—
Description. 3. Sudbury (Ont.)—Industries.
4. Sudbury Region (Ont.)—History. 5. Sudbury Region
(Ont.)—Description and travel. 6. Sudbury Region (Ont.)
—Industries. I. Mulloy, Mike. II Sudbury and
District Chamber of Commerce. III. Title
F1059.5.S85M68   1986   971.3'133   86-5653
ISBN 0-89781-177-1

© 1986 by Windsor Publications, (Canada) Ltd.
All Rights Reserved

Published 1986
Printed in Canada
First Edition

CONTENTS

CHAPTER I
THE BIRTH OF SUDBURY   10

CHAPTER II
ETHNIC COMMUNITIES   22

CHAPTER III
THROUGH THE WARS   32

CHAPTER IV
CULTURE AND THE ARTS   44

CHAPTER V
PROMINENT PERSONALITIES   58

CHAPTER VI
SPORTS AND RECREATION   70

CONCLUSION   102

CHAPTER VII
PARTNERS IN PROGRESS   104

PATRONS   155

BIBLIOGRAPHY   156

INDEX   158

ACKNOWLEDGMENTS

No author writes a book by himself, and this is particularly true in our case. Without pictures, comments, advice, and oral information from a host of people, the book would have been but a shadow of its present self. Among those we wish to thank are: Tony Beljo of the Croatian community; Super Bertuzzi at the Caruso Club; Maurice Clément at the Centre des Jeunes; Eleanor Connors of Gilbert and Sullivan fame; Guy Despatie, who provided information about his talented agricultural family; Fred Hackett, who agreed to read the manuscript and enrich it with the perspective of a long-time historian and resident of Sudbury; Brian Hart and the staff at Huntington who contributed pictures; Inco and its employees, particularly Alex Gray who took us underground to the salad mine, Peter vom Scheidt who helped locate pictures and provided a financial subsidy on Inco's behalf, and Tom Peters, who discussed Inco's re-greening and agricultural programmes; Bill and Mary Iwanochko, whose Ukrainian pictures add colour to the book; Denise Jones of the West Indian Society; Albert Klussmann and other members of the German community (particularly Gunther Jakelski, Gertrud Jared Lewis, and Karl Sommerer) whose pictures and suggestions proved indispensable; Archie MacKinnon, who took the time to pass along his knowledge of Sudbury's Cape Breton community; the staff at *Northern Life,* particularly Glenn Sirois and Ken Collins, who gave us access to their photo collection and invaluable publicity; Jarl Pernu, who let us use his unpublished memoirs; the late Dennis Roberts, a social worker who was active in Sudbury for more than a third of its history; Spike Hennessy and Nick Evanshen of the Sudbury Regional Development Corporation, who provided both pictures and information; Mike Solski, who gave us the benefit of his extensive photo archives; the staff at the Sudbury Public Library—both at the reference section and at the Mackenzie Street collection; the Sudbury Theatre Centre's Judy Cameron; and George Thomson—a veritable encyclopedia of Sudbury's cultural life.

Many people at Laurentian University were highly encouraging, and those who helped in a practical way included Dieter Buse, who read the early drafts and saved us from many statements for which we might have been sorry; Paul de la Riva and Daniel Roy, who assisted with the research; Paul Copper, Helen Devereux, Joe Shorthouse, and Keith Winterhalder, who helped record aspects of Sudbury's history and pre-history; Tom Kujanpaa, who drew the maps; Mary Catherine Roche at the Media Centre and Jean Baxter at the Communications Office, who provided pictures; and Carl Wallace, who stimulated an interest in Sudbury's past and who offered sound advice regarding the manuscript. Others too gave illustrations and will see their names under the pictures as they appear in the following pages.

Finally, we are grateful to the people of the Sudbury Region whose actions have proven historic and without whom there would have been nothing to write. It goes without saying that we accept responsibility for the accuracy of this book.

Graeme S. Mount
Michael J. Mulloy
Sudbury, Ontario
January 1986

An early band in Copper Cliff, circa 1900. Courtesy, Inco Triangle

INTRODUCTION

The name "Sudbury" signifies a bad joke for many Canadians. In 1977 immigration officers at Toronto's international airport burst into laughter when a history professor from Trinidad told them he was on his way to Sudbury. When residents of Sudbury identify themselves as such, total strangers respond with comments that range from "I'm glad I don't live there" to "Oh! I feel so sorry for you." Air Canada once told a travel agent in Los Angeles, "Sudbury is a blight on the face of the earth." As recently as 1984, when a professor was picking up concert tickets he had reserved in Hamilton, Bermuda, the man behind the counter became hostile and said, "You're from Sudbury—that bloody awful place. . . . I'm from Canada and can say what I think." The Canadian Broadcasting Corporation, *Maclean's* magazine, and the *Globe and Mail* occasionally have articles or news items about the regreening of Sudbury and improvements in the city's quality of life, then a few days later carry a sly dig that completely ignores the previous report.

One cannot deny that Sudbury has suffered some of the worst environmental damage in Canada. Travellers on the main line of the Canadian Pacific Railway or on Highway 17—the principal artery between Manitoba and Quebec—have seen some of the worst of it. The farmlands and green forests of other parts of Northern Ontario used to give way to miles and miles of barren rock. If the skies were grey, the impact could be so depressing that twenty years ago one Toronto coroner, noted for exaggeration, declared Sudbury "unfit for human habitation."

Yet, newcomers to the city are happily surprised to discover the reality considerably better than the image, and some families have chosen to reside in Sudbury for generations. During the summer, people of all ages enjoy the beaches of Lakes Ramsey and Nepahwin, both within walking distance of the downtown. For those with cars, other attractive lakes lie within fifteen minutes of the city centre. The shores of the lakes are green, not barren, and many people have established residences there. In winter, snow remains white long after a snowfall, and cross-country ski trails within the city limits lure thousands of people each weekend. Golf courses, tennis courts, hiking trails, indoor and outdoor skating rinks, curling rinks, swimming pools, and gymnasiums offer a wide range of recreation throughout the year.

Sudbury's cultural amenities are also substantial. Primary, secondary, and post-secondary schools, colleges, and universities offer instruction in both English and French. One of the most pluralistic cities in Canada, Sudbury hosts musical groups ranging from Scottish pipe bands to Croatian and Ukrainian choirs. Each July 1, Canada's national holiday, the Sudbury Regional Multi-Cultural Centre arranges a wide variety of ethnic music and foods, from German and Finnish to Indian and Chinese. The Canadian Broadcasting Corporation's two Sudbury outlets, CBCS in English and CBON in French, reach an audience scattered from Mindemoya and Britt in the south to Attawapiskat in the north, and from Mattawa on the Quebec border to Sault Ste. Marie and Lake Superior in the west. The Sudbury Theatre Centre offers English-language plays, musical dramas, and dinner theatre of a professional calibre throughout the year, and le Théâtre du Nouvel Ontario caters to the cultural needs of the city's French-speaking residents. Most shopping areas include a bookstore, and the Sudbury Public Library lends books in English, French, and various European and Asian languages. There are museums—including one on John Street with rotating exhibits, and one at the flour mill on rue Notre Dame that specializes in French Canadian folklore, both within walking distance of the downtown core. A few blocks downhill from John Street and on the shores of Lake Ramsey is the enormous Science North, a world-class science museum that opened in 1984. In addition to educating Sudburians, Science North attracts some of the millions of tourists that drive within a few blocks of it on the Trans-Canada Highway each year. The St.

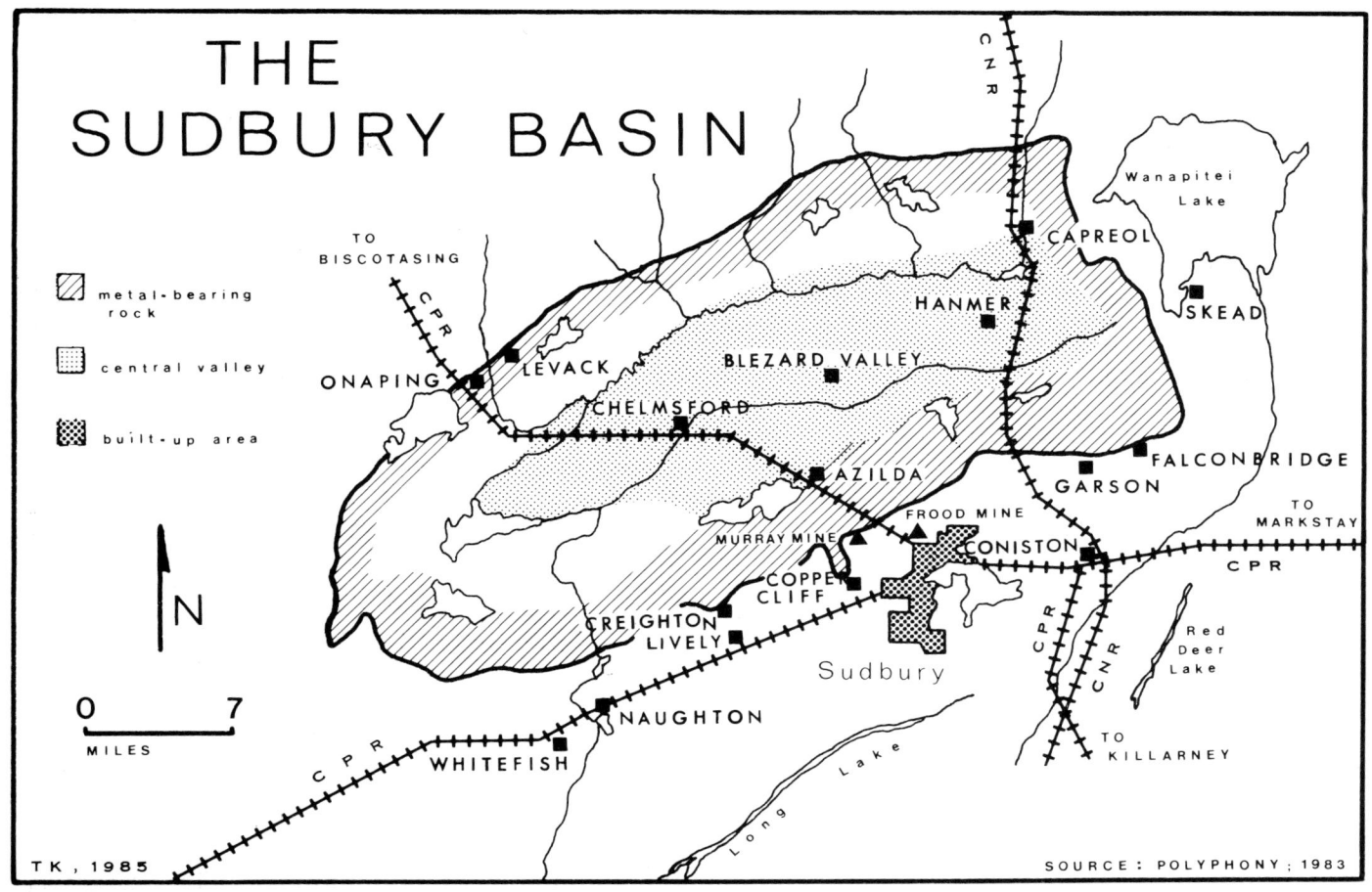

This map provides an overview of the Sudbury Basin's many communities and mining regions. Courtesy, Thomas Kujanpaa

Andrew's Concert Series and the Sudbury Symphony Orchestra bring professional musicians to the city. Residents of other parts of Northern Ontario come to Sudbury to shop or to benefit from medical services not available in their own communities, and whatever their tastes, they can usually find something of interest.

The Sudbury Region includes communities which legally lie outside the city of Sudbury. Economically, nevertheless, the region is a unit. People live in Copper Cliff and work in Sudbury and vice versa. Farmers of the Hanmer and Blezard Valley areas sell their produce on the Sudbury market; others whose work is in Sudbury live in Hanmer or Blezard Valley either to enjoy the country living or to take advantage of the real estate rates, which are lower than those in the city. While the Canadian Pacific Railway serves the region through Sudbury, Canadian National has its local headquarters at Capreol. Sudburians go to Copper Cliff to play hockey, but young people from Copper Cliff go to Sudbury for an education.

The story of the Sudbury area is largely the story of nickel. Nickel guaranteed Sudbury's survival as the railway-building crews moved westward. It shaped and determined the economy, the physical environment, the types of people who would live in the region, and the interests of those people. Even now, as nickel markets shrink and an ever decreasing proportion of the work force works for either of the nickel conglomerates—Inco (formerly the International Nickel Company) or Falconbridge—what happens is largely a response to the declining fortunes of the nickel industry.

This book is designed for two audiences—those who live in the Sudbury region and those who do not. Those who do may appreciate the story of their community's past and its evolution. Outsiders may learn something of the positive side of Sudbury and reasons why people actually live there *by choice.* Perhaps they may be enticed to visit or to invest in the Sudbury Region.

CHAPTER I

Sudbury's story begins with the mining of nickel, which was discovered in 1856. Mining would develop Sudbury from a temporary work camp for Canadian Pacific Railway workers, and ensure its survival through the years. These are Copper Cliff miners in 1893. Note the absence of hard hats—today an essential safety feature—and the use of candles for lighting.
Courtesy, Inco Triangle

The Birth of Sudbury

Those communities in northeastern Ontario which predate Sudbury—Moose Factory, Sault Ste. Marie, Mindemoya, even Mattawa and North Bay—had strategic locations on water arteries significant for trade. Sudbury, by contrast, owes its start to a different aspect of its geography—its rocks. Some geologists think that Sudbury's substantial deposits of copper, nickel, sulphur, and other elements were formed about 1.7 billion years ago, when eruptions in the area spewed forth rich lava. The lava then solidified into a boat-shaped basin some thirty-seven miles long and seventeen miles wide. However, other geologists believe that the impact of a meteorite created the basin. Indeed, the Apollo XI astronauts visited the basin before their historic 1969 flight to study the site of a possible meteoritic impact such as they might see on the moon.

Whatever the origins, the basin's rim contains mineral ores, while rich soil conducive to agriculture fills the lower-lying areas. A traveller crossing the basin today will find flat farmland bordered by scenic hills.

According to archaeologist Helen Devereux, who has spent the last seventeen years studying the pre-history of the Sudbury area, the first people known to have lived in the basin were those called Shield Archaic people. They arrived about 8,000 years ago, after the glacial ice had retreated northward. Forests covered the land, and many present-day plant and animal species existed.

Shield Archaic people inhabited much of the Canadian Shield, as far east as Cape Breton, until about 500 B.C. They shaped a culture and society so highly adapted to Northern Ontario that it changed in only a few minor ways before the arrival of Europeans. The people lived along waterways, in small kin-based patrilineal bands, moving seasonally from camp to camp according to the availability of food resources. Their subsistence base was diversified; they fished, gathered wild plant foods, and hunted large game such as caribou, moose, bear, and rabbit. Their weapons consisted primarily of long thrusting spears, with heads of flaked chert (a flint-like stone), polished slate, and hammered native copper. Fish hooks and gaffs were also made of native copper, and perhaps bone. Flaked chert knives and scrapers, as well as other tools, were used. Their clothing consisted of hides and furs, and they probably made birchbark containers, twisted cording, and woven mats. They probably had birchbark canoes, snowshoes, toboggans, and dogs. Most likely they spoke a proto-Algonkian language and are the distant ancestors of the present Ojibwa people who live near Sudbury.

Direct evidence that the Shield Archaic people lived in the Sudbury area has been found in several places. At the Mullola site, a sandy beach near the west end of Long Lake, Devereux found a chert projectile tip and a quartzite flake knife. East of Sudbury, a native copper knife was found at Markstay, and a large chert spear point was discovered at the Desloges site near Garson. On Red Deer Lake, at the Saarinen site, a ground slate gouge (a woodworking tool), along with chert flaking debris, were excavated.

There is at present no direct evidence of occupation of the Sudbury area between roughly 500 B.C. and A.D. 1000. This lack of physical proof, however, may be due to erosion and construction disturbance rather than absence of population. It is abundantly clear that the descendants of Shield Archaic people, called Initial Woodland people, were present throughout much of Ontario. They lived essentially as did their ancestors, except that they had learned to make pottery from fired clay, somewhat conical in shape and decorated around the rim with impressions. Some buried their dead in conical, earthen mounds. They advanced from spears to bows and arrows. Because their sites have been discovered as near as Killarney, it is very likely

The Sudbury Basin's extraterrestrial geology prompted astronauts from the Apollo series to visit Sudbury in 1971 before going to the moon. Courtesy, Inco Triangle

Three women of the Woodland culture are here illustrated making pottery in the Sudbury Basin. The Woodland Indians, dating back to A.D. 1000, were the original inhabitants of the region. Courtesy, Helen Devereux

that they also inhabited what is now the Sudbury Region.

The Terminal Woodland people, descendants of the Initial Woodland group, occupied Northern Ontario from about A.D. 1000. Their way of life resembled that of their well-adapted Archaic ancestors, except that they were influenced by various neighbours to the south, such as the Iroquois. Their clay vessels became globular in shape and bore collars often decorated with straight-line geometric designs. Their small arrow tips lost their notches, and they smoked tobacco pipes. Although they attempted to grow some corn along the north shore of Lake Huron, they were not very successful. Evidence of their presence in Sudbury is scarce: two pottery sherds from a Lake Wanapitei beach bearing fabric-impression decoration.

The settlement of Canadians of European descent in Sudbury dates from the spring of 1883, when the government of Sir John A. Macdonald was building the Canadian Pacific Railway (CPR). Few expected Sudbury to become more than a temporary work camp for railway workers, and in order that they might have some place to eat and sleep the CPR erected the earliest buildings. Once the railway moved its construction camp westward toward Biscotasing in 1885, Sudbury's population dropped from 1,500 to 300. Indeed, that there was any community at all was partially the responsibility of William Allen Ramsay, the engineer after whom Lake Ramsey—despite the change in spelling—is named. He ordered construction of the CPR's right of way farther north than his superior, James Worthington, had intended it to be. It was Worthington who named the site "Sudbury Junction," in honour of his wife's birthplace in England. (Sudbury Junction was five miles east of what is now

THE SUDBURY REGION

Sudbury pioneer Thomas Frood, after whom Frood Mine and Frood Street are named. Courtesy, Inco Triangle

The original railway station at Sudbury Junction, around 1900. A sign at the station indicated that Montreal was 443 miles to the east, Vancouver 2,464 miles to the west. Courtesy, Sudbury Public Library

downtown Sudbury.)

The abundance of unexpected mineral wealth was what assured the Sudbury area of a future. Travellers through the basin, A.P. Salter and Alexander Murray, had discovered copper and nickel near today's Creighton Mine as early as 1856-1857, but there was no development until construction of the railway some twenty-seven years later. CPR blacksmith Tom Flanagan found ore and initially thought he had discovered gold, but Flanagan pursued the matter no further, presumably because he neither knew the value of nickel nor had the connections for marketing purposes. John Loughrin, who cut railway ties, invited three friends— Thomas Murray, William Murray, and Harry Abbott—to join him in Sudbury. As early as February 1884 they staked what became the Murray Mine of the future International Nickel Company (Inco). Charles Francis Crean, an English immigrant in his thirties, earned his living by transporting supplies to the construction camps. Shortly after his arrival on the first train to Sudbury, Crean spotted a yellow rock used as a paperweight in a CPR-owned store. He sent a piece to a chemist in Toronto who identified it as copper. Later Crean saw what looked like copper ore lying on the ground in various places and staked claims for what became the Elsie and Worthington mines. Within Sudbury's first year, Rinaldo McConnell, a timber cruiser, staked property that became valuable to the Canadian Copper Company, one of the ancestors of the International Nickel Company. Thomas Frood, a railway construction timekeeper, saw value in the property that be-

THE BIRTH OF SUDBURY

came the Frood Mine.

Incredibly, in view of its later reputation, Sudbury was once noted for its trees. A thriving lumber industry developed, with William Joseph Bell one of the most successful lumber barons. Bell and his wife, the former Katherine Skead, had a strong sense of responsibility to use their wealth wisely. They donated the land for Bell Park on the shores of Lake Ramsey, where Sudburians today swim and picnic, stroll and slide, listen to concerts and enjoy the scenic beauty. People still recall Katherine Bell and her travels around town by horse and buggy as she delivered turkeys for women to cook for church suppers. In 1901 a local newspaper estimated that 5,000 men worked in the lumber industry near Sudbury; their need for goods and services created additional employment in the town.

Nevertheless, mining rather than lumbering was to dominate the Sudbury Basin's economy. Sudbury itself served as a railway centre, a supply depot for the lumber camps, and a bedroom suburb of Copper Cliff—a town established by the Canadian Copper Company in 1886. There were other minerals, but nickel would prove to be the most valuable.

In 1883 nickel was a little-known commodity, and scientists did not know how to separate it from copper and other elements. Hence fortune seekers did not stampede to the Sudbury Basin as they did in the Yukon gold rush of 1898 or Cobalt's silver experience of 1903. Nickel development would require capital and scientific expertise, and the key individual in providing them was an American, Samuel J. Ritchie. In 1886 Ritchie organized the Canadian Copper Company to develop the Sudbury Basin's copper; he was its first president and Cleveland, Ohio, was the company's headquarters. Encouraged by the Canadian and Ontario governments, which wanted to attract as much investment capital as possible, Ritchie and his Ohio supporters faced minimal restrictions and taxes as they bought mineral patents for one dollar per acre.

Samuel J. Ritchie, the Cleveland entrepreneur whose foresight and connections contributed much to the mining industry's development in Sudbury. Courtesy, Inco Triangle

A naval armaments race provided a market for nickel, and the United States Navy was the first customer. Benjamin F. Tracy, Secretary of the Navy to U.S. President Benjamin Harrison (1889-1893), inaugurated the modernization of the United States Navy. This had become necessary, in Tracy's view, as improvements in artillery had rendered ships vulnerable. With nickel-alloyed steel, a ship's capacity to resist artillery increased significantly. Tracy thus asked his friend, R.M. Thompson, president of the Orford Copper Company of New Jersey, to find a way to separate nickel from copper. Lured by a lucrative contract with the navy, Thompson agreed, and by 1892 Orford had made the necessary technological breakthrough.

THE SUDBURY REGION

Above
The blacksmith crew of the Canadian Copper Company, in the late nineteenth century. Courtesy, Ted Eyre

Opposite page
The Copper Cliff mine in 1888 and the same view in 1973. The Copper Cliff Library is pictured in the bottom photograph. Courtesy, Inco Triangle

By 1898 Grand Admiral Alfred von Tirpitz was masterminding the creation of a German Navy. The British, whose Royal Navy had dominated the seas since the Battle of Trafalgar in 1805, wanted to maintain their lead, and they too built new battleships. The naval armaments race poisoned the international climate and contributed to the rivalry and mistrust out of which developed World War I. However, the race created mining and smelting jobs in Sudbury, especially after the Spanish-American War of 1898. During that conflict, U.S. Navy ships—protected by nickel plating—destroyed most of the Spanish fleets of the Caribbean and the Pacific without the loss of a single ship.

The Canadian Copper Company did not retain its monopoly for long, nor was naval armament the only use for nickel. In 1899 H.H. Vivian and Company came from Wales to initiate operations at the Murray Mine. All attempts failed, however, and the company withdrew in 1894. The British-owned Mond Nickel Company came to Sudbury in 1898, acquired property, and on its own found ways to extract nickel ore. Named for a Swiss businessman, Ludwig Mond, the company mined and smelted primarily for a European market. Massey-

17

THE SUDBURY REGION

Harris, the Toronto-based farm implements company, demonstrated nickel-plated parts on its farm machinery at the Chicago World's Fair of 1893. Civilian and military commodities increased the demand for Sudbury's most important export, from 5,945 tons in 1902 to 24,835 tons—75 percent of the world's production—in 1913.

Environmental damage began in 1888, with the establishment of a smelter at Copper Cliff. In the words of Professor Gilbert A. Stelter, a pioneer in the history of early Sudbury:

While apologists for the mining companies often claim that forest fires which ravaged the area in the late 1880s (usually started by prospectors to enable them to examine the bare rocks for traces of minerals) and lumbering are responsible, the major reason for the moonscape-like appearance of the area was the smelting method known as heap roasting which was in effect until the 1920s. This simply involved piling ore which had a high sulphur content on beds of wood and igniting the whole affair. The piles burned for months, sending off dense clouds of sulphurous fumes.

A reporter from the *Toronto Star* expressed horror at the devastated environment near Copper Cliff as early as 1902.

By that time a number of prominent people had become interested in the Sudbury Basin. Ritchie persuaded Sir John A. Macdonald of nickel's importance to forthcoming armament production, and Macdonald asked Charles Tupper, Canada's High Commissioner in London, to promote the sale of nickel in Europe. As a result, markets for nickel developed in Great Britain, Germany, and France. In 1902 J.P. Morgan's International Nickel Company purchased the Canadian Copper Company and the Orford Copper Company's refinery in New Jersey. In 1901 Thomas Edison visited the basin and searched for nickel. Although he found none, it did exist on the land he staked—just farther under the surface. Later Falconbridge

The Inco train at the Coniston station provided local public transportation at the turn of the twentieth century. Photo by W.G. Gillespie. Courtesy, Albert Klussmann

Nickel Mines was to exploit the same land with considerable success.

A French count, Frédéric Romanet du Caillaud, came to Sudbury in 1902. He bought extensive tracts of land and advertised for French capital and settlers. From 1900 to 1914 the count commuted between Sudbury and Limoges, France, spending summers in Canada and winters on his ancestral estate. A pious man, he saw similarities between the Sudbury landscape and that around the French pilgrimage centre of Lourdes. In 1907 he organized construction of the grotto, twenty feet high and ten feet wide, that remains on the rocks above Lourdes Street. Romanet hoped to sell wood from his land to the mining companies and thought it possible that his lands might contain some mineral wealth. However, settlers from France did not come, and in 1919 his family sold his Sudbury lands.

According to the 1901 census, Sudbury did attract a substantial number of French Canadi-

THE BIRTH OF SUDBURY

Above
This circa 1900 photograph shows a one-horse shay from Turbine to High Falls, a distance of four miles. Courtesy, Inco Triangle

Top
An early form of transportation, circa 1900, on the spurline between the Levack station and the Levack mine. Courtesy, Inco Triangle

19

THE SUDBURY REGION

One of the earliest forms of taxi transportation between Creighton and Sudbury appears in this 1924 photograph.
Courtesy, Inco Triangle

an settlers, as did Mattawa, Sturgeon Falls, and other communities along the Canadian Pacific Railway. Because the CPR's eastern terminus was in Montreal, Sudbury oriented itself toward that city, and many French Canadians arrived from the Montreal area.

Anglophones also had links with Montreal. Presbyterian student ministers, who preached to the railway labourers at Sudbury Junction and other points along the CPR tracks during the summer of 1883, came from Montreal, and the Methodists who arrived the following year belonged to the Montreal Conference of the Methodist Church. Ties with Montreal eventually lessened, however, especially after 1908-1909 when the CPR established a direct link between Toronto and Sudbury.

A third CPR line, begun in 1883 and extending from Sudbury to Sault Ste. Marie by 1888, guaranteed Sudbury's importance as a railway centre, even though the Canadian Northern, now part of the Canadian National system, built its transcontinental line from Montreal through Capreol, some thirty kilometers from Sudbury.

Certain amenities of civilization came to Sudbury with the railway builders, and because of the nickel industry, they were able to stay. The law arrived during the autumn of 1883 in the form of Magistrate Andrew McNaughton, a Scottish immigrant. A dedicated Presbyterian layman, McNaughton guaranteed that Sudbury would be law-abiding. Dr. William H. Howey, McNaughton's contemporary, provided medical care. Streets in Sudbury take their names from McNaughton and Howey, as does the commu-

THE BIRTH OF SUDBURY

nity of Naughton to the west. By 1891 more than 100 farmers had moved into the Chelmsford, Azilda, and Larchwood areas to produce fresh vegetables, meat, and dairy products for the lumbermen, miners, and railway workers. Also by 1891, Sudbury had a weekly newspaper of its own, the *Journal*. Founded by James Orr, the *Journal* carried local news and advertising and offered glimpses of Canadian and international news and commentary, health tips, agricultural and sports reports, and some fiction and humour.

In 1893, with a population of 1,400, Sudbury ceased to be a village and became a town. The town council installed such urban amenities as water, sewers, and electrical services. Fire protection remained minimal in a community of wooden buildings and a volunteer fire brigade. The council instituted controls on the types of animals allowed to roam the streets, and arranged for sidewalks, and, by 1896, a public library.

During the 1890s the Canadian Copper Company had an estimated 500 to 700 employees. Other mining companies had employees of their own, and Sudbury and Copper Cliff acquired neighbouring communities whose economies also depended upon mining: Creighton to the west, site of another Canadian Copper Company mine; and Coniston to the east and Levack to the north, both creations of Mond Nickel.

Although lumbering, farming, and transportation would remain important aspects of Sudbury's economy, by the 1890s it was the nickel industry that was determining the ups and downs of the community. Nickel had tied Sudbury's fate to international markets and armaments developments, factors which would affect the city decisively in the twentieth century.

The Copper Cliff Fire Department, shown here on Serpentine Street in 1904 with its steam-engine pump, was kept busy even during the winter months. Courtesy, Inco Triangle

21

CHAPTER II

Since the late eighteenth century, Highlanders have settled in Sudbury, due to its resemblance in climate and landscape to Inverness. Over the years the Highlanders have maintained many of their traditions. Here, Geoffrey Hervey (left) turns command of the Copper Cliff Highlanders Cadet Corps to Captain Alex Gray (right) October 20, 1973, while Lieutenant Ted Lumley watches. Courtesy, Alex Gray

Ethnic Communities

Some fifteen years ago, a comedy group named "The Jest Society" was touring Canada. Its opening skit purported to take place in an elevator, where two well-dressed travelling salesmen recognized each other as Canadians and embraced.

"You're the first Canadian I've seen in six months," said one.

"Yes," replied the other. "Sudbury's like that."

While the above is an exaggeration, Sudbury has attracted people from many parts of Europe and Asia, and, to a lesser extent, the West Indies. Every group of the Habsburg Empire has representatives in the Sudbury Basin. There are Poles (1,835), Ukrainians (3,395), Germans and Austrians (3,285), Hungarians (355), Czechs and Slovaks (450), hundreds of Serbs and Croats, Italians (8,110)—plus others. No group constitutes a majority, but with 51,415 of metropolitan Sudbury's 148,695 people at the time of the 1981 census, French Canadians formed the largest segment. The 47,690 people of British and Irish

THE SUDBURY REGION

Sudbury's Italian community established the Caruso Club in 1947, the centre for Italian activities. Here the choir sings traditional Italian songs. Courtesy, Inco Triangle

descent ranked next. In addition, greater Sudbury includes 4,490 people of Finnish extraction, 545 Chinese, 355 from India and Pakistan, 255 Greeks, 530 Baltic peoples (mainly Lithuanians and Latvians), and some Vietnamese. The Sudbury Public Library lends books written in English, French, Ukrainian, Finnish, Italian, German, Spanish, Polish, Croatian, and Vietnamese.

A few caveats are in order. Strictly speaking in the Canadian political context, people who speak English and French are considered "founding peoples" rather than "ethnics," and their activities will be discussed in subsequent chapters. Italian and Finnish Sudburians have played a major role in Sudbury's development, and their activities also will appear later.

Sudbury experienced three waves of immigration from continental Europe during the past 100 years. Italians and Poles were involved with the building of the CPR, and by the turn of the century Sudbury had significant German and Italian communities. Finns too had arrived in the basin. The second wave followed the First World War and intensified as United States laws in 1921 and 1924 made migration to that country—especially by people from southern and eastern Europe—more difficult. Finally, hundreds of thousands of Europeans—many of them refugees but some simply people in search of a better life—came to Canada after World War II, and thousands of these settled in Sudbury. As the city's economy grew and changes in Canadian laws permitted increased Asian migration in the 1960s, Sudbury's Indian and Chinese populations grew dramatically. The 1961 census indicated 492 Asians in metropolitan Sudbury; the 1971 census counted 1,210; and the 1981 census reported the same number (Asian-Arabs, 310; Chinese, 545; Indo-Pakistanis, 355). By 1981 there were also Thais, Vietnamese, and Iranians lumped together with non-Asians under "other . . . origins."

Certain tendencies have been common to most of the ethnic groups. Their collective cultural lives have revolved around their own places of worship and community centres. Apart from the Asians—who, in many instances, came to Sudbury as professional people—first-generation immigrants came to Sudbury because the mines, forests, and railways offered employment to those lacking investment capital and language skills. Their children and grandchildren have become successful lawyers, doctors, teachers, engineers, building contractors, and business people. In those cases where the second and third generations married within their own ethnic tradition, people managed to preserve their own language and culture to a greater extent than in cross-cultural marriages. When people married out of culture, marriage partners invariably used English or French—usually English—as the household language, and the offspring assimilated into the dominant culture.

Other factors favoured eventual assimilation. The city's school systems—public, separate, and university—have used only English and French as languages of instruction. Weekly classes in other languages offered by various ethnic communities could not by themselves compete. Daily newspapers and radio and television programmes received in Sudbury have, with few exceptions, been available only in English or French. Weekly newspapers in other languages, whether printed in Sudbury or imported from elsewhere, simply could not counterbalance the impact of the English- and French-language media. Laurentian University and the ethnic communities have offered films in languages other than English and French, but those films have been fewer in number and have played for shorter runs than films in either of Canada's official languages.

The reception that immigrants received has been a mixed one. During World War I, Croatians, Ukrainians, Slovaks, and others from the Austro-Hungarian Empire became "enemy aliens" subject to various forms of legal harassment. Some of Sudbury's Croatians actually moved to the United States—which remained neutral until 1917—in order to escape the pressure. During World War II, Germans, Austrians, Czechs, and Slovaks had to register as enemy aliens under the Defence of Canada Regulations, because their homelands were part of the German Reich on September 10, 1939, when Canada declared war. Although some of these people considered their places of origin victims, not accomplices, of Nazi aggression, they faced possible internment if they failed to register. Italians joined the list of enemy aliens in 1940 when Mussolini's Italy entered the war as an ally of Germany.

Sudbury's treatment of its Chinese community during the 1920s is perhaps its biggest embarrassment. During that decade bigotry thrived on the North American continent, and Sudburians were not immune. In the aftermath of World War I, neither Canadians nor American authorities welcomed foreign immigrants, and in both countries the Ku Klux Klan attracted new members and influenced elected politicians.

Sudbury's problem began on February 4, 1922, when the *Sudbury Star*—which first appeared in 1910 and by 1922 published on Wednesdays and Saturdays—carried a story about three unnamed white girls in their late teens. Two had been waitresses in Chinese restaurants, one a frequent customer. One waitress had offered sexual favours to the London Cafe's male customers in exchange for sums that ranged from five to thirty-five dollars. The second waitress needed unspecified medical attention. The customer, charged with "loitering around Chinese cafes and public places and

The Sudbury Town Council banned stalls or partitions within Chinese restaurants in 1922, in response to the report of two waitresses' molestation. The council also nearly banned the restaurants from hiring women. Photo by Harry Young. Courtesy, Harry Young

with having no visible means of support," joined the other two at Toronto's Mercer Reformatory. In each instance, the *Sudbury Star* reported, the women claimed "molestation at the hands of the Chinese employees of the cafes at which they worked and frequented."

Infuriated, Mayor Robert Arthur, who was a medical doctor, met with the town councillors to crack down on all Chinese restaurants and guest houses in Sudbury. Exhibiting hostility and contempt toward the Chinese and a most patronizing attitude toward women, Sudbury's lawmakers voted unanimously on February 6 to forbid women from working in Chinese restaurants or lodging houses, and to outlaw stalls or partitions which might separate one part of a restaurant from another. Teenagers were meeting behind the partitions with members of the opposite sex, and Sudbury's elected representatives sought to eliminate opportunities for privacy. It did not matter that Sam Chew, owner of the London Cafe, had operated two restaurants and lodging quarters over a seven-year period without a single conviction; that an investigation had cleared Chew of any wrongdoing; that Chew had fired a cook whom he discovered to be living in a common-law relationship; and that other Chinese restaurateurs were guilty of nothing more than guilt by association.

Significantly, the resolution as finally passed made no mention of "white" women, as distinct from other women. The *Sudbury Star* explained that Indian girls also worked in Chinese restaurants, and the councillors believed "that Indian or any other girl was entitled to the same protection as were white girls."

Five days later, the council met again for a special Saturday session to discuss whether or not it was legal to forbid Chinese restaurants from hiring women. The councillors found a solution to the problem: they would remove the clause from the by-law, but order local police to warn Chinese restaurateurs not to hire women. Council had authority to revoke restaurant licences suddenly and without explanation, and police were to warn the Chinese restaurant owners that it would do so to any establishment with white female employees.

During the session Mayor Arthur voiced second thoughts about the cost of removing restaurant stalls. It was unfair, he suggested, that the Balmoral Cafe, which had done nothing wrong, should have to spend $4,000 to renovate. Councillor Lauzon and the majority disagreed. There should be no "discrimination," they said; all Chinese restaurants must be handled the same way.

The problem intensified. Sam Chew, whose London Cafe had employed the prostitute waitress, lost his licence effective February 19. Council gave him one week to dispose of his investments, including the New Ontario Cafe, which had an estimated value between $40,000 and $50,000. Chew nevertheless continued to operate his restaurants as usual until he was fined for operating a cafe without a licence. He then sold his properties. Because the council gave no official notice that restaurateurs must remove the partitions and dismiss their female employees, some did not. Newspaper reports and the grapevine were not, they thought, reasons in themselves for disruption. Then on March 27, citing "moral grounds," Sudbury authorities gave owners of five Chinese restaurants an ultimatum: dismiss all female help within a week, or close. While the women lost their jobs the next day, the cafe owners applied to the courts for an interim injunction, which, once granted, permitted them to remain in business—at least for a while.

On April 13 the Chinese community and Sudbury's town council reached an agreement. The restaurateurs would allow the injunction to expire, would pay their own court costs, and would individually write to the council promising not to hire any women. In exchange, the council would allow the restaurateurs to keep their licences.

Fortunately, Sudbury has advanced since 1922. In 1982 voters elected a resident of Chinese descent, Peter Wong, to a three-year term as mayor, and in 1985 they elected Wong to a second term. Hundreds of Asian people—from the Indian subcontinent and Southeast Asia as well as from China—have settled in Sudbury and most have lived their lives without controversy.

Above
The Chinese community's float in the 1967 parade for Canada's centennial. Photo by Harry Young. Courtesy, Harry Young

Top
Chinese women march in honour of the centennial. Photo by Harry Young. Courtesy, Harry Young

THE SUDBURY REGION

Music is an important part of the Croatian tradition in Sudbury. The Croation Kolo and Tamburitza Sudbury chapter, established in 1930, includes twenty boys and thirty girls from ages five through twenty-two. Courtesy, Sudbury Croatian Community

Sudbury's ethnic groups have displayed a deep sense of loyalty to Canada. People of German and Italian extraction served overseas with the Canadian forces. On September 21, 1939, seventy people from Hungary met at All People's Church, a United Church mission organized in 1931 to serve the needs of continental Europeans, and declared their loyalty to Canada regardless of whatever course of action Nazi Germany might force their homeland to adopt. A one-time student at Sudbury High School (now Sudbury Secondary), Joseph Zdyb, won the Polish Distinguished Flying Cross. The Croatian Orchestra performed at a dance on February 9, 1940, while Yugoslavia was still neutral, to raise money for the Canadian Legion. The Legion wanted to buy educational and recreational amenities for servicemen. Croatians also bought Victory Loan Bonds in substantial numbers. Sudburians of all backgrounds, Finnish to French Canadian, Amerindian to Anglo, suffered battlefront casualties. Northern Ontario Ukrainians staged Sudbury's first parade of 1940, from St. Mary's Church to the Cenotaph, pledged their loyalty to the Allied cause, and boasted that they had stifled Communist Ukrainian elements. The Chinese community played a large role in the 1941 Victory Loan Campaign, and on New Year's Eve, 1941, published a full-page advertisement in the *Sudbury Star* quoting Rudyard Kipling and depicting Winston Churchill and Chiang Kai-Shek as the great men who would lead the Allies to victory.

Canadian though they are, Sudbury's ethnic peoples have retained an interest in their homelands and have carried some of the controversies of Europe to northeastern Ontario. Italians were the only significant group of Sudburians other than French Canadians to vote negatively on April 27, 1942, when the Canadian government asked voters to release Prime

ETHNIC COMMUNITIES

Minister Mackenzie King from his promise not to introduce conscription for overseas service. The Croatian community, which never calls itself "Yugoslav," is not on speaking terms with the local Serbs. Among the Finnish population there have been conservative, Protestant (United Church, Pentecostal, or Lutheran) "White Finns" and left-wing, anti-religious "Red Finns," who had separate newspapers and community halls. During the Depression of the 1930s, some Red Finns actually left Sudbury to create a socialist utopia in Soviet Karelia. These ideological differences originated in Finland.

Sudbury's Finnish population demonstrated a profound attachment to Finland during the winter of 1939-1940 when the Soviet Union invaded its smaller neighbour. Even before the Soviet attack, Sudbury Finns had organized the Sudbury District Finnish War Aid Association, and its coffee parties proved particularly successful. With donations from one dollar per cup of coffee, the association raised $1,200 within a few weeks. Nor were coffee parties the only means of fundraising. Spectators paid admission to a Sampo Hall ski demonstration in February 1940, and proceeds went to the war effort. The same month, Mr. and Mrs. Arne Kastern of Broder Township hosted a chicken dinner for the benefit of the Finnish War Aid Society, and the society organized a benefit concert. The programme included a forty-voice Finnish choir. Before the fighting stopped, Sudbury's Finnish community was able to contribute $17,000 to the cause.

Like the Finns, Sudbury's Ukrainians have

Members of Sudbury's Ukrainian community's Dnipro Choir observe the choir's fiftieth anniversary, July 31, 1982. The choir has performed in Toronto's O'Keefe Centre, Ottawa's National Arts Centre, in Buenos Aires and Caracas, as well as throughout Northern Ontario. Courtesy, Mary Iwanochko

been divided. As residents of the Austro-Hungarian Empire, most of the earliest arrivals belonged to the eastern rite of the Roman Catholic Church, and they opened their first parish, St. Nicholas, on Poplar Street in 1909. In 1921 political activist Mykolal Hucaliuk arrived from Winnipeg and organized a branch of the left-wing Ukrainian Labour Temple Association, later the Ukrainian Labour-Farmer Temple Association (LFTA), which, by 1925, had two halls—one on Spruce Street in Sudbury and one in Coniston. The Ukrainian Catholic Church did not approve, and Church people and Temple people regarded each other with disdain, hostility, and contempt. Sudbury's left-wing Ukrainians, who labelled the other group "Fascist," argued that the Ukraine was part of the Soviet fraternity of republics, in voluntary association with its larger Russian counterpart. The right-wing Ukrainians called the leftists "Communists" and claimed that Russians controlled and misruled the unfortunate Ukraine. These ethnic and ideological differences proved important in the Cold War era, especially during the struggle between the Mine-Mill and Steelworkers unions in the nickel industry.

Most immigrants arriving from the United Kingdom and Ireland spoke English, but many from the Scottish Highlands were more familiar with the Gaelic language. Cape Breton Island had attracted many Highlanders in the late eighteenth and the nineteenth centuries, and in the twentieth century, hundreds of their descendants—particularly of those who lived in Inverness County—moved to Sudbury. They acclimated quickly, since Sudbury's climate and landscape closely resemble those of Inverness. People from Cape Breton came in two waves—one during the 1930s and another after World War II. Given the strategic importance of nickel, Sudbury was one of the few communities in Canada which had job opportunities for the unemployed during the 1930s. Some Highlanders had been coal miners on Cape Breton Island, and they adapted to the nickel mines of the Sudbury Basin. Others had been farmers or fishermen on Cape Breton, but they also became miners in Sudbury. The Cape Bretoners in Sudbury have managed to maintain many of their island's traditions. Each June they have a lobster boil, and their *ceilidhs* feature Highland dancing and "Down East" music. They watch Cape Breton movies, organize Gaelic-language classes, and they have sent relief money to Glace Bay.

In the years since World War II, ethnic Sudburians have really come into their own. People with Italian, Slavic, and Finnish surnames have operated successful businesses to a greater ex-

After teaching for nine years on Cape Breton Island, Archie F. MacKinnon migrated to Sudbury in 1936. Since 1979 he has taught Gaelic-language classes for the Sudbury Cape Breton Club. In 1982 he was awarded the first "Archie F. MacKinnon Shield" by the club for his Gaelic recitation.
Courtesy, Archie F. MacKinnon

ETHNIC COMMUNITIES

The Copper Cliff Highland Band, founded in 1928, marches past the Nickel Range Hotel on Elm Street after winning the provincial cadet championship in 1970. William Livingstone, founder of the band, moved to the Sudbury Basin from Ayrshire in southwestern Scotland. His son and namesake, William Livingstone, Jr., later won bagpipe competitions at Inverness, Scotland. Courtesy, Sam Laderoute

tent than in earlier years, and to an impressive extent by any standard. They have entered the professions—architecture, teaching, engineering, and medicine. Some have had successful political careers. Judy Erola, of Finnish extraction, was a cabinet minister from 1980 to 1984 during the administrations of prime ministers Pierre Trudeau and John Turner. Joe Fabbro, of Italian background, served two terms as mayor of Sudbury, from 1964 to 1965 and again from 1968 to 1975. He then became chairman of the Regional Municipality of Sudbury, a kind of super-mayor of the communities in the Sudbury Basin. The Province of Ontario created that post effective in 1972 to handle certain common services for the several separate communities. Nor was Fabbro the only ethnic Sudburian to hold that post. His immediate predecessor was George Lund, his successor Delki Dozzi. John Rodriguez from Guyana first won election as member of Parliament for the Nickel Belt constituency—parts of suburban Sudbury and rural areas of the Sudbury Basin—in 1972, won reelection in 1974 and 1979, lost to Judy Erola in 1980, but returned to defeat her in 1984.

Nickel attracted people to Sudbury, and it created an economy that could support others, both migrants and their descendants. As Sudbury developed, an increasing number of jobs outside the nickel industry became available. Many recent immigrants, in fact, have had no experience in the nickel industry. Yet, because there would not have been as large a community to which to migrate without the mines, even these last must acknowledge their indirect dependence upon nickel.

Sudbury has offered opportunity to a wide range of people. Political refugees, the unemployed, and the upwardly mobile moved to the nickel city from other continents and from other parts of Canada. Some stayed only a short time before returning to their place of origin or moving elsewhere, while some became permanent residents. To a considerable degree, almost all have assimilated, but their surnames, ethnic choirs, community halls, and centres of worship serve as reminders of Sudburians' many roots.

CHAPTER III

During World War II many Sudbury women volunteered for the Canadian Women's Army Corps (CWAC) and comparable branches of the navy and air force. The women's primary role was the performance of non-combat duties in Canada and Europe in order that men might be released for combat. Here officers inspect an army auxiliary of women preparing for duty at the Grey Street Armoury. Courtesy, Molly Downe

Through the Wars

Nickel is a strategic material, and until the late 1970s when world nickel markets became glutted, Sudbury's prosperity varied in direct proportion to the seriousness of conflict and potential conflict elsewhere. When there was war or danger of war, Sudbury boomed. When peace seemed secure, the local economy did not fare as well. During periods of prosperity, residents of less prosperous areas of Canada moved to Sudbury to share any opportunities which war and the threat of war might provide, and those already in the Sudbury Basin made the most of the situation. Usually they regarded Canada's war effort as their responsibility, and they volunteered for the armed forces and worked hard to produce nickel. Not surprisingly, however, nickel workers thought that they should share any profits made from the metal's production, and during World War II they unionized in order to realize this goal.

In many respects, Sudburians' attitudes toward each conflict resem-

THE SUDBURY REGION

bled those of their peers in other parts of Canada. In 1899 Great Britain went to war with two republics in southern Africa, the Transvaal and the Orange Free State. Because of Canada's constitutional position at the time, Canada was automatically at war. The impact upon Sudbury appears to have been minimal, although a Methodist clergyman, the Reverend Alex B. Johnston, preached sermons on the subjects "The evils of war" and "Are we justified in the present struggle?" The titles indicate some degree of controversy within Sudbury, as indeed there was across Canada.

World War I was a much more serious matter. Again, Canada became involved as soon as Great Britain entered the war in August 1914. Between that time and November 1918, when hostilities ceased, eighty-five Sudburians died in battle. Given that the census of 1911 reported 4,150 people living in Sudbury, the casualty rate was substantial. War did benefit the town's economy, nevertheless. Nickel production soared from 45,517,937 pounds in 1914 to 92,507,293 pounds in 1918. During the same period copper production rose from 28,948,211 pounds to 47,074,475 pounds. The 1921 census reported 8,621 people in Sudbury itself, with thousands more in the basin communities of Copper Cliff, Capreol, and Chelmsford.

Like urban Anglophones elsewhere, Sudbury's Anglophone establishment was highly supportive of the war effort. In its last issue before the federal election of December 17, 1917—essentially a referendum on conscription—the *Sudbury Star* urged voters to support the pro-conscriptionist Unionist candidates (an alliance of Conservatives and pro-conscription Liberals) against the anti-conscription Liberals. "Your birthright is at stake," warned the *Star* on its front page December 15. "Are we to become ignominious puppets or stand Britains [sic] four square to all the winds that blow free and untrammelled for Liberty, Honor, Justice, and Sovereignty of the State?" The Reverend William McDonald of St. Andrew's Presbyterian Church, five of whose young men died because of the conflict, compared the war dead who had resisted the Kaiser to heroes from the Book of Daniel who had resisted Nebuchadnezzar, king of Babylon. The Sudbury District

Copper Cliff around 1909. Because of the large immigrant population, the area below the smokestack was called "Little Italy." At the turn of the century, Copper Cliff's population was greater than Sudbury's. The lack of vegetation was due to smelting. Courtesy, Sudbury Public Library

34

of the Methodist Church voted unanimously to support conscription for overseas service and sent a copy of the resolution to the Prime Minister, Sir Robert Borden.

Across the country, French Canadians and farmers exhibited less enthusiasm. Francophones who volunteered often could not understand English-language commands from Anglophone officers and then faced disciplinary action. In 1912 Ontario's Conservative government led by Premier Sir James Pliny Whitney had introduced Regulation 17 into the provincial legislature. When it became law, Regulation 17 banned French as a language of instruction in Ontario's schools. To many French Canadians, the Germans—far away in Europe—seemed a lesser threat than the Anglophone majority in Ontario. Farmers were reluctant to leave their land, buildings, animals, and equipment to fight in Europe. Unlike workers in the nickel industry, who could return to more or less what they had left behind, farmers had investments to protect. Many of the farmers in the Sudbury Basin were also Francophones.

Sudbury's Francophones did fight. The eighty-five war dead included such surnames as Bélanger, Bonhomme, Ethier, Gatien, Lagacie, Lecour, Matte, Prévost, Sauvé, Savard, and Thérriault. Yet, the French-speaking people of the Sudbury area—like French-speaking people elsewhere in Canada—tended to oppose conscription.

At the time of the 1917 election, Sudbury was part of Nipissing constituency. Sudbury itself voted Unionist by a narrow margin, and Copper Cliff by a wider one, both reflecting their French Canadian proportions. Such French Canadian communities as Hanmer, Verner, Sturgeon Falls, and Mattawa voted heavily Liberal. Unionist C.R. Harrison defeated his Liberal opponent E.A. Lapierre by a narrow margin, 6,411 to 6,367. Canada as a whole returned a Unionist government by a more decisive margin, 153 to 82, with most of the Liberals elected in the province of Quebec.

Another issue, which became controversial elsewhere but had its origins in Sudbury, involved nickel. Canadians feared that nickel might reach Germany or its allies through the United States, which remained neutral until April 1917. Since there were no nickel refineries in Canada at the time, nickel matte from Sudbury went to refineries in Great Britain and the United States, which then exported it to other countries. Twice in 1916 a German cargo-carrying submarine, the *Deutschland,* left Baltimore with shipments of nickel, which might or might not have been of Sudbury origin. Prime Minister Borden thought that they were, and the Canadian public was irate that nickel produced in Sudbury might have been used to enable Germans to kill Canadians. Fortunately, the amount of nickel involved was small, 240 tons on the first shipment and 350 tons on the second shipment.

To avoid such a dilemma in the future, a royal commission, appointed by the provincial government to study the nickel industry, recommended in March 1917 that a nickel refinery be established in Ontario. Consequently, Inco built a refinery at Port Colborne, Ontario, near the Welland Canal, which connects Lake Erie and Lake Ontario.

A drop in the demand for nickel following the war hurt Sudbury's economy, but by the 1930s a number of factors, not all of them military, had revived the demand. New, improved consumer products, in addition to the ambitions of Mussolini and Hitler and the ensuing armaments race, enabled Sudbury to emerge from the Depression more quickly than the rest of Canada. Canadians moved to Sudbury from places where the unemployment rate was considerably worse—from Saskatchewan, where educational authorities could not afford to pay schoolteachers; from Manitoba, where the prairie drought hurt farmers and grain shippers; from Cape Breton Island, where residents were, and still are, among the last to benefit in prosperity and the first to suffer in adversity. Sudbury's population, 18,518 in 1931, grew to

THE SUDBURY REGION

32,203 by 1941, and many who came to Sudbury at that time have remained. By 1935 Sudbury's nickel output was breaking new records.

With increasing nickel production, however, came increasing environmental damage. Air pollution from the nickel industry killed vegetation, which led to extensive soil erosion. As travellers approached Sudbury by rail or by road they observed miles of barren landscape that resembled that of the moon. Individuals with a low tolerance to sulphur often complained of eye and lung irritation and the chemical's foul smell. In addition, those buying homes in the Sudbury area had to agree to absolve the nickel companies from responsibility for damage to their gardens and yards as a result of air pollution.

From 1909 local farmers continually complained that the nickel companies' emissions damaged their crops, and they often took the companies to court. To avoid legal battles with the farmers, the Canadian Copper Company in 1915 relocated its roasting yards farther away from farming and residential areas. In 1921, after Ontario elected its one and only farmers' government (the United Farmers of Ontario, 1919-1923), the cabinet passed the Damage by Fumes Arbitration Act, which relieved the courts of responsibility. Under the act, the government would appoint an official sulphur fumes arbitrator whose decision would be final. The government would also hire an agricultural expert to assist the farmers in preparing their cases.

The Conservatives returned to office in 1923, and during the following year they revised the Damage by Fumes Arbitration Act. Those changes remained in effect until 1970. According to Laurentian University history professor R.M. Bray, the provincial government

was again authorized to appoint a sulphur fumes arbitrator and make awards not subject to appeal. Farmers were required to notify not only the offending company but also the arbitrator within seven days of a visitation of sul-

Above
Spring floods were common until the 1930s when dams were built, due to the Junction and Nolin creeks often overflowing their banks. This picture shows the stables where Palm Dairies kept the horses which pulled milk wagons. Civic Square now occupies the site pictured above. Photo by Charlie Workman. Courtesy, Michael J. Mulloy

Top
Here pictured is a Beech Street flood, looking west from the front of St. Mary's Roman Catholic Church, circa 1930. Photo by Charlie Workman. Courtesy, Michael J. Mulloy

THROUGH THE WARS

new jobs between December 1939 and April 1944. Falconbridge enjoyed a similar boom. In 1947, according to Inco's chairman and president, Robert C. Stanley, "Sales of nickel . . . were the highest of any peacetime year except 1937." In fact, the *Triangle* reported that underground development, almost all of it in the Sudbury Basin, totalled 54,790 feet—more than ten miles—in 1947. A company history claims that Inco's profits shrank each year, from $36,847,466 in 1939 to $25,010,938 in 1945, because the company had to produce quickly, regardless of cost, and not by the most economical means possible. Moreover, the more nickel it produced by such means, the less there would be for more profitable exploitation in peacetime.

Nevertheless, the demand for nickel provided obvious economic benefits for the city. By December 1939 unemployment had almost disappeared, and Sudbury's welfare budget was

phur fumes, and it was then the responsibility of the arbitrator to undertake immediately an investigation of the damages. This was the most important change in that it meant there would have to be a permanent, full-time arbitrator living in Sudbury who would be able to survey damages as soon as they happened. Farmers still were given until November 1st of the year in question to lodge a complaint with the arbitrator, at which point the arbitration process went into effect. The act did specify, however, that this process could at any time be stopped if the two parties arrived at satisfactory settlement on their own.

The nickel companies contributed a maximum of $5,000 per year to cover costs, including the arbitrator's salary.

Sudbury boomed during World War II and the Cold War that followed. The International Nickel Company's internal newsmagazine, *The Inco Triangle,* reported the creation of 5,000

King George VI and Queen Elizabeth (the present Queen Mother) leaving Inco's Frood Mine during their 1939 visit to Sudbury. Queen Elizabeth was the first woman permitted to go underground into any of Inco's mines. Photo by Canadian National Railways. Courtesy, Inco Triangle

THE SUDBURY REGION

A crowd gathered in front of the Sudbury Post Office to await passage of the royal visitors, June 1939. The decorations were put into place for the occasion. The post office stood at the corner of Durham and Elm, where Woolworth's has its store today. Photo by Michael J. Mulloy. Courtesy, Michael J. Mulloy

minuscule. In April 1940 Inco contributed $15,000 to the YMCA's financial campaign and Inco employees donated an additional $3,000. By the summer of 1940 there was a labour shortage. In the January 1 to June 15 period of 1940, city tax collections jumped $100,000 above the level of the previous year. Christmas sales set a new record. Sudbury banks reported higher bank clearings ($53,155,916) for 1940 than for any year since 1930. Customs Revenues for 1941 set an all-time record, and Sudbury's municipal tax rate for 1942 was its lowest since 1931.

Nor were miners the only people to find employment. Demand for lumber increased to the point where by late 1941 there were not enough men available to keep pace with the orders. A factory opened to produce skis for soldiers at the front and received all the orders it could handle.

Women also found new roles. Although they performed traditional activities—knitting and sewing, collecting blankets and clothing, playing bridge to raise funds for war work, preparing food for charities and soldiers on leave, canvassing for funds—they also entered fields previously reserved for men. On April 20, 1940, the *Sudbury Star* carried a story about

THROUGH THE WARS

Here pipers entertain the crowds awaiting the royal visitors in 1939. Sudbury's first royal visit attracted record-breaking numbers of observers. Photo by Michael J. Mulloy. Courtesy, Michael J. Mulloy

public school board, while another set a precedent by signing the nomination papers of E.A. Whissel, an aldermanic candidate in Fournier Ward. Mrs. D.W. Ward won the school board seat in Ryan Ward, while Mrs. George Locke failed in her bid in McCormick Ward. At a St. George's Day banquet on April 23, 1941, a United Church clergyman and orator, the Reverend Norman Rawson, praised women for entering the labour force and suggested that more should do so in order that men could be free to enlist. Actually, the reversal of roles worked both ways. Boys at the College Street Public School knitted scarves and other items for Canada's soldiers. However, Sudburians' changing lifestyles carried a price tag. By 1944 the city

the Women's Auxiliary Motor Service. Its task was to qualify women for "men's work," and two nights earlier the women had had their first lesson "in the care and operation of heavy motor vehicles." Two months later twenty-eight women completed the course and earned the right to drive and repair cars, trucks, tractors, and ambulances. Other Sudbury women then undertook and completed the course. Soon, eighteen-year-old Anne Graf was driving a truck for Buron Grocery and Meat Market, and other women were ushering at theatres or announcing the station identification for the city's radio outlet, CKSO, the *Sudbury Star* reported. In fact, CKSO hired women for all but technical work, and Inco went further, hiring women for electrical, mechanical, and other technical positions. The CPR followed suit and hired women mechanics.

Women showed interest in other endeavours outside the home and received encouragement to do so. Two women ran for positions on the

These CWAC women were photographed circa 1940. Courtesy, Molly Downe

39

THE SUDBURY REGION

had one of the highest rates of venereal disease in the Province of Ontario, although Dr. W.J. Cook, medical officer of health, thought it had one of the highest recovery rates too.

Unfortunately, World War II meant more to Sudbury than a series of golden opportunities. It hit the city at a very personal level. Kathleen Ferguson of Copper Cliff and two of her children, Kathleen, 9, and Margaret, 3, were passengers aboard the British liner *Athenia,* torpedoed on the first day of the war. The Sudbury Children's Aid Society sought homes for forty children evacuated from Great Britain, and Sudburians responded with enthusiasm. Inco's 11,000 employees joined other Canadians in registering with authorities so that the federal government could make the most efficient use of available manpower, and children received encouragement to spend their pennies on war savings certificates. Boys boxed during their summer holidays, charged admission to the fights, and forwarded the proceeds to the Red Cross. Girl Guides had a bake sale and fishpond, again to raise money for the war effort. People of all ages played bingo so that they might raise funds to buy cigarettes for servicemen. There was a camp for interned German prisoners-of-war west of Sudbury, and excitement vied with apprehension when prisoners escaped. In April 1941 about 170 servicemen staged a mock occupation of Sudbury as part of their training, and by September of that same year, Sudburians had salvaged sixty tons of scrap material for war purposes. The city had blackout drills, and a sub-regional office of the Wartime Prices and Trade Board located in Sudbury. The Sault Ste. Marie-Sudbury Regiment held a training camp at Minnow Lake during the summer of 1942.

The Russo-Finnish War, fought during the winter of 1939-1940, also had a direct effect upon Sudburians, Finnish and non-Finnish. Some Finnish Sudburians had relatives in the war zone, and Inco had an operation at Petsamo and Kolosjoki, in the part of Finland overrun by Soviet forces. Fortunately, all of Inco's Canadian employees managed to flee the war zone with their families and return safely to Canada. There was general relief when Mrs. I.J. Simcox, formerly of Copper Cliff and wife of Inco's general manager at Petsamo, called early in December 1939 to say that everyone had reached Kirkenes in Norway. Eventually the Soviet Union compensated Inco for its lost property.

While Sudburians kept themselves busy and the nickel industry boomed, pockets of poverty managed to persist. When Rotarians were distributing pre-Christmas charity in 1943, they discovered considerable "ill health and squalid living conditions." A month later, Sudbury experienced a diphtheria epidemic, resulting largely, according to Dr. Cook, from "poor housing conditions and overcrowding." The *Sudbury Star* lamented the lack of adequate heat and ventilation in many homes.

Sudbury's labour force had felt shortchanged by any boom during World War I. In 1919 Frederick Eldridge, a machinist, won loud approval when he told some of his fellow workers:

The workers do not get enough of what they produce ... I advocate government ownership of everything: mills, mines, factories, smelters, railroads, etc. That is the only solution of the problem and I am only one of hundreds of workmen in Sudbury that think the same thing.

Their sons and successors were even more outspoken during World War II. Employees at Inco and Falconbridge took steps to gain what they considered their fair share of the prosperity while nickel was in high demand.

It was no simple matter to introduce a union. Previous attempts had failed, and Inco was willing to go to some lengths to prevent one from establishing itself. First, in 1942 it organized and subsidized its own "company union," the United Copper Nickel Workers Union, nicknamed by opponents "The Nickel Rash." Then, according to various sources, when the International Union of Mine, Mill

THROUGH THE WARS

and Smelter Workers (Mine-Mill), an affiliate of the Congress of Industrial Organizations (CIO), came to Sudbury, Inco management hired goons to raid Mine-Mill offices and intimidate Inco employees who showed an interest in it. The goons assaulted union people and destroyed union property, and the police never prosecuted them, although their identity was known. The media were strongly opposed to unionization, as were the churches and the courts. In 1943 the CIO endeavoured to organize a parade, supposedly on behalf of the 1943 Victory Loan campaign, but the Sudbury police commission denied permission. Magistrate J.S. McKessock opposed Mine-Mill's application on the grounds that "there was no point in inviting trouble," and Judge E. Proulx said that while a Victory Loan parade might be justifiable, a union parade was unnecessary. In fact, Inco had allies throughout the city. One union organizer, Bob Miner, tells of his problems in finding accommodation once he mentioned his name to prospective landlords.

Much of the credit for organizing the union goes to Robert H. Carlin, who came to Sudbury from Kirkland Lake in 1942. A wartime Mine-Mill strike in the Kirkland Lake gold mines had been a spectacular failure, and Mine-Mill needed new members. Sudbury had the potential, and if Mine-Mill was successful, it would control the work force of an essential component of the Allied war effort. Carlin came as a stranger to Sudbury and used his anonymity to promote the union. He called it "CIO" rather than "Mine-Mill" because the CIO's prestige among workers was higher, and he placed CIO pamphlets by the toilets in a beer parlour. Then, unrecognized, he sat near the washroom door to watch the men's reactions as they emerged. One day he followed an apparently responsive individual onto a streetcar and to his home, where he introduced himself and discussed union activity. One contact led to another until a certification vote was held at Inco on December 17, 1943, and at Falconbridge three days later. Mine-Mill won decisively. At Inco, 6,913 voted for Mine-Mill and 1,187 for the "Nickel Rash." Of the 959 voting at Falconbridge, 765 favoured Mine-Mill over the Falconbridge Workers' Council. Contracts followed in 1944. Because wages were frozen by wartime regulations, Mine-Mill was limited as to what it could do for its members, but it made progress on matters related to grievance procedures, seniority, and time spent on the job.

Nevertheless, Mine-Mill had its share of controversy. Throughout the decade there was constant hostility between Carlin and James Kidd for leadership of the Sudbury Local, 598. Above all, there was the Communist issue.

During the period from 1945 to 1949, numerous Soviet takeovers and attempted takeovers occurred in Europe. Stalin and the Soviet Army occupied or seized control of eastern Germany, Poland, Bulgaria, Hungary, Romania, and Czechoslovakia. During World War II the Soviet Union had been an ally, and the presence of Communists among Mine-Mill leaders was of marginal importance. Soviet and Western interests coincided, and a strike at Inco or Falconbridge would have been as critical to Soviet interests as to Canadian or American interests. After the war, however, the Soviet Union became a threat. Nobody knew the extent of Stalin's ambitions, but neither his blockade of West Berlin through the winter of 1948-1949 nor the presence of Communists in Mine-Mill proved very comforting.

Even from the perspective of retirement in 1980, Carlin failed to appreciate the importance of the Communist issue. To him, and apparently to Reid Robinson, one of Mine-Mill's international organizers and a suspected Communist, communism was irrelevant. A person's political affiliation did not matter; willingness to work on behalf of improved conditions for the union membership was what counted. If anyone, Communist or not, had good ideas and would endeavour to implement them, Carlin would regard him as an ally. Though he maintains that he was never any-

THE SUDBURY REGION

Lieutenant Peter G. Chance of Ottawa presents the bell of the corvette HMCS Copper Cliff *to Copper Cliff Mayor E.A. Collins May 22, 1946. According to the* Inco Triangle, *the* Copper Cliff *"saw plenty of action" in the North Atlantic during World War II. Photo by* Inco Triangle. *Courtesy, Sudbury Public Library*

thing other than a Socialist, Carlin repeatedly refused opportunities to dissociate himself from Communists, communism, or even Soviet policy. However, his unwillingness to antagonize his Communist allies and supporters rendered both him and the Mine-Mill union controversial, embarrassed friends, divided the union, and lessened its influence. In 1948-1949, the Canadian Congress of Labour (CCL) used Mine-Mill's unauthorized criticism of an affiliated union's newly negotiated contract as a pretext for its expulsion, and thereafter CCL affiliates felt free to raid Mine-Mill in search of members. Thereafter, too, Mine-Mill would be on its own in the event of a strike, less powerful to negotiate a strong contract for its members.

With regard to the politics of war (on the federal level), Sudbury voted strongly Liberal during the decade. Dr. J.R. Hurtubise of Sudbury, the incumbent, had no difficulty defeating Conservative candidate Onesime Larocque of North Bay in a two-way fight for the Nipissing seat in 1940. With Dr. Hurtubise's appointment to the Senate, Leo Gauthier, another Sudbury Liberal, easily won the seat. Redistribution then gave Sudbury a seat of its own, and Gauthier won it in 1949. This meant that Sudbury always supported prime ministers Mackenzie King and Louis St. Laurent.

On April 27, 1942, Sudbury voters approved Prime Minister King's request that voters release him from his promise not to introduce conscription for overseas service. Those who said "Yes" in Sudbury numbered 8,180, while the "No" forces mustered 4,949 votes. French Canadians and Italians appeared the most reluctant, while other Sudburians voted overwhelmingly in the affirmative. Largely Anglo-Saxon McCormick Ward voted "Yes" by a margin of 2,406 to 605. Ryan Ward, populated by immigrants from the Ukraine, Finland, Poland, and Czechoslovakia, also voted "Yes"—4,229 to 1,563. French Canadian Fournier Ward voted "No" by a margin of more than two-to-one. Copper Cliff voted in the affirmative, 1,203 to

Able Seaman John Hughes of Sudbury (centre) shows Copper Cliff Mayor E.A. Collins pictures of the corvette HMCS Copper Cliff, *as Hugh Watson watches. Hughes spoke highly of the generosity of the people of Copper Cliff, who had sent gifts to the ship, christened in honour of the town. Photo by* Inco Triangle. *Courtesy, Sudbury Public Library*

42

Sudburians gather in the streets to observe V-J Day, August 14, 1945. White's Meat Market stood where Cole's Bookstore now has its Elm Street outlet. Photo by Harry Young. Courtesy, Harry Young

479, but those who cast their ballots at the Italian Hall polling station voted 365 to 193 in the negative. Sudbury's "Yes" vote was less substantial than the nearly 84 percent average across Ontario, but the city's French Canadians were more numerous than in most parts of the province. Quebec voted "No" by almost 72 percent.

The same hesitation toward war was evident even at the provincial level. When the provincial Liberal government of Premier Mitchell F. Hepburn asked the Ontario legislature to censure the federal Liberal government for its failure to carry out the war with sufficient diligence, Northern Ontario MPPs were not among the forty-four ayes. Three of the ten nays came from Northern ridings, and Sudbury's Liberal MPP, J.M. Cooper, joined six other Northerners in absenting themselves at the time of the vote.

Yet, according to the Royal Canadian Legion, 489 young men from Sudbury died in action during World War II. One of them was Sudbury's Flying Ace, Theo Doucette, winner of the Distinguished Flying Cross. An additional 337 suffered injuries, and sixty spent time as prisoners-of-war. Such was the general relief when the war ended on August 15, 1945, that Sudbury witnessed a V-J Day riot. The *Sudbury Star* reported:

Sudbury's riot was the only one in Canada to mark V-J Day. This morning it was estimated that at least $40,000 damage was done, and the figure may exceed this as the result of looting of supplies at the city's liquor, beer and wine stores and shattered glass plate windows said to number 40. Constable Robert C. Ford, of the RCMP, is in [the] hospital, two other police were slightly injured, and 28 men are under arrest.

German prisoners of war returning to Europe in 1946 reported that in their travels across Canada, only Winnipeg and Sudbury gave them hostile receptions.

Since World War II, only one Sudburian serviceman has lost his life in battle. James Beaudry was a casualty of the Korean War, the only military conflict since 1945 in which Canada was a belligerent.

War, then, had a direct bearing on the people of Sudbury. It provided economic opportunities, as it did elsewhere, and it aroused both patriotism and doubts. Unionization, achieved during World War II, was to have long-term consequences for the city. Nickel workers led the way, and others, from municipal employees to teachers, eventually unionized as well.

CHAPTER IV

The ballet is just one of the Sudbury Region's many cultural offerings. Here, the Ida Sauvé Dance Company's 1983 performance of "Terrestrial Cat People." Courtesy, Northern Life

Culture and the Arts

The smaller cities of Canada have always had difficulties maintaining a high level of the classical arts. Residents of Regina or Sudbury who want to participate in or observe professional theatre, symphony music, opera, or ballet usually must wait for opportunities and take what is offered. Choice is limited, especially when, like Sudbury, the city in question is neither a capital city nor a rival to the capital (like Calgary or Saskatoon). However, this does not mean that those arts are absent. Indeed, Sudbury offers a rich popular culture of clubs, crafts, and amateur entertainment built upon a long tradition of ethnic groups, churches, and unions that constructed their own halls and encouraged creativity. That culture and the arts in Sudbury have developed to the extent they have is a tribute to the city's people.

Culture has taken many forms in Sudbury, and participants in the arts speak and sing in many languages. One of the most remarkable features of Sudbury life has been the survival of the French language,

THE SUDBURY REGION

Sudburians have usually been able to find a place to dance or see a movie; if not, they make their own entertainment. Jarl Pernu, a Finnish immigrant who began to work for Falconbridge in 1932, gave an example of the homemade humour which defused tense situations. Forty men slept in one bunkhouse, he recalled, with the double-decker beds crowded together. The manager, Ernie Craig, had a huge St. Bernard named Barney. In Pernu's words:

One night we put Barney, who was a peaceful old slob of a dog, into a rough guy's bunk, and

The Chorale des Benevoles' performance at the Centre des Jeunes. Founded in 1950 by Albert Regimbal, S.J. Groulx, and Jacques Groulx, the centre was Ontario's first French-language cultural centre. It is now one of many in the province and serves both young and old. Courtesy, Centre des Jeunes

Sudbury's secondary school teachers, members of the Ontario Secondary School Teachers Federation, went on strike in February 1980 and remained off the job until well into the spring. Here they picket at Civic Square where the Sudbury Board of Education has its offices. Courtesy, Northern Life

despite a series of restrictions which culminated in Regulation 17. Until 1970, French was not the main language of instruction in any of Sudbury's secondary schools, and yet there were people anxious to read French-language books and newspapers, listen to French-language radio, watch and participate in French-language plays, and attend classes in which French was the medium of instruction. Those people are living evidence of the determination of Franco-Sudburians to retain their language. A recent study, in fact, reveals strong opposition within the District of Sudbury, as elsewhere in Northern Ontario, to enforced anglicization.

CULTURE AND THE ARTS

we covered him up. The fellow came in. It was pretty dark, and he started roaring about someone in his bunk. Well, he kind of cooled down when I told him it was a new guy, big and tough, with the reputation of being real handy with a knife.

The guy sat up all night. In the morning, old Barney got up, stretched, jumped down and ambled out. Later the fellow got a laugh out of the joke, but that morning he was ready to kill the bunch of us.

Some individuals have operated at a highly sophisticated level and made their art a source of income. Artists Nellie Keillor Lowe, Ivan Wheale, Albert Klussmann, Anna Jalava, Frank Homer, and Charlie Rapsky have made an impression across Canada with their paintings. Stone-carver Peter Ellero, an Italian immigrant whose family had been working at the craft for five previous generations, arrived in Sudbury in 1960. At first he had to work full-time in the mines and cut monuments and curling stones after his shift had ended. Before long, however, his reputation was such that he and his twelve-year-old son, Fred, established Peter Ellero and Son, Limited, a stone-carving business. The two Elleros created and offered for sale shelves of stones shaped into birds, animals, lamps, vases, and games. In 1985 they opened an outlet in Ottawa. Charles Paxy has achieved a wide reputation for his wood carvings of miners and mining machinery.

While some artists have thrived as individuals, others have found greater satisfaction in group activities. By 1920 the Methodist Church had a Sunday School orchestra which featured young people who could play a wide range of wind instruments. The congregation of St. Andrew's United Church helped finance Wesley Hall, a new wing which opened in 1941, through the sale of tickets to plays. The Sudbury Little Theatre Guild began in 1948, and at one point managed to stage four plays each year. This indicates commitment and dedication on the part of the actors, producers,

The Sudbury Methodist Church, erected in 1908, became the Cedar Street United Church when Methodists and Presbyterians united. Later an annex to St. Andrew's United Church on Larch Street, the building continued as Wesley Hall until 1939. At that time, St. Andrew's sold it to the Bell Telephone Company and the church built a new adjacent facility.
Courtesy, Northern Life

and stagehands, all of whom had other employment and regarded the guild as recreation. In 1949 the guild hosted the first Northern Ontario Drama Festival, a bilingual event in which three local groups besides the guild itself—the Alerts Athletic Club, College Sacre Coeur, and the Finnish community—participated. Other entries came from Sault Ste. Marie, North Bay, Kirkland Lake, Timmins, and South Porcupine—a not inconsiderable feat for these last two since Highway 144 had not yet been built between them and Sudbury. The festival, which

THE SUDBURY REGION

The Sudbury Theatre Centre began modestly in 1972. Since then it has become one of Canada's fastest growing regional theatres. Here, Bert Meredith presides over the court during the production of Witness for the Prosecution. *From left to right, the other actors are: Peter Small, Larry Aubrey, Vernon Chapman, Brian Kelly, and Donald Saunders. Photo by Gerry Hess. Courtesy, Sudbury Theatre Centre*

rotated throughout northeastern Ontario, became an annual event. In addition to its role as a cultural medium, the Sudbury Little Theatre Guild offered a forum where newcomers to the city could meet new friends and become part of community life. Some of its people, including Bert Meredith, Bill Hart, Wilf Davidson, Judy Erola, and Sonja Dunn, benefitted from adjudicators' comments and became professional actors, producers, and television personalities.

In 1970 Francophones founded a theatre of their own, le Théâtre du Nouvel Ontario (TNO), the first French-language theatre in Ontario. Since 1975 it has operated from La Slague, and its repertoire includes both local productions and plays and casts from outside the city. Its goals include the promotion of interest in the arts, specifically in Franco-Ontarian literature, theatre, and music, and the advancement of French-language theatre in Canada. Since a financial crisis in 1981, the TNO has enjoyed a boom. Between 1982 and 1984, revenues from ticket sales quadrupled. In 1983-1984, the TNO staged 160 performances of four different plays in New Brunswick, Quebec, Ontario, Manitoba, and Saskatchewan. Because of recent successes, the TNO receives grants from the federal and provincial governments.

The TNO has a sense of responsibility toward the wider community. It produces shows for children, both Francophones and Anglophones who are trying to learn French. In order to reach a larger audience, it has even performed one controversial play, *Les Rogers,* in an English-language translation. One feature, *Nickel,* dealt with Sudbury life in 1932.

By 1972 theatre buffs wanted professional theatre in Sudbury, and they organized the Sudbury Theatre Centre (STC). It began modestly but has become a smashing success, due in no small part to the talents and imagination of director Tony Lloyd. By September 1982, with the inaugural of the first season inside its own $2.2 million complex on Shaughnessy Street, the STC had 3,800 subscribers, as compared to 300 its first year. The first play in the new building was the musical *Oliver,* which had a cast of seventy-five, including fifty-five local children. Directed by Tony Lloyd, *Oliver* ran for more than five weeks, with every performance sold out. With more than 4,000 current subscribers, the STC claims the highest per capita subscription rate of any regional theatre in Canada.

The STC has diversified. Besides musicals, mysteries, comedies, and thought-provoking dramas, it annually offers two dinner theatres and a Young Company production. In addition to seven plays during the regular season, it has performances throughout the summer months and sponsors a drama programme for youngsters. In January 1985, it launched the STC

CULTURE AND THE ARTS

*In 1952 Local 598 of the Mine-Mill Union hired Weir Reid, former program director for the central YMCA in Toronto, to direct the Mine-Mill Camp on Richard Lake, south of Sudbury. This 1956 picture shows Reid (right) with some of the campers.
Courtesy, Mike Solski*

Touring Company for children and young people. Over the following four months, the touring company gave 110 performances before 30,000 spectators throughout northeastern Ontario.

Long before there was professional theatre, Sudbury's miners displayed a significant appreciation of the arts, quite apart from their own ethnic activities. In 1952 Local 598 of the Mine-Mill union appointed Weir Reid—experienced as a programme director of the central YMCA in Toronto—as director of its cultural and athletic affairs. The union arranged for the Royal Winnipeg Ballet to perform in Sudbury on January 29 and 30, 1954, and both performances were sell-outs. One week before its projected Sudbury visit, the ballet suddenly announced that it would not be coming. According to Mine-Mill organizer and historian Mike Solski, the State Department threatened the dancers with a warning that if they performed under the auspices of Mine-Mill, suspected of Communist leanings, they might not be as free to tour the United States. Nevertheless, Soviet artists and American vocalist Paul Robeson, also in trouble because of his alleged political views, did indeed perform in Sudbury under Mine-Mill auspices in the mid-1950s. In addition, Mine-Mill sponsored dance classes, amateur theatre, and its own highly acclaimed film, *Salt of the Earth,* about a strike by Mexican-American members of a Mine-Mill local in New Mexico.

If the miners had their union, affluent and well-educated Anglophones had the Canadian Club, which sponsored speakers. The Sudbury Chapter, founded for women in 1920, had 200 members by 1937. Sons and husbands of members could attend meetings, but men were not eligible for membership in their own right until after World War II. Travelogues and women's topics ("How Canadian women can best serve their country today," 1931; "What women can do to make democracy work," 1946; "A housewife in Britain today," 1947) were particularly popular. On April 16, 1944, Dorise Nielsen, a member of Parliament, stressed "women's efforts must not end with this war, ... we are citizens, not just homemakers." Charlotte Whitton, a future mayor of Ottawa and a frequent speaker at the Canadian Club, made one of her Sudbury visits on February 14, 1946. On that occasion she asked the question "Are Canadian women political flops?" and answered in the affirmative. Whitton found it less than satisfactory that there was only one woman in the House of Commons, while barely half a dozen held seats in all Canada's provincial legislatures.

Members of the academic community, journalists, military officers, and diplomats addressed the Canadian Club on such topics as the rise of Hitler, the League of Nations, the Spanish Civil War, the independence of India, and nuclear weapons. Expatriate Russian nobility discussed their former homeland. In an address on December 8, 1933, entitled "The New Canadian," Count Paul Nicholas Ignatieff, once a minister of education under Czar Nicholas II, emphasized that "Russians were not Europeans but somewhat Asiatic." On November 22, 1934, the Baroness de Hueck, who had established residence in Toronto, noted forty-eight Communist newspapers in that city, twelve of them published in English. Writers, including poet E.J. Pratt and editor B.K. Sandwell (of *Saturday Night* magazine) came to Sudbury under the auspices of the Canadian Club, as did Paul Martin, long a federal cabinet minister, and John Diefenbaker (in 1946), a future prime minister. On February 6, 1947, Claire Wallace, a CBC broadcaster, attracted an audience in excess of 600. There was even one Dick Bird, who, on March 22, 1945, spoke about bird life in Canada.

Topical speakers continued to be popular. M.J. Coldwell, leader of the CCF party, told an audience of Liberals and Conservatives why the federal government ought to own the natural gas industry. Then he and members of the audience adjourned to the home of Bill Luke, public relations officer of Northern Ontario Natural Gas, for refreshments. Fidel Castro's ambassador to Canada presented an optimistic account of the 1959 Cuban revolution to the Canadian Club. An officer of Birks who had helped appraise the jewels owned by the Shah of Iran gave a slide presentation on that monarch's assets. Jean Lesage, Quebec's premier from 1960 to 1966, described changes taking place in that province under his leadership.

The Canadian Club attracted hundreds, but the Falconbridge Lecture Series has reached thousands, in part because there is neither ad-

Dr. Lois Wilson, activist for nuclear disarmament and a strong supporter of Amnesty International, was one guest speaker in the Falconbridge Lecture Series April 4, 1984. As president of the World Council of Churches for North America and co-director of the Ecumenical Forum of Canada, her topic was "The Ecumenical Movement in the 1980s: A Challenge for Human Community." Photo by Laurentian University. Courtesy, Laurentian University

CULTURE AND THE ARTS

Vancouver scientist Dr. David Suzuki delivers a lecture in the Falconbridge series, "Science in the 1980s: The Challenge for Education." Courtesy, Laurentian University

mission nor membership fees and in part because its speakers have access to Laurentian University's spacious Fraser Auditorium. It also helps that some of the speakers have addressed the audience in the French language. The series began in 1978, after a tragic accident in which four Falconbridge officers died while flying from Sudbury to Toronto. Falconbridge Nickel Mines established a trust fund in their honour, which sponsors the speakers. Famous American speakers have included chemist Linus Pauling, economist John Kenneth Galbraith, and physician Benjamin Spock. On October 20 and 21, 1983, Stanford University's Paul Ehrlich gave two frightening speeches, "The Ecology of Nuclear War" and "Extinction." The last surviving Father of Confederation, former Newfoundland Premier Joseph Smallwood, came to Sudbury, as did Quebec separatist and singer Gilles Vigneault. Scientist/educator David Suzuki and playwright Mavor Moore came within one year of each other, while comedian Johnny Wayne chose to address an audience "On being Canadian—and other difficulties." A few months later, novelist/poet Margaret Atwood read some of her works. Ken Dryden, Montreal lawyer and former goalie for the Montreal Canadiens, had tremendous appeal during his two speeches, "The Future of Professional Sport in Canada" and "What the Canadians have to do to beat the Russians." Historian/educator Jill Conway delivered three lectures, including "Women in History."

For a quarter century, from the early 1940s until 1969, the Sudbury Community Concert Association brought instrumentalists and vocalists to perform. Many—including soprano Lois Marshall, who came to Sudbury in 1961—were soloists, but there were some world-class groups: de Paur's infantry chorus, a group of thirty-five black veterans who had given more than 2,000 concerts for American forces from Iwo Jima to Berlin during and after World War II (in 1949); the Trapp Family Singers (1950); boys' choirs from Tucson, Arizona (1954) and Columbus, Ohio (1960); the Vienna Academy Chorus (1957); the Obernkirchen Children's Choir (1968-1969); and others. Then, in 1969, the cost became prohibitive as greater opportunities for artists of such calibre developed in larger population centres. No hall in Sudbury had sufficient audience capacity to draw the revenues needed to hire such artists.

Yet, other types of performances did survive. The University Women's Club attracted live opera to Sudbury. In 1979 St. Andrew's United Church launched its St. Andrew's Concert Series of five performances each year, with tickets sold on a subscription basis. Among the artists

The Von Trapp children wave farewell toward the end of the Sudbury Theatre Centre's 1982 performance of The Sound of Music. *From left to right: Allison Lloyd, Theresa Stewart, Peter Roman, Stacey Yagnych, Tami-Lyne Mayrand, Eric Moses, and Margaret Anne Park. Photo by Gerry Hess. Courtesy, Sudbury Theatre Centre*

who have packed the house are singer Maureen Forrester and The Canadian Brass. Popular vocalists from Stompin' Tom Connors to Reg Schwager (a one-time resident of Sudbury now with the David Young Trio) have included Sudbury in their Canadian tours. Franco-Sudburians gather at La Slague in the centre of the city for performances by classical and contemporary musicians and singer-songwriters.

Each summer, the Northern Lights Festival Boreal attracts talent from near and not-so-near. Nancy White, a Toronto-based satirical folksinger, has commented of Festival Boreal:

It was one of the first festivals I ever played at . . . I thought it was one of the best and most exciting, particularly because it was bilingual. It was amazing to watch the organizers and performers switch back and forth from French to English without a break.

Ken Whitely, another Toronto performer at Northern Lights, found that he encountered more French Canadian talent in Sudbury than in any other community. Elsewhere, performances were given in one language or the other, but not in both languages.

Unpaid volunteers have created music in Sudbury and they have made serious commitments to practise and to perform well. The Sudbury Male Chorus of the 1950s, limited by

CULTURE AND THE ARTS

its constitution to a maximum of forty members, sang songs from around the world—Negro spirituals, "The Road to the Isles," selections from *My Fair Lady,* sacred music, and classical pieces. In 1960, after a decade of concerts, record making, and successes at Kiwanis Music Festivals, it had to disband because of declining membership. In 1976 the Sudbury Philharmonic Society divided into two specialized groups, both of them still active: the Bel Canto Chorus and the Sudbury Symphony Orchestra. The chorus has performed works ranging from Handel's *Messiah* to Rogers and Hammerstein's *The Sound of Music,* and has sung in English, French, German, and Latin. The Sudbury Symphony Orchestra gives four concerts per year, and its Christmas performance, usually at St. Jean de Brebeuf Church, is a community event. Before sell-out crowds, the orchestra plays Christmas music while choirs from the city's ethnic communities sing appropriate songs from their European homelands. Other concerts of the Sudbury Symphony Orchestra feature itinerant artists whom the orchestra accompanies. A group of male and female vocalists, the Sudbury Chamber Singers, formed in 1975, gives from four to six concerts per year. The choir performs music from the Renaissance to the present.

Organized informally in 1953, the Sudbury Symphony Orchestra incorporated in 1975. Here on the tenth anniversary of the incorporation, conductor Metro Kozak assumes his position before a dress rehearsal. The Sudbury Symphony has travelled throughout Northern Ontario, and played for the Queen during her visit of October 1984. Photo by René T. Dionne. Courtesy, René T. Dionne

THE SUDBURY REGION

Members of the first Board of Regents, Huntington College, Laurentian University, 1960-1961. Standing: Reverend Frank Stymiest, Walter Muncaster, Norman Grant, Thornley Virene, Dalton Caswell, Reverend Norman Hillyer, Norman Wadge. Seated: Chester Jury, Reverend Alvin Kennard, Walter Tate, Principal Edward Newbery, President Earl Lautenslager, Don Best, Thomas Palmer. Courtesy, Huntington College

Secondary schools also have their bands. In late March 1985, more than 1,000 young musicians from thirty-five secondary schools converged upon Sudbury's Lockerby Composite School for an unprecedented Northern Ontario Band Festival. Bands from Lockerby and Lasalle Secondary School won numerous awards and, by unanimous decision of the three judges, received invitations to participate in the National Stage Band Festival in Quebec two months later. Later that same spring, the Lockerby Composite School Concert Band and the Lockerby Jazz Ensemble participated in the New England Festival of Music at Boston, Massachusetts.

Laurentian University helps to promote music and the theatre arts, and the Roman Catholic Church deserves credit for serving as midwife at the university's birth. Until the late 1950s, Sudbury's college-level students either had to go to school elsewhere or study through extramural programmes such as those offered by Queen's University in Kingston. Queen's offered summer courses which northern residents with teaching jobs could attend, and it sent professors to lecture to classes in distant parts of the province. Then in 1957 Jesuits—in Sudbury since the 1880s—extended their College Sacre Coeur (a secondary school founded in 1913) and established the University of Sudbury. The Resurrectionist Fathers at North Bay moved at once to create North Bay College within the walls of their secondary school in that city, Scollard Hall. In 1958 laymen and clergy of six Northern Ontario presbyteries of the United Church of Canada agreed that they should develop a university in northeastern Ontario; from their efforts came Huntington College, named for a pioneer Methodist in the region. During this time the Anglican Church of Canada also showed interest in establishing

CULTURE AND THE ARTS

a university. Because this was a period of university growth across Ontario, the Progressive Conservative government of Premier Leslie Frost (1949-1961) proved cooperative. The province would not finance three separate denominational universities, but it would accept an arrangement whereby the three churches were partners in a secular university. By the terms of the Laurentian University Act of 1960, the churches could teach religious studies and other designated subjects within their own particular colleges. Most subjects, however, would be the responsibility of professors recruited by the non-denominational university itself, and the church colleges would send their students to study with them.

At first it appeared as though North Bay, rather than Sudbury, would be the seat of the university. (At one point Sault Ste. Marie had similar ambitions.) The Roman Catholic Church had interests in both cities, whereas key United Church people favoured North Bay. *The United Church Observer,* official newsmagazine of the denomination, favoured North Bay, and the Reverend Earl Lautenslager, minister at the largest United Church in the Sudbury area, went on record as saying that he expected the university to be in North Bay. The *North Bay Nugget* put forward a number of arguments. North Bay was at the time the hub of northeastern Ontario; until 1970, anyone travelling from Kapuskasing, Cochrane, or Timmins to points south had to pass through North Bay. It would be unusual to locate a university in an area of environmental devastation such as Sudbury, wrote the *Nugget's* editors, and unwise to build it in a community so dependent upon one industry, nickel. Sudbury had suffered from a devastating ninety-day strike in the nickel industry in 1958, and its nickel resources were finite. Would it not be wise, they wrote, to build the university in a community with a more diversified economy?

There are several reasons why Sudbury became the site of Laurentian University. The church colleges had to federate with one an-

The Reverend Earl Lautenslager, an ardent fisherman as well as the first president of Huntington College, attends a ceremonial farewell in his honour before leaving Sudbury in 1963. Shown, from left to right: Reverend Edward Newbery, first principal of Huntington College; Reverend Ernest Long, secretary of the General Council of the United Church of Canada; Lautenslager; Reverend Claude de Mestral from Rouyn-Noranda; and Reverend Elton Van Goudoever of Capreol's United Church. Courtesy, Huntington College

other, and the Congregation of the Resurrection at North Bay, with commitments to the University of Waterloo, was not as free as Sudbury's Jesuits to federate with Huntington. Another factor was the leadership of Earl Lautenslager, back for a second term as minister at St. Andrew's United Church in Sudbury from 1954 to 1963. A dominant personality with tremendous powers of persuasion, he mobilized his own congregation behind the university. St. Andrew's alone contributed $175,000, more than any other single congregation. Besides, Sudbury had by far the largest population of any community in the area to be served, and it

THE SUDBURY REGION

may have helped that one Sudbury-area constituency, Nickel Belt, had a Progressive Conservative member in the provincial legislature, Rhéal Belisle, while a Liberal represented Nipissing (the North Bay area). Certainly, after the legislature approved Laurentian University for Sudbury in 1960 it rejected a private member's bill from Liberal Leo Troy to allow North Bay College to grant degrees. (Nipissing University College, which offers some university-level courses in North Bay, must do so on conditions imposed by the senate of Laurentian University in Sudbury.) The ability of giant corporations like Inco and Falconbridge to assist did not pass unnoticed; North Bay had no such corporate giants to support it. It should be noted, however, that Inco did not announce its $2,500,000 contribution—the largest it had ever made to a university—until September 15, 1962, some time after the decision to locate in Sudbury. Publicly at least, Inco neither lured the university to Sudbury through a substantial grant nor threatened to withhold the money if authorities decided to build in North Bay.

Each of the church colleges has made a significant contribution to the arts: the Roman Catholic University of Sudbury in the study of folklore; Huntington College in the field of music; and Anglican Thornloe College in the field of theatre. At the University of Sudbury, professor Germain Lemieux, a priest, has a collection of 600 French Canadian stories in thirty volumes. The tales originated with Franco-Ontarian pioneers who settled between Mattawa and Sault Ste. Marie and at other places north of the French River. Father Lemieux wants succeeding generations to appreciate traditional folklore, and to that end he has published each story twice—one in standard French, and one in the original slang. The collection's files indicate ninety-two names of storytellers, most of them residents of Ontario. Folklorists continue to interview pioneers and expand the holdings.

Laurentian University's Huntington College, which has had a conservatory of music since 1978, helps to train singers and instrumentalists, and it has provided musical directors from its teaching staff: Metro Kozak of the Sudbury Symphony Orchestra; Robert Hall and Susan Marrier of the Bel Canto Chorus; Dr. Douglas Webb of the Sudbury Chamber Singers. Since 1981 the Huntington Conservatory of Music has staged an annual Summer Music Programme, a seven-day music camp with a wide range of instruction. Because younger musicians lack the wind to perform from 9:00 a.m. to 5:00 p.m., their activities are shorter than the senior and intermediate programmes, designed for people of high school age, university age, and beyond. There is a beginner programme for the uninitiated, as well as a more challenging one for the highly experienced. People who just want to experiment may rent an instrument for the week. Prominent musicians descend upon Sudbury for the Summer Music Programme, and bursaries and scholarships are available to participants.

Thornloe College, founded by the Anglican Church in 1961 and a part of Laurentian University since 1963, has taken a deep interest in theatre arts. Throughout the academic year, the Thornloe Players—most of them university students—entertain the university community and the public at large, but between 1981 and 1985, Thornloe organized the Sudbury Summer Theatre, a professional body. Students received salaries to study and perform drama and appeared on stage as often as ninety times per summer. They performed in such diverse locations as the Canadian National Exhibition and Ontario Place in Toronto, tourist areas of the District of Muskoka and Manitoulin Island, and on stages, in shopping centres, and even in backyards. Professor Stanley Mullins of Laurentian University's English department and Bill Hart, a professional actor who directs the university's media centre, have provided direction for the young actors.

The university also operates the Laurentian University Museum and Arts Centre on John Street, located in the former mansion of lum-

CULTURE AND THE ARTS

ber baron William Joseph Bell. The museum has a permanent collection of 500 works by Canadian artists, who themselves span 130 years of history and range from Euro-Canadian and Amerindian to Inuit. The Laurentian University Museum also displays exhibits which rotate more or less every second week. These include works of local artists, exhibitions of a national or international nature, and historic—and even prehistoric—material. Pamela Krueger, its director, estimates that more than 18,000 people visit the centre each year.

Sudbury has other museums as well. The most famous is Science North, which opened in 1984. It hosts a display of animal and plant life, computers which visitors can handle, and exhibits in the fields of physics, chemistry, and geology. The Flour Mill Heritage Museum specializes in Franco-Ontarian culture and traditions and houses antique furniture and implements that early Francophones in the District of Sudbury would have used. The Copper Cliff Museum also displays antiques, set in an early settler's log cabin. The Anderson Farm at Lively depicts life on a pioneer Finnish homestead.

In cultural matters as in other aspects of community life, nickel has been important. The nickel industry attracted the heterogeneous labour force which created a pluralistic society in Sudbury. The Mine-Mill Union sponsored and promoted the arts. The nickel companies have also invested time and money in cultural pursuits. People who served those working in the nickel industry made their own contributions, singing in choirs, performing in plays, serving on library boards, and inviting speakers and musicians. By the late 1970s and 1980s, as the nickel industry employed fewer people, Sudbury's artistic and cultural activities assisted the city's survival. Through the arts, as through medical and shopping facilities, Sudbury became a regional hub and service centre, a place where outsiders came for entertainment and where residents happily remained.

The Thornloe Players and the Thornloe Summer Theatre frequently perform outdoors. Here, the Thornloe Players at the 1980 Festival Boreal. Photo by Brian Hart. Courtesy, Thornloe College

CHAPTER V

Sudbury's Frank Cochrane helped plan the Conservative victory in Canada's 1911 federal election. Left to right: Robert Borden, the Conservative leader and, following the election, prime minister of Canada; Edmund Bristol; Frank Cochrane; Joseph Octave Reaume; and James Pliny Whitney, premier of Ontario. Courtesy, Public Archives of Canada

Prominent Personalities

Sudburians have achieved prominence in a number of fields. They have become cabinet ministers, at both the provincial and the federal levels. They have gained fame in business and labour. They have taken advantage of the nickel industry's environment to research regreening and subterranean food production, and to develop world markets for secondary industry. Nickel has often been a factor which, directly or indirectly, affected the career patterns of prominent Sudburians.

It is impossible to include in this chapter every Sudburian who has lived a useful life. Several politicians, medical personnel, clergy, teachers, miners, social workers, and civil servants have devoted their lives to ceaseless, selfless service, but only a few have become household names outside Sudbury. This chapter attempts to deal with those few.

The first cabinet minister to come from Sudbury was Frank Cochrane, who served at both the provincial and federal levels. The

THE SUDBURY REGION

Thirston "Rusty" Blakey, a veteran bush pilot with Austin Airways, started his career with the company in 1937. In 1946 Austin purchased the Norseman BSC, a superior bush plane built by Canada Car, and for twenty years Rusty flew it as far afield as James Bay and Hudson Bay. With the advent of airstrips in the north, Rusty started charter flights out of the Sudbury area with Beaver aircraft. Courtesy, Northern Life

founder of a chain of hardware stores, Cochrane was elected mayor of Sudbury in 1897, 1898, and 1902. In that year he sought a seat as a Conservative in the Ontario legislature without success, as 1902 was a Liberal year, both province-wide and in Nipissing, the constituency of which Sudbury was a part.

In 1905 Conservative fortunes changed. Under the leadership of James Pliny Whitney, the Conservatives won Ontario's general election, and Premier Whitney selected Cochrane—acclaimed in a by-election as Conservative MPP in East Nipissing—to be his Minister of Lands, Forests, and Mines. In 1908 he won election as MPP for Sudbury. This was the first election in which Sudbury had its own seat in the legislature, and Cochrane won it by a margin of 1,492 to 888 over his Liberal opponent, C.V. Price.

As a member of the Whitney cabinet, Cochrane made a significant impression. It was during his term of office that the Whitney government extended the Temiskaming and Northern Ontario Railway (now the Ontario Northland Railway) to meet the newly constructed Transcontinental line (now part of Canadian National). The cabinet decided to name the community which formed at the junction Cochrane, in honour of Northern Ontario's cabinet minister.

Having campaigned actively for the federal Conservatives and against Reciprocity with the United States in the federal election campaign of 1911, Cochrane accepted an invitation into federal politics. He won an acclamation for Nipissing's federal seat, and once again a newly elected Conservative prime minister, Sir Robert Borden, appointed him to the cabinet. As Minister of Railways and Canals from 1911 to 1917, Cochrane promoted the refining of Sudbury nickel within Canada rather than in New Jersey. For economic reasons as well as for national security, he wanted Canadians to have the refining jobs, which became available when Inco opened its refinery at Port Colborne in 1918. Poor health forced Cochrane to retire in 1917, and he died in 1919.

The next provincial cabinet minister from Sudbury was Charles McCrea, a lawyer and a Conservative. McCrea first won election to the Ontario legislature in 1914 and remained an MPP until the Conservatives lost office in 1934, when he lost his seat. Appropriately for someone from Sudbury, he too served as Minister of Mines from 1923 to 1934, when his

PROMINENT PERSONALITIES

status as an MPP coincided with periods of Conservative government. Prominent Ontario historian Joseph Schull has termed McCrea and the premier who invited him into the cabinet, George Howard Ferguson (1923-1930), as "friendly to [mining] entrepreneurs. . . ."

Yet a third Conservative from Sudbury, Welland Gemmell, became Ontario's Minister of Mines in 1949. Gemmell, the first cabinet minister actually born in the area, captured the Sudbury riding in 1948 and won reelection in 1951. A merchant and former municipal politician, he succeeded Leslie M. Frost as Minister of Mines when Frost became Premier of Ontario. In 1952 he became Minister of Lands and Forests, a position he held until his death two years later.

Sudbury's only other cabinet minister at the provincial level has been Progressive Conservative Jim Gordon, MPP for Sudbury since 1981 and a one-time mayor of Sudbury (1976-1981). The election of May 2, 1985, marked the beginning of the end for Premier Frank Miller's Progressive Conservatives, who lost their majority and won only 52 out of 125 seats in the legislature. They also saw eight cabinet ministers go down to defeat in their own constituencies. Forced to reorganize, Premier Miller invited Gordon to become Minister of Government Services. His tenure as a cabinet minister lasted but a few weeks, as the thirty-eight Liberals and twenty-five New Democrats elected on May 2 joined forces six weeks later to defeat the Miller government and end forty-two years of Progressive Conservative government.

The fact that all four provincial cabinet ministers from Sudbury have been Conservative may give the misleading impression that the city is a hotbed of conservatism. It is not. In the fifteen general elections since McCrea's last victory (1929), Sudbury has voted Conservative (or Progressive Conservative) five times, including 1948 and 1951 when it returned Welland Gemmell and 1981 and 1985 when it returned Jim Gordon. It has voted Liberal five times and Cooperative Commonwealth Federation/New Democratic Party (CCF/NDP) five times. By 1955 the population of the Sudbury Basin had grown to the point where it acquired a second MPP, the member for Nickel Belt. Nickel Belt has voted Conservative four times, CCF/NDP five times. In 1967, the area acquired a third seat, Sudbury East, which Eli Martel (now NDP House Leader) has carried for the NDP through six elections. As the CCF/NDP has never formed a government in Ontario, none of its members could become cabinet ministers. Similarly, Elmer Sopha, a Sudbury lawyer who won three of the Liberal victories in Sudbury riding (1959, 1963, 1967) did so when his party was in opposition. Given that Ontario's Conservatives have held office for all but eighteen years of the twentieth century, Conservatives who did win a seat in Sudbury stood a much better chance of entering the cabinet than did anyone else.

Sudbury has also had some prominent people at the federal level. Jim Jerome, a lawyer and a Liberal, benefitted from the wave of Trudeaumania in 1968 and first won election as Member of Parliament (MP) that year. He was reelected in 1972, 1974, and 1979. In 1974 Prime Minister Pierre Trudeau nominated him Speaker of the House of Commons, a position he held for the life of that Parliament. During that term, Inco and Falconbridge began to encounter a glut on world markets of the minerals the Sudbury Basin was producing, and the results were devastating. Inco's unionized workers, by then members of local 6500 of the United Steelworkers of America, went on strike for higher wages September 15, 1978, and remained off the job for more than eight months. It was not their fault, they said, that Inco had taken money generated in Sudbury and invested it in a Guatemalan enterprise which was proving less than successful. The miners demanded higher wages and, citing market conditions, the company would not or could not comply. When the strike ended, Inco eliminated thousands of jobs, through early retirement when possible and otherwise through layoffs.

THE SUDBURY REGION

Thomas "Spike" Hennessy, general manager of the Sudbury Regional Development Corporation, has served the community in a variety of ways. He helped select the site of Civic Square while city engineer and director of Public Works (1953-1970). He also directed planning for a major north-to-south arterial road along Paris, Drinkwater, and Notre Dame streets. Despite considerable controversy, he piloted construction of a sewer tunnel through five miles of solid rock. Courtesy, Thomas Hennessy

Below
Members of the Sudbury City Council, 1982-1985. Standing (left to right): Sterling Campbell, Frances Galdarelli, Gary Peck, Diane Marleau, and Ted Nicholson. Seated: Ricardo de la Riva, Bill Sutton, Mayor Peter Wong, Ron Symington, and Bob Fera. Courtesy, Northern Life

People who did not work in the nickel industry felt the impact. Merchants had fewer customers. As laid-off parents moved out of town in search of employment elsewhere, there were fewer children in classrooms, and school boards gave redundancy notices to teachers. Homes went onto the market, and there were few people to buy them. It appeared that for the foreseeable future Inco would not be in a position to give Sudbury the prosperity it had enjoyed as recently as the early 1970s (during the Vietnam War), when the demand for nickel was high and Inco was looking elsewhere in Canada for labourers.

Jim Jerome, MP for Sudbury, used his connections in Ottawa to alleviate the situation. He persuaded Prime Minister Trudeau's Liberal government to build a Taxation Data Centre in the city. Charged with responsibility for the income tax returns of most Ontario residents, the data centre would become one of the area's largest employers. Shortly before the federal election of 1979, workmen delivered a few steel beams to the playing field at the corner of Lasalle and Notre Dame, site of the forthcoming data centre.

For a while, the data centre's development appeared doubtful. Sudbury reelected Jim Jerome and the area's other federal constituency, Nickel Belt, returned a prominent New Democrat, John Rodriguez. Nationally, the Liberals lost the election and resigned. No party managed to win a majority of the seats in the House of Commons, but the Progressive Conservatives, led by Prime Minister Joe Clark, had the largest bloc of seats, and they formed a minority government. Members of Prime Minister Clark's cabinet talked of economy, fiscal restraint, and cancellation of "unnecessary" public works projects authorized by the Liberals.

Fortunately, the Clark government decided that it needed Jerome. A speaker cannot vote, except to break a tie, and the cabinet considered the neutralization of a Conservative MP too high a risk under the circumstances. It made sense to deprive an opposition party of a voting member, and the obvious choice was the man with experience, Jim Jerome, speaker of the previous House of Commons. Needing Jerome's cooperation, the cabinet decided that plans for the data centre were "too pregnant to be aborted." Jerome became speaker for the duration of that short-lived Parliament, and construction began on the data centre. Operational by 1981, it hired hundreds of people on a full-time basis, and it employs additional help in the early months of each year when Canadians are paying their income tax. By 1985 the federal government had become the fifth largest employer in the Regional Municipality of Sudbury; the Taxation Data Centre alone had 700 permanent and about 1,800 part-time employees.

The Clark government found itself in the midst of constant controversy from the date of its inception in June 1979. Barely six months later, even with Jerome as speaker, the Progressive Conservative cabinet lost a vote of confidence in the House of Commons and asked the governor-general to dissolve the House. The Liberals won the ensuing federal election of February 1980. Speaker Jerome thought it inappropriate, under the circumstances, to contest the election as a partisan Liberal and retired from the political arena. Doug Frith, chairman (or super-mayor) of the Regional Municipality of Sudbury since 1977, held Jerome's Sudbury seat for the Liberals. In an election which saw Liberals sweep every seat across northern Ontario from Quebec to the Manitoba border, Liberal Judy Erola defeated John Rodriguez in Nickel Belt.

At once Prime Minister Trudeau invited Erola into his reconstituted cabinet. A local television personality, she could communicate effectively, but she became highly controversial. Presumably because she was from Sudbury, she became Canada's Minister of State for Mines, to the dismay of many a male chauvinist. Soon she also became Minister Responsible for the Status of Women and in January 1983 won *Chatelaine* magazine's award as "Woman of the Year." *Chatelaine* regarded Erola as a cred-

THE SUDBURY REGION

Prime Minister John Turner campaigned in Sudbury weeks prior to the federal election of 1984. Turner lost the election, retaining only forty seats for the Liberal party across Canada, but one of them was Doug Frith's in Sudbury.
Courtesy, Inco Triangle

ible candidate for the Liberal leadership once Prime Minister Trudeau stepped down.

Then things started to go wrong. Erola voiced her opinion that a childless woman who stayed at home as a full-time housewife was not a very useful person. Many disagreed with her remarks, while others misinterpreted them. The Trudeau government reluctantly agreed to a request from Washington to permit testing of the air-launched cruise missile over Canadian territory, where physical conditions resembled those of Eastern Europe. Unlike Erola, many Sudburians thought that the cruise missile was either useless or dangerous and wanted no part of the tests. In June 1984, supporters of Project Ploughshares (named for the biblical ideal of beating swords into ploughshares) promoted a petition against the testing. Anxious to collect as many signatures as possible before Trudeau's successor—Prime Minister John Turner—called an election, canvassers went from door to door, set up tables at local churches, and sought signatures in other forums. Roman Catholic parishes (particularly St. Patrick's which, under the leadership of the Reverend Donald McMillan, collected more than 300 signatures), women's and professional groups, unions, and small businesses cooperated. Jim Grassby—himself a prominent Liberal—helped with the necessary fundraising. By the time Prime Minister Turner asked the governor-general to dissolve the House of Commons early in July, Sudburians had responded emphatically. In proportional terms, no place surpassed Sudbury in terms of the number of signatures collected. In absolute numbers, only Toronto, Montreal, Vancouver, and Winnipeg had more. By contrast, Erola was emphatic in her defence of the tests.

Finally, by the time he left office late in June 1984, Prime Minister Trudeau himself had become highly provocative, and his successor, John Turner, proved unable to salvage traditional Liberal support. Across Canada in the election of September 4, 1984, the Liberals lost all but thirty-nine of their seats while gaining only one new constituency. Erola was one of the casualties, personally defeated by her old nemesis, John Rodriguez.

Sudburian Doug Frith never was part of the Trudeau cabinet, and this may have been advantageous for him. He was free to be among the first to suggest that Trudeau had outlived his usefulness as Liberal leader and ought to retire. He disagreed with the decision to permit cruise missile tests over Canada. Yet, he did support the candidacy of John Turner for the Liberal leadership in 1984, and Turner supported the cruise tests. In turn, when he became prime minister, Turner appointed Frith to the cabinet as Minister of Indian Affairs and Northern Development. The glory was short-lived. Barely two months after his assumption of office, Prime Minister Turner led his party to its worst electoral defeat in Canadian history. Doug Frith, one of forty Liberals to win a seat in the debacle of September 4, 1984, did survive, and he became health and welfare critic of what remained of the Liberal caucus.

Another elected representative who made an impression outside the Sudbury area was Bob Carlin of the Co-operative Commonwealth Federation (CCF). A key organizer in 1943 when the International Union of Mine, Mill and Smelter Workers won the loyalties of Inco and Falconbridge employees, Carlin served two terms as Sudbury's MPP. Winning almost 60 percent of the popular vote in a four-way race, he entered the Ontario legislature in the general election of 1943. This was the election in which the CCF won thirty-four seats, ten of them in Northern Ontario, and came as close as it ever did to forming the government of Ontario. The Conservatives with thirty-eight MPPs formed a minority government, and the Liberals lagged behind with fifteen seats.

The provincial election of 1945 saw Carlin again sweep to victory, this time despite a general CCF collapse. The CCF held only eight seats in the entire province and forfeited the role of official opposition to the Liberals. As an MPP, Carlin lashed out against Inco's air pollution and called for stricter controls over the company. In doing this, he found himself accused by Mines Minister and future premier Leslie M. Frost of threatening employment in Sudbury and failing to represent the true interests of the workers. Carlin eventually became an embarrassment to his own party. Asked on the floor of the legislature to dissociate himself from certain Communists in the Mine-Mill union, Carlin refused. As far as he was concerned, anyone—whether Communist or otherwise—with good ideas and a willingness to implement them was an ally. Carlin's refusal

Jean Chretién (far left) joins Roger Regimbal and other Franco-Sudburians in celebrating the relocation of the Centre des Jeunes to the Empire Building in 1967. Chretién, at the time a junior cabinet minister, eventually held major cabinet positions under Prime Minister Pierre Trudeau and later became a major contender to succeed the prime minister.
Courtesy, Centre des Jeunes

proved untimely—it came at the very moment of the 1948 pro-Soviet coup in Czechoslovakia.

Under the circumstances, the CCF decided that someone else would have to be its candidate next time. Yet, Sudbury voters evidently did not share the concern of the rest of the world that Bob Carlin and his friends might paint the world red. Running as an Independent, Carlin came a close second in the election of 1948. Undoubtedly he would have won had the CCF vote not been divided between himself and the official candidate, Victor Whalen. Welland Gemmell benefitted from the split.

The Mine-Mill union, although branded as Communist-influenced and expelled from the Canadian Congress of Labour, continued to represent Inco and Falconbridge workers for another decade. Then, despite a shortage of money in its strike fund, Mine-Mill failed to negotiate a contract with Inco in 1958 and

THE SUDBURY REGION

called a strike. The strike lasted from September 24 to December 22, when a combination of desperation on the part of the union membership and pressure from the community forced the union to accept a company offer which many regarded as only a slight improvement over pre-strike offers. Mine-Mill's leadership suffered a loss of confidence among certain members, and this, along with suspicions of Communist influence, aided those who sought to replace Mine-Mill with the United Steelworkers of America (USW). Even Bob Carlin turned against Mine-Mill. In 1962 Inco workers voted 7,182 to 6,951 to break their ties with Mine-Mill and join the USW, which had greater financial resources and more support from the rest of organized labour. Spared the 1958 strike, Falconbridge workers remained with Mine-Mill.

Whether the change of union was worthwhile is still in dispute. Mike Solski, president of the Mine-Mill local at Inco during the 1958 strike, thinks not. In a recent book he observes that when Mine-Mill negotiated for Inco workers, they had the second highest wage levels in Canada. The best-paid workers were also members of Mine-Mill, in Trail, British Columbia. Shortly after the USW assumed responsibility, the wages of Inco workers fell to fifteenth place. USW supporters can take comfort from the fact that, with its greater resources, the USW has managed to survive several strikes (including those in 1969 and 1978-1979 which were considerably longer than the 1958 strike) without any mutiny.

Indeed, during the 161-day strike of 1978-1979, Dave Patterson—president of local 6500 of the USW (the Inco local)—won reelection to the post. In 1981 he was elected as director of District 6 of the USW of America, whose 100,000 members include mine, smelter, and steel workers throughout Ontario.

Among businessmen, Sudbury's most famous is, undoubtedly, Paul Desmarais. Born in Sudbury in 1927, he made his name in the field of transportation. In 1916 his grandfather had established the Sudbury-Copper Cliff Suburban Electric Railway Company, a streetcar line between Sudbury and Copper Cliff. On his death, the grandfather divided his estate between a business partner and two relatives. After World War II, the Desmarais family bought out the partner and converted the streetcars to buses. Within a short time, Paul's father gave him the bus company. As more and more people bought their own cars, the demand for bus travel declined, and the company could not make ends meet. Fearing that unreliable bus service from Sudbury to its Copper Cliff mines would jeopardize production, Inco bought part of Desmarais' assets for $138,000. He used some of that money, along with a bank loan, to purchase the Gatineau Bus Company of Ottawa-Hull in 1955. Gatineau Bus made a profit, and Desmarais' fortunes took off. Twenty years later, Desmarais' investments were so extensive that author/editor Peter C. Newman could write, "It is difficult for the ordinary Canadian to exist a week without enriching Paul Desmarais . . ."

Politicians, union leaders, and businessmen are by no means the only prominent Sudburians. Increasingly the medical profession has been establishing the city's name, in fields of mental health, heart surgery, and cancer.

As late as 1950, North Bay had the only mental health facilities north of Orillia. That year, Dr. Thomas Dixon—son of a pioneer doctor at Sudbury's St. Joseph's Hospital and himself a native Sudburian—graduated in psychiatry and agreed to open an out-patient clinic in his home town. Assisted by a psychologist, Dennis Roberts, Dr. Dixon worked out of the office of the Medical Officer of Health and then, within a few weeks, out of six rooms at the newly completed Sudbury General Hospital.

The response was tremendous. People came to Sudbury from Thunder Bay, Timmins, and Parry Sound. There were suicidal people who needed referral to North Bay, couples with marital problems, and individuals seeking voca-

PROMINENT PERSONALITIES

St. Joseph's Hospital in Sudbury, circa 1912, at the north end of Elgin Street. The original section, to the right, dates from 1898. St. Joseph's Hospital has since closed; several specialty hospitals now service the region. Courtesy, Michael J. Mulloy

tional guidance. The Children's Aid Society wanted consultations, and courts and local doctors made referrals. The need for in-patient facilities became so obvious that the Sudbury General Hospital built a new wing for psychiatric services. The Sudbury Algoma Hospital followed in 1952; it remains the principal child-care psychiatric centre in Northern Ontario.

Unlike Dr. Dixon, Dr. Paul Field is not a native of Sudbury, nor even of Canada, but he has made a tremendous improvement in the quality of life for many people. Born in Wales and trained as a heart and lung surgeon in the United Kingdom, Dr. Field first came to Sudbury in 1955. He became a fellow of the Royal College of Surgeons, Edinburgh (1961); a fellow of the Royal College of Surgeons of Canada (1962); a fellow of the American College of Surgeons (1965); and in 1966, Dr. Field obtained a fellowship in cardiovascular and thoracic surgery. Two years later he performed Canada's first open-heart bypass operation.

Since then he has conducted 250 such operations annually at Memorial Hospital.

The results of Dr. Field's operations have been spectacular. A survey of his patients in 1979 revealed that those who survived coronary bypass operations had a much lower rate of heart attack than heart patients without such surgery. Eighty percent of his patients were able to resume normal lives, even when "normal" meant a return to strenuous positions within the mines and mills of the nickel industry. Before Dr. Field's arrival, only 10 percent of the heart patients could undertake such work. His surgery has also lessened the patients' dependence on drugs. Before their operations, Dr. Field estimated that 80 percent of his patients were using nitroglycerine. One year after surgery, only 5 percent were taking it. In 1978 Memorial Hospital became the regional cardiovascular centre for northeastern Ontario.

The arrival of Laurentian Hospital's oncologist, Dr. Robert Corringham, in the mid-1980s brought tremendous hope to cancer patients throughout northeastern Ontario. Until Dr. Corringham's arrival, they had gone to Toronto for treatment, often on a long-term basis and at a point in their lives when they and their loved ones most wished to be together. It was frequently inconvenient and expensive for relatives to stay in Toronto for protracted periods, and many relatives could not afford the stay. The opening of the cancer treatment centre eased the problem, not only for Sudburians but for other northerners to whom Sudbury was less distant than Toronto.

During his first year (1984-1985), Dr. Corringham's case load rose to more than 500, considerably higher than the projected 300. When funds to provide additional staff did not materialize after nine months, Dr. Corringham presented his resignation, effective August 1, 1985. Happily for all concerned, on June 14, during the last week of his administration, Premier Frank Miller announced the availability of money to hire two additional cancer specialists, and Dr. Corringham rescinded his resignation.

67

Inco and Laurentian University have pioneered food production in Inco's inactive mine tunnels. Professor Joseph Shorthouse has been testing the growth of vegetables with underground light. Pictured are Peter J. Beckett (left) and Professor Shorthouse in Inco's Creighton Mine. Courtesy, Joseph Shorthouse

Scientists have also made significant contributions to the local quality of life. Professors from Laurentian University's biology department approached Inco during the winter of 1977-1978 to request the company's cooperation in developing subterranean food production. The professors thought it might be feasible to take advantage of the heat from the earth's core and, with the addition of light, grow food in an abandoned tunnel. Inco accepted the idea, agreed to provide the necessary artificial light, and provided agriculturalist T.H. (Tom) Peters and Alex Gray (the Inco gardener) to work alongside Professor Joe Shorthouse and assistant Doina Serbanescu. Experiments at the Creighton mine demonstrated that it was feasible to produce cucumbers and lettuce, although there were problems with tomatoes. Dr. Peters suggests that the experiments, now being repeated at a potash mine at Allan, Saskatchewan, indicated that it is economically viable to grow certain types of food in active mines. The cost of operating the hoist, however, would make operations in an inactive mine more expensive than the cost of trucking comparable salad products from Florida to Sudbury. The technology gained from the research is now available to miners who work in Arctic locations, where the cost of transportation is higher than in the Sudbury area, and Inco too is capitalizing upon it. With a biannual planting of 30,000 seedlings for trees in the Creighton mine, Inco can now meet its own reforestation requirements.

Inco and Laurentian University's biology department have cooperated on other projects. The first of these began as an Inco project in 1957, three years before the founding of the university, but as it progressed, the company and the university exchanged information. Before 1957 Copper Cliff suffered dust storms as the wind blew over its tailings—thousands of acres of waste rock from which minerals had been extracted. The dust blew into the homes of Copper Cliff residents and interfered with the smooth operation of Inco's machinery. Inco pioneered experiments in the development of vegetation which might grow amid, and then contain, the tailings. Various species of pine and spruce trees proved most suitable, and since 1976 the company has annually planted between 5,000 and 15,000 seedlings with a 60 percent success rate. By 1985 jack pines—the

PROMINENT PERSONALITIES

most adaptable of the trees—were reaching heights between four and five meters. Birds moved into the newly forested areas, and by 1981 bird censuses established the presence of waterfowl, shore birds, and other bird species previously unseen in the Sudbury area.

Another cooperative endeavour has been the regreening of areas close to Sudbury and along the highways approaching the city. Aware of public concern and the possibility of government action, Inco established monitoring stations as early as the 1940s to determine levels of sulphur dioxide emissions. By 1972 there were ninety-two such stations scattered throughout Northern Ontario, enabling the company to know the extent of damage for which it might or might not be responsible. The government of Ontario had stations of its own, but Inco located some on sites where the government had none, and it made its findings available to the provincial government. Inco also conceived the idea of the superstack, which would avoid concentrations of sulphur dioxide at ground level. The outside of the superstack was complete in 1970, the same year that a control order from the provincial government limited Inco's emissions from its Copper Cliff smelter to less than 4,720 tonnes per day. By 1983 the maximum permissible was 1,770 tonnes per day. (Falconbridge had a maximum limit of 930 tonnes per day in 1969, and 420 tonnes in 1982.) Inco's superstack became operational in 1972.

In December 1985 Ontario's newly elected Liberal government announced the toughest crackdown to date upon Inco's sulphur dioxide output. Concerned about the resulting acid rain, Environment Minister James Bradley ordered the province's worst polluters—Inco, Ontario Hydro (in Toronto), Algoma Steel (in Sault Ste. Marie), and Falconbridge—to reduce their emissions to 665,000 tons per year by 1994, a 67 percent reduction from the 1.9 million tonnes permissible in 1980. Bradley imposed the heaviest cut of all upon Inco, the largest polluter in North America, with instructions to cut by 77 percent. Charles Baird, Inco's chairman and chief executive officer, expressed concern that the costs might render Inco less competitive in world markets and force further layoffs from a payroll which had already fallen from almost 40,000 in 1976 to fewer than 15,000 in late 1985. (Falconbridge suffered a similar decline in the work force over the same period.)

Yet, despite their economic problems, the nickel companies and the Laurentian biology department continued to make progress in regreening. The cost of bulldozing some of the devastated areas seemed prohibitive until biology professor Keith Winterhalder thought of using school children to carry lime and fertilizer on an experimental basis. In 1975 elementary school pupils from St. Hubert's Separate School spread lime and fertilizer along Highway 144, and two years later pupils from St. Paul the Apostle Separate School did likewise near Coniston. Public money provided the financing. The experiments proved so successful that secondary school and university students subsequently found summer employment doing those same jobs on a larger scale. The federal government paid their wages, while the nickel companies were among those providing equipment.

With exceptions, it is the nickel industry that has dominated the lives of most Sudburians. The four longest serving cabinet ministers—Cochrane, McCrea, Gemmell, and Erola—were Ministers of Mines. Jim Jerome's greatest claim to fame locally arose from the Taxation Data Centre, which softened the blow from layoffs in the mining industry. Bob Carlin and Dave Patterson worked with miners, and Paul Desmarais transported them to and from work. Scientists have engaged in projects designed to offset the damaging effects of the mining industry and to exploit the positive. Sudbury's medical community has served the mining and nickel-producing people of the area and has improved their quality of life. The story of Sudbury's people is indeed intertwined with the story of mining.

CHAPTER VI

Bell Park on Lake Ramsey around 1930. The buildings offered privacy so that men and women could change their clothes. Photo by Michael J. Mulloy. Courtesy, Michael J. Mulloy

Sports and Recreation

Sudbury has always been strongly inclined toward sports and recreation. Such a tendency is evident from the many facilities that have permitted many local athletes to attain a high level of excellence.

Lacrosse was popular in the late 1880s, but it never regained its earlier popularity after a decline in the 1920s. Baseball's apparent ubiquity may explain why several of the local teams have managed to win provincial and national titles. Football has been played in Sudbury since the 1920s with the formation of the successful Sudbury Hardrocks and Spartans. Among the talented Sudburians to have played with a pigskin were Murray Mulligan, who played for the Toronto Varsity and Argonauts in the 1940s and 1950s; Mike Kovac of the Montreal Alouettes; Gene Cappeletti of the Hamilton Tiger Cats, Philadelphia Eagles, and Montreal Alouettes; Randy Fournier of the Ottawa Roughriders; and Kari Yli-Renko, who played for the Chicago Blitz of the World Football League. The best local player was Jim Piaskoski, an Ottawa defensive

THE SUDBURY REGION

Sid Forster, the highly successful coach of the Sudbury Spartans football team, anxiously watches his players.
Courtesy, Northern Life

lineman who won several all-star nominations and twice played on winning Grey Cup teams.

Immigrants have dominated Sudbury soccer, and their high calibre is obvious. The Sudbury Falcons and Falconbridge played at the provincial and national levels in the 1930s, and the German Olympias advanced to the eastern Canada semi-final in 1958. Since the 1960s, the best local squad has been the Sudbury Italia Flyers, Ontario Cup winners and Canadian finalists in 1964, while the Sudbury Polish White Eagles matched the Flyers' feat in 1969. From 1965 to 1969, Carmen Santoro entered the Italia Flyers into the professional National Soccer League, and from 1975 to the early 1980s the Sudbury Cyclones participated in this league. Recently the top local team has been the Laurentian University Voyageurs, a team that won several provincial titles and two national university titles, one in 1971 and one in 1983. Oscar Albuquerque graduated from the Voyageurs into the Major Indoor Soccer League, where he has become one of the best competitors and most highly paid players. At the junior soccer level, Mike Krauss and Dr. Ricardo de la Riva began in 1965 to change the ethnic atmosphere of soccer by building a Canadian image in the new Sudbury Minor Soccer League. Nowadays soccer appeals to Canadian-born players.

Curling was popular in the 1890s after the opening of the Martin's Rink in 1892 and the Young Street Rink the following year. By 1927, due to the quality of its organization, Northern Ontario won permission to participate in the Canadian Brier; it remains the only entry which does not represent an entire province. Over the years, Sudbury rinks have participated in ten national briers and have hosted the National Curling Brier twice, in 1953 and in 1983.

Hockey players have benefitted from the proximity of many frozen lakes, rivers, ponds, and boarded rinks during much of the year. Success has followed local teams: the Sudbury Senior Wolves and the Sudbury Junior Wolves, who won the 1932 Memorial Cup; the Sudbury Falcons, 1936 Allan Cup finalists; and the Frood Tigers, a team that won the Allan Cup and supremacy of Canadian amateur hockey in 1937. Other teams that have brought honour to the city include the Copper Cliff Redmen, who advanced to the Memorial Cup finals in 1937, and the Sudbury Wolves who, with the permission of the Canadian Amateur Hockey Association, represented Canada and won the world amateur championship in Czechoslovakia. In 1948 the Sudbury Wolves won a silver medal when they again participated in the world championship, this time in Stockholm. From 1959 to 1962, the Sudbury Wolves participated in the Eastern Professional Hockey League as an affiliate of the Toronto Maple

SPORTS AND RECREATION

Leafs and Detroit Red Wings. Since 1972 the Sudbury Junior Wolves have been a part of the Ontario Major Junior Hockey League.

Many talented players from Sudbury have played in the National Hockey League (NHL). Sam Rothschild, the first Jewish player in the NHL, played for the Montreal Maroons and the New York Americans from 1924 to 1928. Other prominent local players include W.T. "Shorty" Green, inducted into the Hockey Hall of Fame, and Redvers "Red" Green and Alex McKinnon, leaders of the first and only players' strike (1924-1925) against the Hamilton Tigers organization.

Hector "Toe" Blake played for the Montreal Maroons and Montreal Canadiens following his Memorial Cup victory in 1932. During his brilliant career, Blake played alongside the legendary Maurice "Rocket" Richard and Elmer Lach on the famous Punch line, won the scoring championship in 1938-1939, and received the Lady Byng Trophy in 1945-1946 for his sportsmanship and high level of play. Blake later coached the Canadiens to eight Stanley Cup victories. In 1966 he was inducted into the Hockey Hall of Fame. Another local hockey great was Art Ross, remembered each year with the Art Ross Trophy—awarded to the league's top scorer.

Bill Durnan, another member of the Hockey Hall of Fame and a former Wolves player, guarded the net for the Montreal Canadiens from 1943 to 1950. He won the Georges Vezina Trophy, given to the league's best goaltender, six out of seven years, including four in succession. Other local players include George

Opened in October 1983, the Valley East Recreation Centre offers swimming, fitness programmes, and squash to residents of the Sudbury Region on a year-round basis. Internationally renowned squash players frequently give exhibitions at the centre. Courtesy, Ron Mulholland

THE SUDBURY REGION

Above
The Sudbury Soccer League executives, 1965. Seated (left to right): George MacDonald; President Paul Salfi; past-president Bill Gaylor; Vice-President Angus MacDonald; and Treasurer Frank Pierce. Standing: Nike Krauss and Dr. Ricardo de la Riva, executive councillors. Courtesy, Northern Life

Left
The Sudbury District Junior Soccer League was highly active by 1966, just one year after it was started. Here, Bob Gills (striped shirt) of the Garson Gunners eludes Freddie De Luca of the Sudbury Police. Courtesy, Inco Triangle

Opposite page
Dr. Ricardo de la Riva poses with the Steelworkers Pee-Wee Soccer Team of 1968. Local 6500 of the United Steelworkers of America, as well as several small businesses in the Sudbury area, sponsor soccer teams. Courtesy, Ricardo de la Riva

SPORTS AND RECREATION

Kennedy, captain of the Toronto Maple Leafs in the 1950s and 1960s; Doug Mohns, a Boston Bruins player from 1953 to 1975; Gerry Pappin of the Chicago Black Hawks; and Eddie Giacomin, who won the Georges Vezina Trophy with the New York Rangers in the early 1970s before finishing his playing days with the Detroit Red Wings.

More recent local talent to play in the NHL include Dale McCourt, the 1977 Rookie of the Year; Mike Foligno, who played for the Detroit Red Wings and the Buffalo Sabres; Randy Carlyle, who won the James Ross Trophy as the league's best defenceman in 1980-1981 with the Pittsburgh Penguins before playing with the Winnipeg Jets; and Ron Duguay, who began his career with the New York Rangers in 1977 before being traded to the Detroit Red Wings, and represented Canada in the 1981 Canada Cup Tournament. Other quality players include Al Secord, an NHL player since 1978 who scored more than fifty goals during one season with the Chicago Black Hawks; Jimmy Fox, an offensive player for the Los Angeles Kings; and Dave Taylor of the Kings, who, in 1984-1985, was one of the league's best paid players. In the past Taylor played on the offensive triple crown line, and in 1984-1985 he acted as captain of Team Canada during the world championships held in Europe.

Some other Sudburians in the NHL include Alger "Al" Arbour, who, following his playing days, coached the New York Islanders to four successive Stanley Cups from 1980 to 1983;

75

THE SUDBURY REGION

As part of Sudbury's centennial celebrations, the city hosted the National Curling Brier in March 1983. The Ed Werenich team representing Ontario went on to capture the 1983 Labatt Tankard. Later the team won the world curling title known as the Silver Broom. Courtesy, Northern Life

Ron Wicks and Dave Newell, league referees in the 1980s; and several other players who resided in Sudbury during their playing days with the Sudbury Wolves in the Ontario Major Junior Hockey League. Such players include Don Beaupre, a brilliant goaltender for the Minnesota North Stars in the 1980s; Eric Vail, the 1974 Rookie of the Year with Atlanta; Dave Hunter, a double Stanley Cup winner with the Edmonton Oilers in 1983-1984 and 1984-1985; his younger brother, Dale Hunter, who in 1980 joined the Quebec Nordiques, where he has become a crowd favourite.

Sudbury has also had facilities necessary for figure skating. Many Sudburians have excelled: Ann Aubin in the 1940s; Joyce Salo from 1949-1951; Joy Barnard in 1958 and 1959; Nelson Bellmore from 1961 to 1963; the skating pair Gertie Desjardins and Maurice Lafrance, who won the national title in 1960 and in 1962 placed sixth at the world championships in Prague, Czechoslovakia. Sue Carscallen represented Canada at the 1976 Olympics in Innsbruck, Austria, where she placed fourteenth in the dance pairs, and in 1977 she placed sixth at the world championships in Tokyo.

The top speedskaters from the region are Frank Stack, Florence Hurd, and Alex Hurd—all of whom came to Sudbury in the 1930s to find work. All three had previously dominated different national and North American meets and participated in the 1932 Olympics in Lake Placid, New York, where both men were medal winners.

Owing to the presence of a strong Finnish community, Sudbury has produced several national level cross-country skiers: Arnold Back, the 1936 national champion; Lauri Tulkki, a 1937 provincial winner; and Paul Jansson, who was second at the 1939 Dominion Championship, first at the 1941 International Ski Classic in Duluth, Minnesota, and first at the 1949 Ontario Championship. A few years later, Lauri Huuki won the 1948 and 1949 Canadian races. In 1956 Bob Gray won the national junior championship, while Lynn Cullis captured the 1961 Canadian four-way combined alpine titles before becoming a member of the national team.

Sudbury cross-country skiers were at their strongest in the 1950s and 1960s. Arvo Ayranto won the Canadian championships in 1954, 1956, 1957, and 1958 and placed twenty-seventh at the 1958 World Cross-Country Ski Championships in Finland. In 1956 Antero Rauhanen won the Ontario men's race and came in second at the national fifteen-kilometer race. During his successful career, Rauhanen won thirteen Canadian titles, of which four were for the fifteen-kilometer race from 1958 to 1961. He won other fifteen-kilometer victories in 1963, 1966, and 1967, in addition to the thirty-kilometer race in 1960, 1961, 1963, 1966, and 1967. Rauhanen also won the fifteen- and thirty-kilometer events at the North American championships in 1957, and the thirty-kilometer race at this same championship in 1965. At

SPORTS AND RECREATION

After a successful period with the Wolves, Sudbury's Mike Foligno won the Ontario Hockey Association scoring crown in 1979, then played with the Detroit Red Wings and the Buffalo Sabres. He still plays with the Sabres and helps operate the Megasport school which trains the young in hockey.
Courtesy, Northern Life

the world championships in Poland in 1962, Rauhanen placed in the top thirty, while in Oslo in 1966 he placed fifty-ninth. In 1983 and 1985 this local champion participated in the Canadian Masters, where he won the fifteen- and thirty-kilometer events.

The list of prominent local skiers includes Matti Maki, a national level skier, who was on the winning three-man team in the 1968 North American championships, and Perry Sakki, the Canadian junior cross-country ski champion in 1980 and a member of the national junior team. Eric Rauhanen, son of Antero Rauhanen, has been the best Canadian biathlon skier from 1983 to 1985, with good placings in the ten- and twenty-kilometer races. In 1982 Eric Rauhanen placed in the low forties in the ten-kilometer race at the world championships in the USSR, while his younger brother Kenneth Rauhanen, who had placed third in the Canadian junior championships, won the 1984 Ontario University cross-country championship. The most recent discovery is Darren Derochie of Onaping Falls, who in 1984 was chosen to participate in a programme aimed toward preparation for the 1988 Winter Olympics in Calgary. In 1984-1985 Derochie won two golds, a silver, and a bronze at the national junior championships. Lately Sudbury has hosted two talented skiers—Reino Keski-Salmi, who died in a helicopter crash during the summer of 1985, and Cam Bryson, the Canadian junior biathlon champion in 1980.

From 1940 to the 1960s, there were several talented local basketball teams—the Sudbury Merchants, the Sudbury Incos, the YMCA, the International Hotel, and the Helpert Pistons. In the 1970s, a successful women's team appeared. The Laurentian University Voyageurs, led by the coaching of Norm Vickery and the play of Sylvia Sweeney of Montreal, won several national titles. In the 1980s, under a new coach, this team has performed almost as well. In 1984-1985 Carol Hamilton led the varsity team, was chosen as the top female player in the Canadian university circuit, and was selected to play with the national team training for the 1988 Olympics in Seoul, South Korea.

Other impressive local players include Gary Silc, who played for the Detroit Pistons; John McKibbon, a participant in the 1960 and 1964 Olympic Games in Tokyo and Rome; and Eli Pasquale, Canada's team leader on the court during the 1984 Olympics in Los Angeles. Prior to the 1984 Games, Pasquale was drafted by the Seattle Supersonics of the National Basketball Association.

Boxing gained popularity and acceptance at the turn of the century. Among the local pugi-

THE SUDBURY REGION

Above
Cross-country skiing is very much a part of the Finnish tradition in the Sudbury area. The competitions, known as "loppets," have since become a Sudbury tradition. Antero Rauhanen displays in this 1967 photograph the perfect stride during a race. Courtesy, Antero Rauhanen

Top
This picture depicts the Inco Loppet of early 1976. Courtesy, Inco Triangle

lists, a few talented individuals stand out: Johnny Teale, the 1940 Canadian amateur welterweight champion; Jack Thibeault, the Canadian heavyweight champion; Cliff Beckett, who twice challenged Sugar Ray Robinson; and Alex Mason, the 1949 Canadian welterweight champion. Another local boxer, Gordon Wallace, the 1949 Canadian and British Empire light heavyweight champion, defeated Ron Barton in 1955 for the British Empire championship. More recently, Bill Rannelli won a bronze medal at the 1978 Edmonton Commonwealth Games.

Finns have influenced amateur wrestling. Among the top wrestlers is Karl Lehto, who never lost a bout in America and who defeated the Canadian light heavyweight champion in 1921. Other wrestlers came in the 1930s in order to obtain employment in the mining sector; these include Nick Choma and "Chip" Chaplain, the 1939 Canadian middleweight champion. The greatest local wrestler was Matti Jutila, who won his first Canadian middle-

SPORTS AND RECREATION

Downhill skiing has long been a popular winter sport, thanks to the many hills in the Sudbury Region.
Courtesy, Northern Life

weight division title in 1957 in Greco-Roman and freestyle wrestling. During his career, Jutila won a silver medal in Perth, Australia, during the 1962 British Empire Games; was champion at the 1962 North American championships; and was a silver medalist at the 1963 Pan American Games in Sao Paulo. At the 1964 Olympics in Tokyo, Jutila managed to pin the reigning world champion, M.E. Saifpour of Iran. In 1979, Marcel Demore, a young local wrestler, captured a bronze medal at the world amateur wrestling championships in San Diego.

Local weightlifters have also experienced success. Aldo Roy, the 1984 Canadian Olympic weightlifting coach, won his first Dominion title in 1960, while his brother Ralph was second behind fellow Sudburian Murray Veno. Both brothers starred at the Canadian level, and in 1962 Aldo Roy finished eighth at the Commonwealth Games. Three years later he participated at the world championships in Iran. In 1967 he placed sixth at the world championships in Mexico and fifth in the Pan American Games at Winnipeg while Ralph placed eighth. At the 1968 Olympics in Mexico City, Aldo was fifteenth; a year later he participated at the world championships in Poland.

Kevin Roy, son of Ralph, took a gold medal at the 1979 Canada Winter Games, and a fifteenth, an eighteenth, and a ninth placing at the 1978, 1980, and 1981 junior world championships. In 1979 Roy's effort turned to gold in the America Cup and later in the 1980 Pan American championships, while in 1982 Roy set a new junior Commonwealth record with a 336-pound snatch. He also won a bronze medal at the 1982 Commonwealth Games in Brisbane. In 1983 Roy won a gold at the Pan American Games in Caracas and, in 1984, placed fourth at both the world championship and the Olympics in the light heavyweight division. Between 1978 and 1981, Rolly Chrétien also won many titles and events.

Since the 1950s many agile badminton players have graduated from Ed Staples' training programme: Ed Hreljac, the 1958 Canadian junior champion; Marie Barbe, the 1956 provincial winner; and in 1972 Ed Jreljac, nephew of Ed Hreljac, who won the Canadian junior doubles title. Lucio Fabris represented Canada in doubles in a 1974 meet in Mexico, won the 1976 Canadian mixed doubles title, and thus managed to compete in the All-England Championship, the World Badminton Championship in Malmo, Sweden, and in Thailand for the Thomas Cup. In 1978 Fabris helped Canada win a silver at the Commonwealth Games in Edmonton.

In 1925 Bill Beaton, later alderman and mayor of Sudbury, established the Sudbury Canoe Club. Through this organization several canoeists have reached the victory podium at the Dominion Championship Regatta. Among the elite paddlers is Don Stringer, who con-

THE SUDBURY REGION

Sports are an important part of student activity at Laurentian University. Here Carol Hamilton of the Laurentian Voyageurs Ladies' Basketball Team dribbles past an opponent during the 1984-1985 season. Photo by Perry Beaton. Courtesy, Perry Beaton

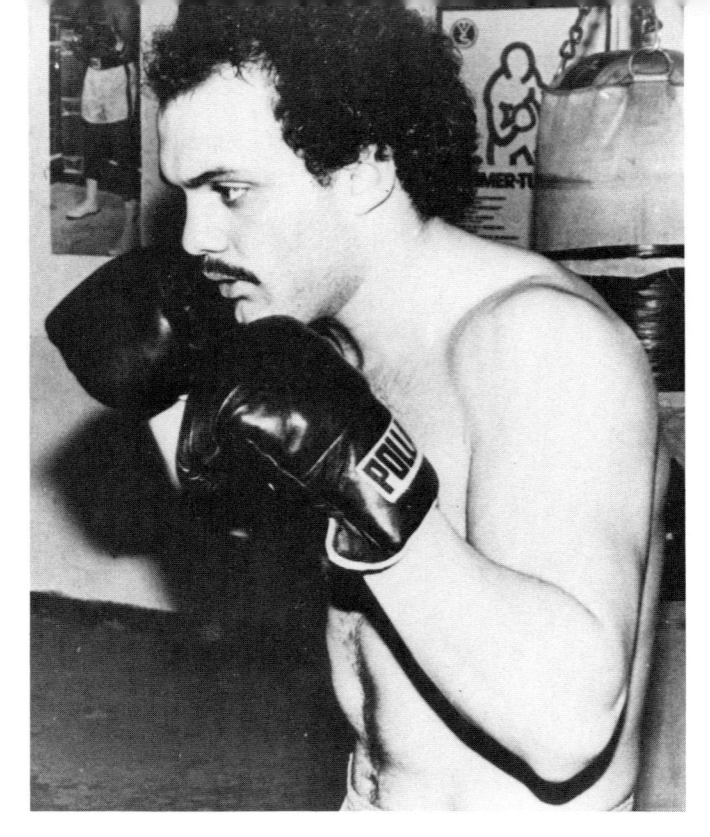

Gordon Apolloni of the Phoenix Boxing Club has been one of Sudbury's most successful boxers from 1973-1980 at both the provincial and Canada-wide levels. He has been a three-time holder of the Canadian Champion. Courtesy, Northern Life

trolled the Dominion championships through the fifties in the single blade event. During his career, Stringer won the 1952 President's Cup Regatta in the United States, set several Canadian records, and won the 1954 North American championships. In the 1956 and 1960 Olympic Games, Stringer placed seventh in the 10,000-meter final.

Two paddlers originally from Yugoslavia, Louis Lukanovich and Tony Petrovia, competed at the International Regatta in the North American championships of 1953 and 1954, while Lukanovich participated in the 1960 kayak tandem in the Olympics. Other talented participants were John Beedell and Joe Derochie (father of Darren Derochie, the cross-country skier) who both raced in the 1958 world championship in Prague, and in the 1960 Olympics, where the pair qualified for the semi-finals.

Sudbury has produced such track and field athletes as Percy Hagarman, who moved to California and in 1906 was named that state's all-round athlete. Hagarman also placed among the top three in the hurdles and the broad jump at the 1906 world championship in Great Britain. Prior to his arrival from Finland, runner Matti Ilomaki had trained and raced with the legendary Paavo Nurmi, the "Phantom Finn." Another Finnish runner, Taavi "Dave" Komonen, won the 1933 *London Free Press* marathon, the 1933 U.S. National Marathon Championship, the 1933 Canadian Marathon Championship, and the U.S. National Twenty-Five Kilometer Championship. Komonen's moment of glory came in 1934 when he won the prestigious Boston Marathon, after finishing

81

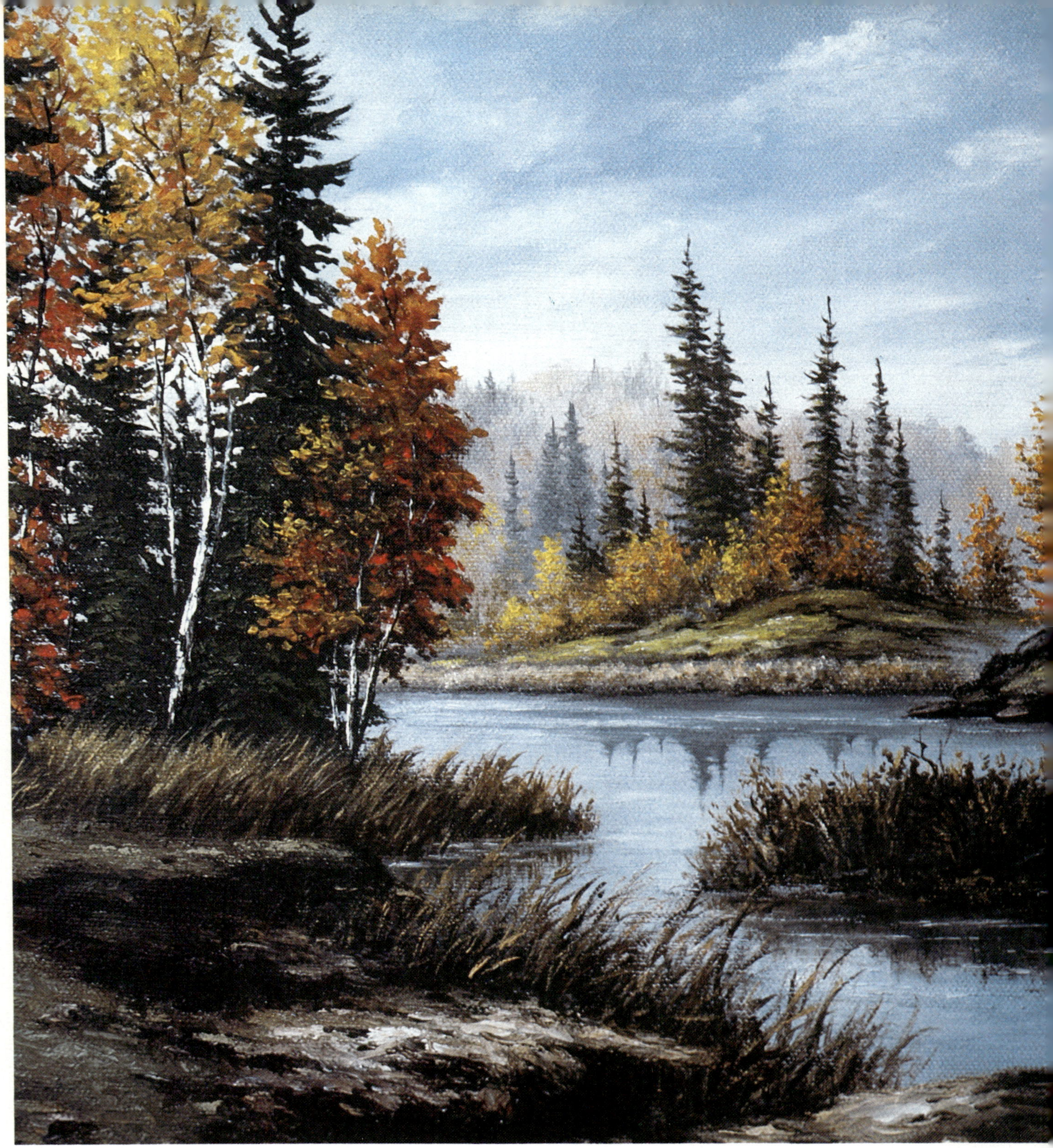

Above
The Sudbury Region has long been an area of fascination for local artist Albert Klussmann. Log cabins like this one were typical during Sudbury's pioneer era. This particular cabin is located in Morgan Township, north of Blezard Valley.
Courtesy, Albert Klussmann

Left
This autumn scene is of a beaver pond north of Capereol.
Courtesy, Albert Klussmann

Preceding page
Klussmann found this late winter scene near Chelmsford.
Courtesy, Albert Klussmann

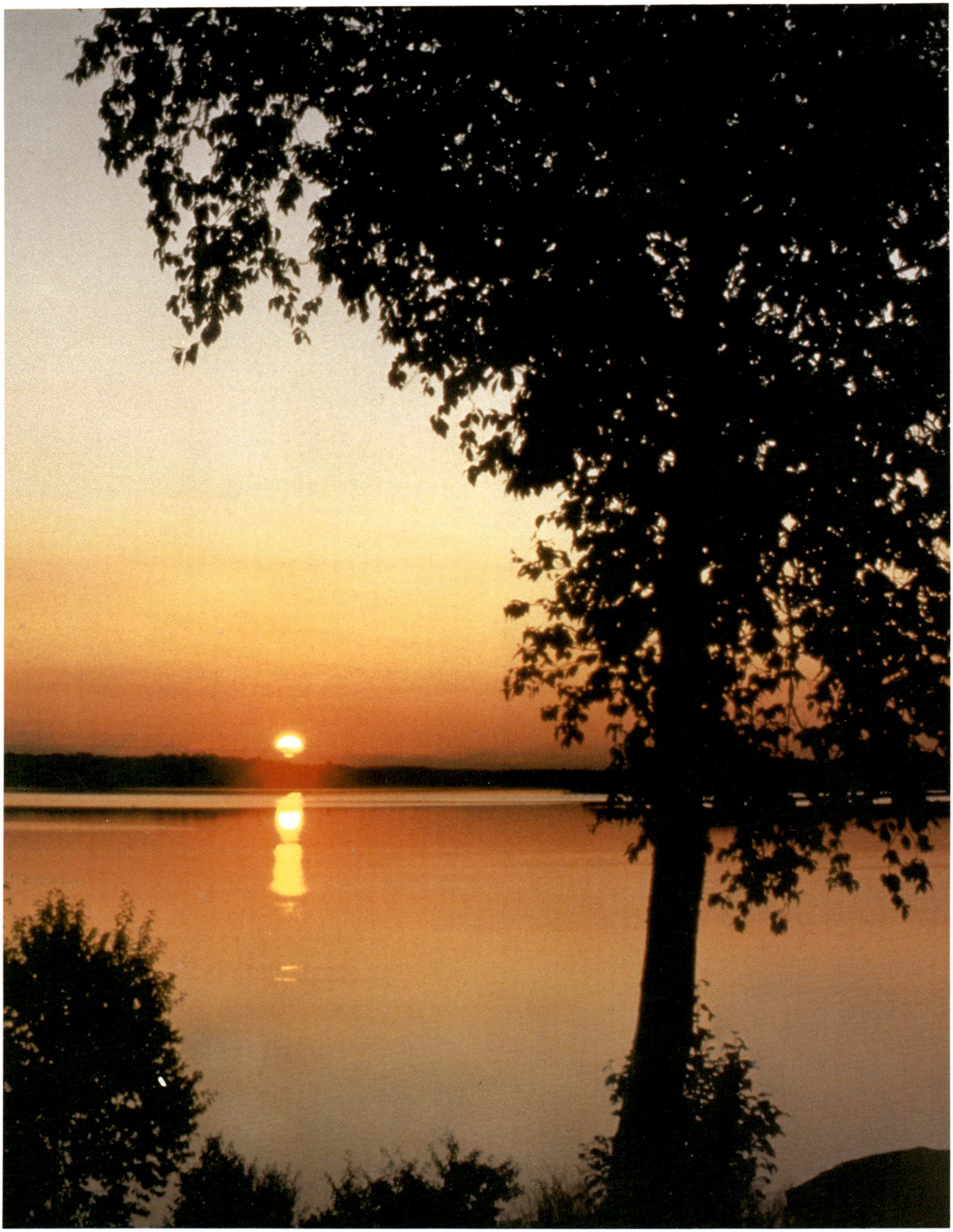

Opposite page
A beautiful sunset over Lake Ramsey. Courtesy, Sudbury Regional Development Corporation

Above
Frost-covered trees at Bell Park present a winter wonderland. Courtesy, Sudbury Regional Development Corporation

86

Opposite page, top
Fountain at Civic Square, downtown Sudbury. Courtesy, Sudbury Regional Development Corporation

Opposite page, bottom
Sailboats on Lake Ramsey, a few blocks from downtown Sudbury. Laurentian University is in the background. Courtesy, Sudbury Regional Development Corporation

Above
From pioneer days to the present, Sudburians have enjoyed sleigh riding as a form of winter recreation. Photo by Graeme S. Mount. Courtesy, Graeme S. Mount

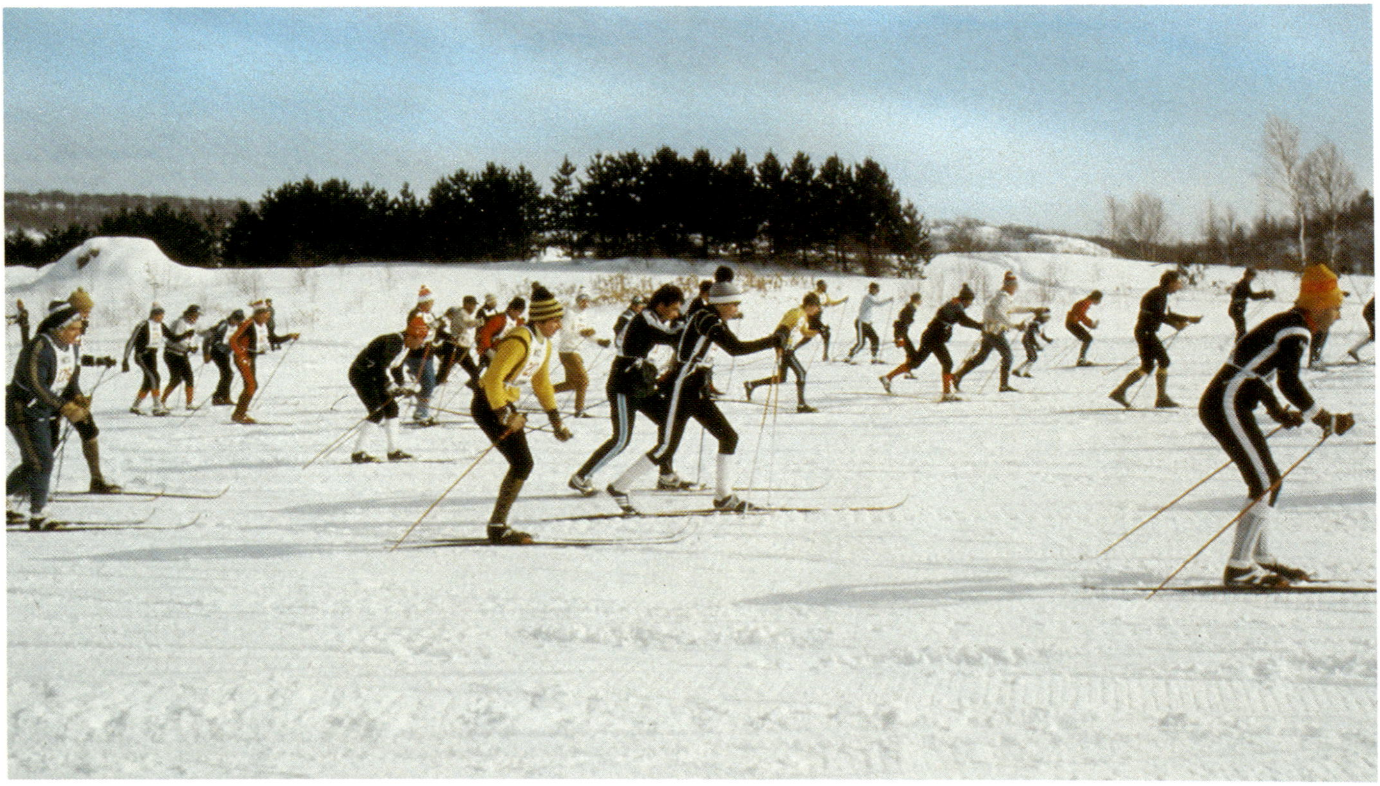

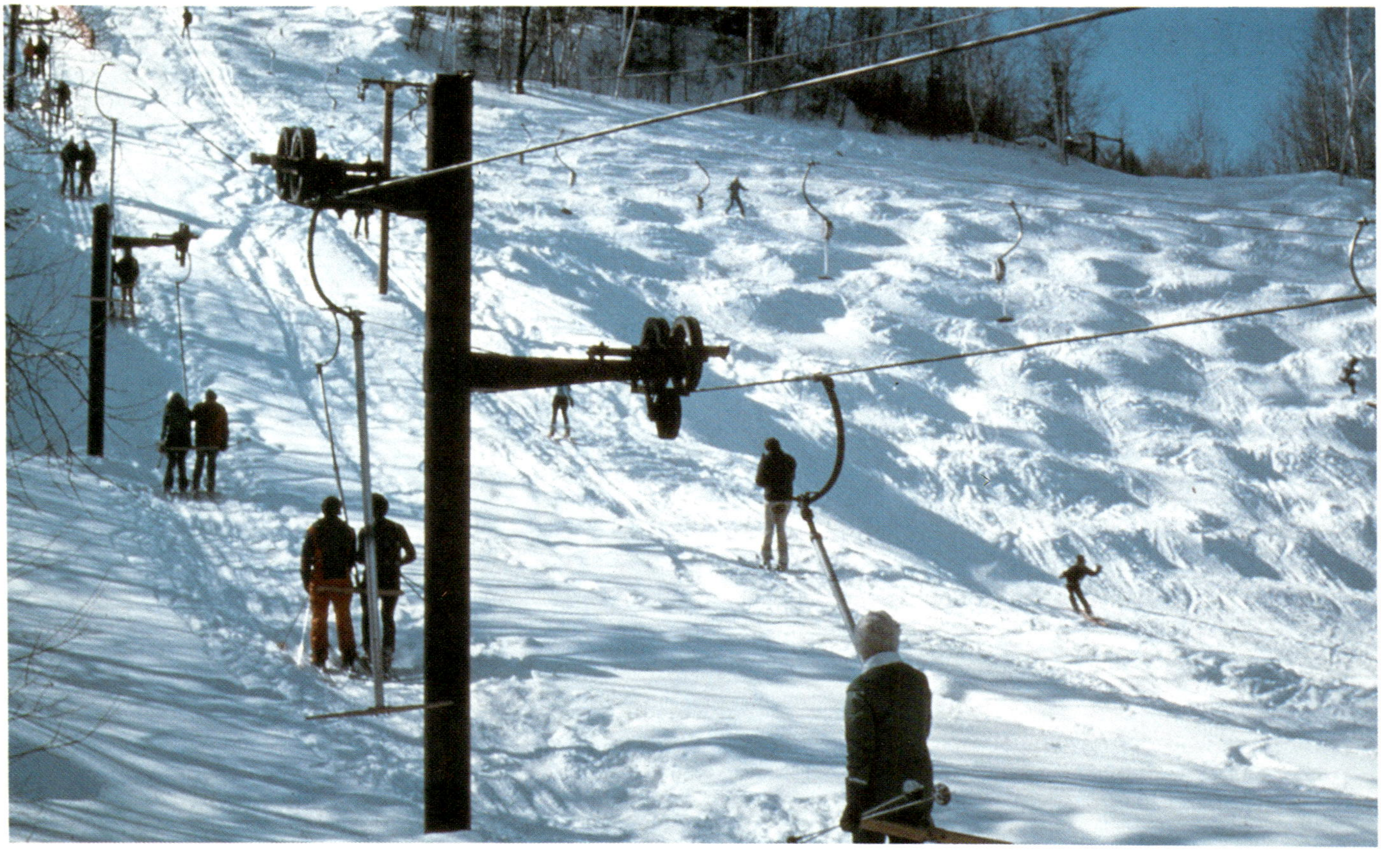

Opposite page, top
A Finnish "loppet" (a cross-country ski marathon) has been part of Sudbury's tradition since the Finnish immigrants' arrival. Courtesy, Sudbury Regional Development Corporation

Opposite page, bottom
The Levack ski hill and twin ski tow, north of Sudbury, is one of the region's many ski stations. Courtesy, Sudbury Regional Development Corporation

Above
Sudbury General Hospital, with Bell Park beach in the foreground. Sudbury offers several specialty hospitals; General Hospital specializes in obstetrics. Courtesy, Sudbury Regional Development Corporation

90

Opposite page, top
Ukrainian dancers have performed annually on Dominion Day since 1967. This 1984 performance was sponsored by the Multi-Cultural Centre. Courtesy, Sudbury Regional Development Corporation

Opposite page, bottom
Ukrainian dancers at Sudbury's Yarmarok Market Place, 1977. Photo by Bill Iwanochko. Courtesy, Mary Iwanochko

Above
Sap flows from maple trees each spring when the temperature rises above freezing during the day, then falls below the freezing point at night. Farms, such as the Despatie farm near Hanmer in the Sudbury Basin, produce sap, which their owners boil into maple syrup. Here, a horse-drawn sleigh makes the rounds of the sap-producing trees to collect the liquid while interested children look on. Courtesy, Graeme S. Mount

Left
View of Inco's smelter complex at Copper Cliff, showing the superstack—1,250 feet in height—and Sudbury in the distance. Courtesy, Sudbury Regional Development Corporation

Below
Highrise apartments on Paris Street, with Lake Nepahwin behind them. In the distance is Laurentian Hospital. Courtesy, Sudbury Regional Development Corporation

Paris Street, downtown Sudbury, at night. Courtesy, Sudbury Regional Development Corporation

Above and opposite page, top
The Science Centre North complex on the shores of Lake Ramsey serves as a museum as well as a site for scientific research. Opened in October 1984, it is run by the province of Ontario. Photos by Pierre St.-Jacques. Courtesy, Department of Regional Industrial Expansion

Right
The "Big Nickel" is the largest nickel in the world and a Sudbury landmark. Science North owns Big Nickel Park. Courtesy, Sudbury Regional Development Corporation

Opposite page, bottom
Science North also provides tours of working mines which have been renovated. Courtesy, Department of Regional Industrial Expansion

95

A suburban home on one of Sudbury's seven lakes. Courtesy, Sudbury Regional Development Corporation

SPORTS AND RECREATION

seventh in 1932 and second in 1933. In 1934 Komonen also won the London Marathon and the U.S. Amateur Marathon. Other Sudbury athletes of this era include Bill Neva, a long distance runner; Leo Tapper, a javelin thrower; George "Spike" Smallcombe, a triple jumper; and Ray Lewis, a sprinter.

Javelin thrower Leo Roininen went to the 1948 Olympics in London. In 1950, after attending the University of Michigan, Roininen won a bronze medal at the British Empire Games in the shot put and a gold medal in the javelin throw. In 1952 Roy Pella attended the University of Michigan and placed fourteenth in the javelin throw at the Olympics in Helsinki, while in 1953 Pella won the Rowell Trophy, given to Canada's outstanding amateur field athlete.

Track and field's growing popularity led to the formation of the Sudbury Track Club in 1963, to the construction of track and field facilities at several schools and at Laurentian University in 1970, and to the creation of the Northland Athletic Club by Terry McKinty. This club's runners have included Johanne Heale, the 1976 Canadian Ladies Marathon winner, and Chris Lavallee, the race's 1979 winner. Among recent Sudbury harriers, Veronica Poryckyj has won many events: the 1978 and 1979 Canadian junior 3,000-meter championships, the 1979 Ontario cross-country championship, and the 1979 Ontario Marathon. One of Canada's best in the 5,000 and 10,000 meters and in the cross-country run is Ray Paulins, who in his 1984-1985 school year set a new Ontario University record by running the 5,000 meters in 14:07.62. Sudbury has also watched the rise of two sprinters: Dave Case, who in 1979 won the junior indoor 200-meter championship and later received a track scholarship; and Marc Poulin, who in 1984-1985 ranked in the national top ten in the 800 and 1,000 meters.

The Laurentian University all-weather tartan track enabled Sudbury to host the 1975 Women's Dual Meet between Canada and East Germany, and in 1976 it attracted the East German Olympic team, which chose Sudbury as its training base prior to the Olympic Games in Montreal. In 1980 the city hosted the first Pan American Junior Track and Field Championship, in which twenty countries and more than 500 athletes from the Americas participated. Top Canadian athletes, including Angela Baily, Ben Johnson, Mark McKoy, and Charmaine Crooks, participated in these games. The future international stars who participated included Carl Lewis, winner of four gold medals in the 1984 Olympics in Los Angeles; Calvin Smith, another world-class American sprinter and 1984 Olympic medalist; and Joaquim Corvalho Cruz, a Brazilian gold medalist in the 1984 Olympics. Sudbury's reputation as a sports community enabled it to host the 1983 Canadian Games for the Physically Disabled.

Among the challenges for Sudburians are the 24-Hour Relay (organized since the mid-1970s) and the Voyageur Marathon. In 1982 Sudbury

Paul de la Riva, a son of Dr. Ricardo de la Riva, participated in the 1983 Beaton Classic, an annual event which involves running, cycling, canoeing, and swimming. Courtesy, Sudbury Fitness Challenge

THE SUDBURY REGION

SPORTS AND RECREATION

hosted its first Iron Man race, called "the Beaton Classic," during which the participants, competing alone or on teams of two or four, would swim 1.5 kilometers, cycle 31 kilometers, paddle 6 kilometers, and run 16.5 kilometers. Bruce Wainman, a local long distance runner, won the event during its first three years. The Iron Man has attracted several of the area's best athletes—Alex Baumann, Ray Paulins, Darren Derochie, Rob Quinlan, and Robbie Wallenius.

Sudburian Natalie Stelmach won the Canadian Women's Snooker Championship from 1976 to 1981. In 1980 this local pool player reached the world's semi-finals, and she won the World Mixed Pairs in 1981.

With the revival of cycling in the 1970s and the formation of the Sudbury Cycling Club in 1974, several athletes have won races under the guidance of Gianfranco Ronchin and, later, Battista Muredda. Such cyclists include Carlo Berardi, the 1976 Ontario Cadet Road Race champ and 1978 Canadian junior cycling champion; Claudio Vennier, the 1977 provincial junior champion; Eddy Fantasia, the 1974 Ontario Summer Games winner; and Paul

Above
In 1980 the first-ever Pan American Games for juniors (ages nineteen and under) took place in Sudbury. Here a runner from Brazil leads his competitors. Courtesy, Sudbury Fitness Challenge

Right
Richard de la Riva, another son of Dr. Ricardo de la Riva, finishes the running portion of the 1983 Beaton Classic. Courtesy, Sudbury Fitness Challenge

Opposite page, top
Literally hundreds of runners participated in the 1981 Ramsey Tour, a 21.2 kilometer annual run in the Ramsey Lake area. Tony Teddy of Sudbury was the winner of this race. Courtesy, Northern Life

Opposite page, bottom
Steeplechase runners hurdle the water jump during a race at Laurentian University, preparing for the Junior Pan American Games in the summer of 1980. Courtesy, Northern Life

THE SUDBURY REGION

Sudbury Cycling Club Coach Battista Muredda gives Gary Trevisiol some tips on competitive cycling. Trevisiol, who has been track-racing since 1974, is Sudbury's top racer. Shortly before this picture was taken in 1982, he placed third in the individual pursuit and second in the points race at a tournament in Edmonton. Courtesy, Northern Life

Girolametto, a participant in the 1976 World Junior Cycling Road Race in Vienna.

The most successful cyclist has been Gary Trevisiol, who was the Canadian junior road race champion in 1976 and 1977. Among his career highlights, Trevisiol had victories at the 1977 Canadian Summer Games and Montreal Grand Prix. In 1979 he participated in the Pan American Games as a member of the four-man pursuit team, won the Canadian Criterium, finished sixth in a world's points race, and represented Canada in the world championship in Holland. In 1980 Trevisiol was a member of the Canadian Cycling Association Olympic team, and in 1982 he raced in the Commonwealth Games in Brisbane. Other events in his career include participation in the 1981 world championships in Prague and Brno, Czechoslovakia, an eleventh-place finish at the Lowenbrau Criterium Series, and a victory in perhaps the oldest continuing bicycle race in America—the 1982 Tour of Sommerville—in a world record time. In 1982 Trevisiol raced at the world championships in England, while in 1983 he was a member of the pursuit team that placed fifteenth at the World Cycling Championship in Zurich. In 1984 Trevisiol placed seventeenth in the individual 4,000-meter pursuit and eighteenth in the points race in the Los Angeles Olympics, while prior to the Olympics Trevisiol participated in the Tour of Texas and the Oregon Stagerace, where he won a stage and placed tenth. He also participated in the Tour du Quebec, during which he won the Saint-Leonard Stage.

The greatest athlete from Sudbury has to be Alex Baumann, who developed into the world's best all-round swimmer from 1980 to 1985 under the guidance of Dr. Jeno Tihanyi. Baumann's first taste of international competition came in 1979 when he took part in the Coca-Cola International Meet in England. That same year Baumann won a gold medal at the Fina World Cup in Tokyo and a bronze at the Pan American Games in Puerto Rico in the 400 individual medley (I.M.). The swimmer set national and com-

Alex Baumann of Sudbury won two gold medals for swimming at the Los Angeles Summer Olympics of 1984. Winning the 200 and 400 individual medley events in record times, he returned home to participate in a ceremony where a park was named in his honour. This picture of August 1984 shows him wearing his two gold medals at the ceremony.
Courtesy, Northern Life

Alex Baumann celebrates yet another record-shattering triumph at the Los Angeles Olympics, August 1984, as he wins one of his gold medals. Photo by Lazi Perenyi. Courtesy, Lazi Perenyi

monwealth records in the 400 I.M. in 1980, the same year that he would have participated in the Moscow Olympics that were boycotted. Baumann showed in 1981 that he was definitely the world's best all-round swimmer by setting world records in the 400 I.M. in 4:17.41 and the 200 I.M. in 2:01.42. He then lowered the 200 I.M. mark again in the 1982 Brisbane Commonwealth Games, where he also won a gold medal in the 400 I.M. His best performance took place at the 1984 Olympics in Los Angeles, where he won the 400 I.M. and the 200 I.M. Following the games, Baumann received a hero's welcome in Sudbury, the Order of Canada award, and the Canadian Male Athlete of the Year citation.

Other Sudbury swimmers to have attained a high level of excellence include Jody McPhee, a gold medalist in the women's 200 I.M. during the 1977 Canada Summer Games, and Robbie Wallenius, who received a swimming scholarship at Arizona State University, swam the 200-meter backstroke at the 1979 Soviet-Canadian meet in Moscow, placed seventh in the Pan American Games, and swam in the 1982 Commonwealth Games in Brisbane. Jennifer Campbell was part of the national team in 1981 and participated in the 1982 Commonwealth Games, where she was fifth in the 200 I.M. and in the 200-meter backstroke.

Since its birth in 1883, Sudbury has had a very rich sports history. Over the years several local individuals have excelled and brought honour to the community, and it is clear that athletic activities will continue to be important to Sudburians in the future.

CONCLUSION

Nickel has been the dominant force in Sudbury life. For nine decades it provided an economic base, and even in the tenth decade the nickel companies remained the city's largest employers. Many who did not work in the nickel industry served those who did. The nickel industry lured thousands of people to Sudbury, and as it became less labour-intensive, people knowledgeable about the nickel industry promoted and developed mining machinery. In fact, the Ontario government spent $20,500,000 to create an Ontario Centre for Resource Machinery, designed to take advantage of local expertise and to help Sudbury diversify its economic base.

Secondary industry was difficult to develop in the Sudbury area when the nickel mines were expanding and looking for workers because, until the last decade, Inco and Falconbridge could lure workers with higher wages than most manufacturers could offer. Potential new industries could not or would not compete. Now, however, Sudbury has a pool of available labour, skilled in mining technology and aware of the kind of machinery most suitable for operations in mines. It is economical for companies that produce mining machinery to locate in Sudbury, because they can test their equipment in Inco's North Mine (near Copper Cliff), rather than operate from Southern Ontario. Toronto-based companies face expense and inconvenience if they must test their products in a distant community, and it is not feasible to build a test mine in Southern Ontario. The North Mine, by contrast, is a living laboratory. Because of these considerations, the Ontario Centre for Resource Machinery can assist manufacturers of forestry and mining equipment in a significant way. It provides funds to companies seeking to improve existing machinery or to design new machinery for Canadian and foreign markets, and it has had some successes. Four mining companies—Gardner-Denver Canada Incorporated (an American company), Miltor (a British company), Tamrock (a Finnish company), and Continuous Mining Systems Limited (wholly owned by Inco)—have established their Canadian headquarters in Sudbury. As the demand for Sudbury's nickel and copper diminishes, the region's future may rest increasingly with manufacturers of mining machinery who can test and produce locally and then export around the world. Tamrock, for example, recently received a multi-million-dollar contract to supply rock-drilling equipment to India.

According to T.L. "Spike" Hennessy, general manager of the Sudbury Regional Development Corporation, 124 manufacturing companies provided 2,500 full-time jobs in the Sudbury region by the end of 1984. Twelve of those companies, offering 147 new jobs, arrived in 1984, Hennessy said. This, of course, is essential, as Inco's unionized work force has dropped from more than 18,700 to fewer than 8,000 within the past fifteen years, and its total number of employees (management, technical, and labourers) has fallen from almost 40,000 in 1976 to fewer than 15,000 in 1985. The worst may yet come. In the words of *New York Times* reporter Andrew H. Malcolm, "Inco plans to drop permanently one worker every day over the next four years at a time when, on the average, three young workers join the city's labor market every day." The story at Falconbridge is similar, as layoffs (often disguised as "early retirements") have occurred frequently since 1978.

It was through the nickel industry that Sudbury made its impact upon the world, long before its emergence as a centre for the production of mining machinery. Each generation of the twentieth century has sent a Minister of Mines either to Queen's Park or to Ottawa. While visitors remember with horror the devastated landscape created by the mining industry, they can now observe regreening processes fostered by Inco and Laurentian University. Inco and Laurentian also worked together in the study of subterranean food production, a procedure that may enhance the name of Sudbury in distant places and which would have been impossible without the nickel industry.

In many ways, positive and negative, Sudbury

has been a "typical" Canadian city. More cosmopolitan than most, it does nevertheless reflect the Canadian mosaic. Often represented in federal and provincial governments by cabinet ministers, it reflects trends in other parts of the country. Yet, on occasion, as when it defied the Diefenbaker and Mulroney sweeps of 1958 and 1984 or sent Elmer Sopha to chop logic with John Robarts' Progressive Conservatives at Queen's Park, it has gone its own way. To a point, Canada is tolerant of diversity and non-conformity, and that has been true of Sudbury. Sudbury has been vulnerable to nickel markets, controlled by outside forces over which it has little control, but to some extent, that is the story of Canada. And Sudbury is one of the largest urban areas where both Canada's official languages are widely used and where bilingualism is a definite advantage on the job market.

Sudbury, past or present, has not been perfect. It has, however, offered hope, opportunity, and a satisfying way of life. With the passage of time the community has become increasingly sophisticated and diverse, and appears likely to continue along those lines.

Downtown Sudbury: St. Andrew's United Church is in the left background, Civic Square in the centre, and the Sudbury Theatre Centre is in the foreground. Photo by René T. Dionne. Courtesy, Inco

CHAPTER VII

A circa 1890 view of the Canadian Copper Company's smelter at Copper Cliff. The company, which began in 1886, became part of International Nickel Company, now Inco. Courtesy, Inco Triangle

Partners in Progress

Since the birth of Sudbury in 1883, the community has had its ups and downs. Once railway building in the immediate area was complete, work crews moved westward to Biscotasing, and with them went a substantial part of Sudbury's population. Only the presence of mineral wealth enabled Sudbury to survive, and while the mines have been the area's largest employers, their output and labour requirements have varied with world market conditions. There were labour surpluses during the Depression, and since the Vietnam War, layoffs and early retirements have concerned employees and other people with an investment in the community. The solution has been a diversification of the economy.

There have been several reasons why Sudbury is surviving the present crisis. First, Sudbury has had a labour force skilled in mining and capable of adaptation to the production of mining machinery. Second, the region sits at the junction of two transcontinental railway lines. Trains moving west from Montreal or north from Toronto on Canadian National Railways and Canadian Pacific must pass through Sudbury or Capreol on their way to Western Canada. As a result, westbound trains often merge in the Sudbury area and eastbound trains divide, and the Sudbury Region is the most important railway centre between Toronto and Montreal in the East and Winnipeg in the West. Third, a network of highways combined with the largest population base in northeastern Ontario and a central geographic location has contributed to Sudbury's development as a supply and service centre. People come to the region for medical care, university education, or shopping, and patronize hotels, restaurants, and entertainment centres. The Trans-Canada Highway and its alternate route from Montreal and Ottawa pass through Sudbury, bringing hundreds of thousands of potential tourists into the area every summer. Greyhound Bus Lines, Air Canada, and Air Ontario also have their northeastern Ontario headquarters in Sudbury. Finally, both the federal and provincial governments have invested heavily in the community, making it the unofficial capital of northeastern Ontario.

Mining remains the largest single source of employment, but Sudbury is no longer an overgrown mining town. Primarily a service centre, it offers its residents a wholesome lifestyle. Lakes within the city itself and throughout the region enhance the beauty and recreational opportunities. One can work at any of a wide range of occupations within easy distance of his or her place of residence, then enjoy organized sports, cultural activities, or wilderness solitude. One of Canada's most cosmopolitan cities, Sudbury offers food and merchandise from all parts of the world.

The following section details some of the industries, businesses, and institutions that make up Sudbury's heritage and strength. Through their participation they have helped to support this important literary and civic project. Their histories are worth telling, for they provide the foundation for Sudbury's future, and demonstrate that even in hardship there is progress.

THE SUDBURY REGION

SUDBURY & DISTRICT CHAMBER OF COMMERCE

Located at 40 Elm Street West since 1984, the Sudbury & District Chamber of Commerce is prominently positioned on Sudbury's main street. With "ninety years of promoting private enterprise," the chamber, initially known as the Sudbury Board of Trade, has been an important aspect of local history dating back to 1895.

On March 30, 1895, a certificate of formation of "the Board of Trade of the Town of Sudbury and the Township of McKim" was signed by thirty-four Sudburians. It reads like a Who's Who of the pioneer business community: D. O'Connor (lumberman), James A. Orr (publisher and

The Sudbury & District Chamber of Commerce has been serving the people of the surrounding area from its new office at 40 Elm Street West since 1984.

The Sudbury Board of Trade, predecessor to the present chamber, promoted the Sudbury area with the slogan "We're out after business."

printer), Arthur Ferris (builder and contractor), F. Cochrane (hardware merchant), T.J. Ryan (insurance agent), S. Fournier (insurance agent), M. Allard (manager of MacEwan & Co., a dry-goods merchant), D. Rothschild (merchant), P.S. Frawley (gents' furnishings), F.W. Holloway (mercantile agent), J.S. Gill (jeweller), M. Rothschild (butcher), B. Washburn (merchant), A. Hoffman Smith (broker), Geo. H. Lennon (merchant), W.J.C. Harvey (bank manager), H. de M. Harvey (insurance agent), A.W. Wolter (insurance agent), R. Dorsett (decorator), George Elliott (merchant), Robert Inches (contractor), J.H. Rowat (butcher), Neil McArthur (tinsmith), Francis Cook (mechanic), Arthur Evans (mason), S. Johnson (merchant), James Purvis (hardware merchant), John Frawley (merchant), T.M. Kirkwood (wholesale merchant), Alexander Paul (merchant), James White (butcher), R. Martin (boot and shoe merchant), Wm. Chalmers (merchant), and D.L. McKinnon (merchant). The document was declared before M.C. Bigger, a Sudbury lawyer, by James Purvis, who attested to being secretary of the board. In selecting Frank Cochrane as the first president, Sudbury's merchants astutely recognized his leadership abilities.

In 1942 the board of trade was renamed the Sudbury & District Chamber of Commerce. Continuing to represent the area's businesses would remain the mandate.

Today the chamber is active throughout the region and beyond as a voluntary group representing the business community. An insight into its scope is provided when it is noted that currently the group has ten active standing committees: employment/education, government affairs, membership services, program, public relations, regional committees (Capreol, Rayside-Balfour, Nickel Centre, Valley East, Onaping Falls, and Walden), retail, Sudbury export development, tourism, and transportation.

Whether the issues are recommending the granting of a charter to the Sudbury, Copper Cliff and Creighton Electric Railway (1903) or Reassessment (1985), the board of trade and now the chamber always has promoted ". . . . the Civic, Commercial, Industrial and Agricultural interests of the area. . . ." as its main objective.

Sponsorship is recognized as the catalyst so essential to the furthering of interest in Sudbury's rich heritage. Not surprisingly, the Sudbury & District Chamber of Commerce is the local sponsor of this publication. Over the years the chamber has worked co-operatively with local organizations in promoting regional ventures as they relate to improving the quality of life in the community. The examples of the purchase of the W.J. Bell Mansion as a Canadian centennial project in 1967 or the sculpture project at the corner of Brady and Paris streets as a Sudbury centennial project in 1983 illustrate this point.

MID NORTH MOTORS AND SUDBURY AUTO BODY SUPPLY

Mid North Motors, at 2100 Kingsway, is a tale of two brothers—Ron and Ben Scagnetti—while Sudbury Auto Body Supply, at 178 Thomas, was founded by Galdino Scagnetti. Although the stories of these two businesses span but a few decades, the Scagnettis as a family became involved in the Sudbury area prior to World War I.

Ben Scagnetti, Sr., came to Canada in June 1913 from Italy, opening a general store in Garson the same year. Three years later he married Christina Della Vedova of Creighton. Together they would raise a family of nine—sons Galdino, Ron, Ben Jr., and Fermino, and daughters Mafalda, Lillian, Diane, Argentina, and Inez.

Over the years Ben Scagnetti expanded his business enterprises. A partial listing of operations would begin with a general store in Garson.

In the late 1930s expansion included the opening of the Sudbury Products Company at the corner of King and Laforest, operating as a wholesale grocery dealing in such items as confectioneries, spices, and soft drinks. Actually, prior to their involvement with the automotive industry, the Scagnetti family members were general merchants for a variety of commodities including groceries, feed, coal, wood, dry goods, ice, and real estate.

Gradually Galdino Scagnetti moved from operating Sudbury Products Company at the corner of King and Laforest to establishing Sudbury Auto Body Supply at the same location. Over the years the firm, featuring "complete body supplies," has become the largest body shop supplier in the North, necessitating a move to a new 10,000-square-foot store at 178 Thomas Street. Owner Galdino Scagnetti and his two sons, Brian and Peter, have managed to establish a highly competitive wholesale/retail trade.

Ben Jr. and Ron Scagnetti pursued an interest in the automotive field. In 1951 Ben Jr. operated the sales and service department of a Ford and Triumph franchise in Garson. By 1955 Ron held an American Motors dealership on the Kingsway. A pooling of their resources in 1965 resulted in Ben Jr. and Ron operating from the Kingsway location, offering such franchises as American Motors, Mercedes-Benz, Mazda, and Toyota.

The year 1974 marked a major move for the entrepreneurs with the opening of Mid North Motors—a new General Motors dealership offering GMC trucks, Pontiac, Buick, and Cadillac automobiles. In 1975 the largest GM dealership north of Toronto was officially opened at 2100 Kingsway. Located on a 27-acre site, the dealership has one of the most complete service and body shop facilities in northern Ontario. There are sixty-five employees at Mid North Motors, which has an annual payroll of $1.3 million and annual sales of approximately $20 million.

Ben Scagnetti, Sr., and his three sons—Ron, Ben Jr., and Galdino—have been responsible corporate citizens. Today the three Scagnetti brothers with their various Sudbury businesses employ approximately 100 persons and have an annual payroll of about $2 million, and annual sales of approximately $30 million. Mid North Motors and Sudbury Auto Body Supply are a credit to the community—a testimony to dogged determination first exhibited by Ben Scagnetti, Sr., in 1913 when he began as a general merchant in Garson.

Galdino Scagnetti, founder of Sudbury Auto Body Supply.

Ronald J. Scagnetti, co-founder of Mid North Motors.

Ben F. Scagnetti, Jr., co-founder of Mid North Motors.

THE SUDBURY REGION

CAMPEAU CORPORATION

In recognition of Campeau's long-standing involvement in the community, the New Sudbury Shopping Centre extends the best wishes of the corporation to the people of the Sudbury region.

In October 1984 Campeau Corporation completed extensive renovations on the New Sudbury Centre, including the addition of the "Tastebuds" food court concept.

108

PARTNERS IN PROGRESS

MARCOTTE MINING MACHINERY SERVICES INC.

Raymond A. Marcotte's business venture is tailor-made for the Sudbury Basin. Providing mining machinery services, Marcotte Mining Machinery Services Inc. has a ready market in northern Ontario.

Incorporated on February 1, 1979, Marcotte Mining serves as a recent example of how a need was recognized by an entrepreneur. Raymond A. Marcotte came to Sudbury from Quebec in 1965. Thirteen years as the service manager for a northern Ontario mining equipment company served to provide Marcotte with a general understanding of the mining equipment field.

When his firm opened in the winter of 1979, there were two employees working in a 3,000-square-foot facility. One year later the fledgling venture moved two doors west on LaSalle Boulevard into expanded quarters. Today Marcotte Mining employs thirty-five and occupies a 35,000-square-foot plant.

It is a perceptive businessman who correctly reads the marketplace. Initially, Marcotte Mining met the assembling overload for already established companies. Soon the remanufacturing of worn and/or damaged trackless equipment associated with underground mining became the firm's raison d'être.

Design and development has become an important emphasis of Marcotte Mining. Innovation has become the norm. Recognizing the need for modifications in scoop-trams, the firm has developed a number of alterations that extend the reliability and durability of these vehicles. Accepted design modifications include the oscillating axle, centre hinge, and interface kit. As well, Marcotte Mining has developed a hydraulic portable line borer marketed as "Rambor" and a utility vehicle referred to as "Ramcar."

Ramcar II is designed to meet the unique conditions of underground work. Emphasized is the marked durability and low-maintenance features of Ramcar II. This innovative vehicle, dubbed "the most manoeuvrable and safest ramp machine available today," serves as a cornerstone of the firm.

An interior view of the shop. Scoop-trams are being remanufactured and new drilling equipment is being assembled.

Marcotte Mining is a family operation in the truest sense. Raymond A. Marcotte, Sr., is the president and his staff includes his four sons—Raymond K. Marcotte, Jr., service manager; Pierre F. Marcotte, shop manager; Paul J. Marcotte, vice-president; and John J. Marcotte, purchasing manager.

In 1979 sales for the new firm totalled $380,000. Today anticipated sales approach $5 million. The future augers well for Marcotte Mining. With a continued emphasis on design and development, Marcotte Mining Machinery Services Inc. will help to ensure that Sudbury has a viable, diversified economy. For the local firm established by the Marcotte family, Canada and the world serves as the market—a market of inestimable potential.

Seated in Marcotte Mining Machinery Services Inc.'s latest addition to its product line, the Ramcar III personnel vehicle, (from left to right) are Raymond K. Marcotte, Jr., service manager; Raymond A. Marcotte, Sr., president; and John J. Marcotte, purchasing manager. Standing (left to right) are Paul J. Marcotte, vice-president, and Pierre F. Marcotte, shop manager.

THE SUDBURY REGION

LAURENTIAN UNIVERSITY

Laurentian University celebrated its twenty-fifth anniversary in 1985 but there has been interest in postsecondary education in the Sudbury region for almost a century. Shortly after settlement started in the area, Father F. Hormidas Caron, S.J., obtained land from the Canadian Pacific Railway in 1886 in the hope that a college would eventually be built.

A few years later a petition requesting a college was organized by Father Eugène Lefebvre and sent to Monsignor David Joseph Scollard, bishop of the Diocese of Sault Ste. Marie. As a result, Le Collège du Sacré Coeur (Sacred Heart College) was opened in 1913. The Jesuit-run college provided an eight-year program of secondary and postsecondary courses. The college's charter gave it the right to establish universities in addition to schools and colleges.

During the 1950s interest in a northeastern Ontario university grew and the provincial government, aware of the shortages of university places, began to actively promote the establishment of new postsecondary institutions.

In 1957 the Jesuits established the University of Sudbury. A bill was passed in the Ontario legislature incorporating the new university as allowed in the original Sacred Heart College charter. Meanwhile, a prominent Protestant clergyman, the Reverend Earl S. Lautenslager of St. Andrew's United Church in Sudbury, aware that the United Church of Canada was studying the need for new colleges and universities under church sponsorship, formed the Northern Ontario University Association (NOUA). The object of the association was to found and support a United Church and/or Protestant university in northern Ontario.

Discussions took place between the provincial government and representatives from the churches, including the Anglicans, who were also considering founding their own institution. A major problem for church-run universities was that they were not eligible for provincial funding. A special committee was established, made up of representatives from the three church groups and with R.D. Parker, vice-president of Inco, as chairman. This committee provided a solution to the funding problem by recommending that the three churches seek provincial authority to establish a nondenominational university and that each church establish a federated college within the university, give instruction in religion and philosophy, and provide accommodation for students. Further negotiations followed and eventually the new university, named Laurentian University of Sudbury, was incorporated in March 1960, and the first students were enrolled in the bilingual university in September of the same year. Father Emile Bouvier, S.J., was president and R.D. Parker, chairman of the board of governors.

Dr. J.S. Daniel, Dr. J. Tihanyi, and Alex Baumann enjoying Laurentian's "Welcome Home" after the university's 1984 Olympic triumphs. This Laurentian student, under coach Tihanyi, won two gold medals.

The fledgling university operated at first in rented accommodations. The City of Sudbury provided the necessary money for a new site and soon a massive campaign was under way to raise money for buildings. In September 1964 Laurentian University moved to its new campus. The three colleges, the University of Sudbury, Huntington University, and Thorneloe University, also ran fund-raising campaigns and their buildings were opened in the same decade.

Three colleges, Algoma University College, Sault Ste. Marie; Nipissing University Collège, North Bay; and Le College universitaire de Hearst have become affiliated with Laurentian. L'Ecole normale de Sudbury was integrated with Laurentian as l'Ecole des sciences de l'éducation in 1974. Classes are also given in various towns, and there are distance education courses by correspondence and teleconference. Laurentian University can truly be called a northeastern Ontario university.

Programs have been expanded to keep pace with growth as full-time student enrollment has increased from 200 to over 3,400 on the Sudbury campus, with similar growth in part-time enrollment. Laurentian University, from its infancy, has received tremendous support from the community, and in turn has contributed culturally, socially, and economically to the Sudbury region.

—Gwenda Hallsworth

The 750-acre campus is bordered by lakes and a golf course.

L'UNIVERSITÉ LAURENTIENNE

L'Université Laurentienne vient de célébrer son vingt-cinquième anniversaire en 1985, mais c'est depuis près d'un siècle que la région de Sudbury s'intéresse aux études universitaires. En effet, peu après l'établissement de pionniers dans la région, le Père Hormidas Caron, S.J. avait en 1886 obtenu des terrains de la compagnie de chemin de fer Pacifique Canadien, dans l'espoir d'y construire un jour un collège.

Quelques années plus tard, c'est le Père Eugène Lefebvre qui organise et envoie à Monseigneur David Joseph Scollard, évêque du Sault-Sainte-Marie, une pétition demandant l'établissement d'un collège, et c'est ainsi qu'en 1913 le Collège du Sacré Coeur fut ouvert. Ce collège de Jésuites offrait un programme de huit années de cours secondaires et post-secondaires. Selon sa charte, le collège avait le droit d'établir non seulement des écoles et collèges, mais aussi des universités.

Au cours des années 1950, on s'intéressait de plus en plus à l'idée d'une université du Nord-Est de l'Ontario, et le gouvernement provincial, conscient du nombre restreint de places dans les universités, a commencé à promouvoir activement la fondation de nouveaux établissements d'enseignement post-secondaire.

En 1957, les Jésuites ont fondé l'Université de Sudbury. L'assemblée provinciale de l'Ontario a approuvé un décret incorporant la nouvelle université selon les termes de la charte du Collège du Sacré Coeur. Entre temps, un pasteur protestant connu, le Révérend Earl S. Lautenslager de l'église unie St. Andrew's de Sudbury, qui savait que l'Eglise unie du Canada étudiait les possibilités de fonder de nouveaux collèges et universités sous l'égide d'une Église, a créé l'Association pour une université du Nord de l'Ontario (Northern Ontario University Association, NOUA) dont le but était de fonder et financer dans le Nord de l'Ontario soit une université de l'Église unie, soit une université protestante.

Des pourparlers ont eu lieu entre le gouvernement provincial et les représentants de diverses Églises, dont l'Église anglicane où l'on envisageait également de fonder une université. Un problème considérable se posait: les universités organisées par les Églises ne pouvaient pas recevoir de financement public de la province. On a fondé alors un comité spécial, formé de représentants de chacune des trois Églises et présidé par R.D. Parker, vice-président de l'Inco. C'est ce comité qui a proposé la solution au problème du financement, en recommandant que les trois Églises demandent que la province autorise la fondation d'une université non-confessionnelle; chaque Eglise aurait un collège fédéré où l'on enseignerait la religion et la philosophie, et où logeraient les étudiants. Les négociations ont continué, et finalement en été incorporée sous le nom d'Université Laurentienne de Sudbury. Les premiers étudiants se sont inscrits en septembre de la même année dans la nouvelle université bilingue. Le Père Émile Bouvier, S.J. en était le Recteur, et R.D. Parker était le président du Conseil des Gouverneurs.

Tout d'abord la Laurentienne a utilisé des locaux loués. La Cité de Sudbury a procuré le financement nécessaire pour acquérir un nouvel emplacement, et bientôt on lançait une importante campagne financière en vue de la construction. En septembre 1964, l'Université Laurentienne s'est installée dans son nouveau campus. Les trois collèges, à savoir l'Université de Sudbury, l'Université Huntington et l'Université Thornloe on organisé leurs propres campagnes de financement, et ont aussi inauguré leurs édifices au cours des années 1960.

Trois collèges, le collège universitaire d'Algoma au Sault-Sainte-Marie, le collège universitaire de Nipissing à North Bay, et le collège universitaire de Hearst, se sont affiliés à l'Université Laurentienne. En 1974, l'École normale de Sudbury a été intégrée à la Laurentienne sous le nom d'École des sciences de l'éducation. Des cours sont également donnés dans diverses localités, et aussi à distance par correspondance et téléconférence, et c'est pourquoi la Laurentienne est véritablement l'Université du Nord-Est de l'Ontario.

Les programmes se sont diversifiés à mesure que le nombre d'étudiants a passé de deux cents à plus de trois mille quatre cents à Sudbury, avec une croissance comparable pour les étudiants à temps partiel. Depuis ses débuts, l'Université Laurentienne bénéficie du soutien incomparable de la collectivité, et à son tour elle contribue à la vie culturelle, sociale et économique de la région de Sudbury.

—Gwenda Hallsworth
Traduction par Françoise Arbuckle

L'Université Laurentienne a pour mission de fournir une éducation de niveau universitaire aux deux groupes linguistiques qui forment le Nord-Est de l'Ontario.

Son Altesse Royale le duc d'Edimbourg parcourant les sentiers de l'Arboretum de l'Université Laurentienne, 1984. Le président du Conseil des gouverneurs, monsieur Normand Forest, et le recteur John Daniel accompagnaient son Altesse pendant la visite.

THE SUDBURY REGION

FALCONBRIDGE LIMITED

For more than a century the mineral riches of the Sudbury Basin have been recognized. Indisputably, an integral part of the mining chapter in the region is Falconbridge Limited. Though the story of Falconbridge as a corporate entity dates to August 28, 1928, the actual tale began to unfold in 1901.

Thomas A. Edison of Orange, New Jersey, invented the nickel-iron storage battery, taking out a U.S. patent in 1901. During that year he came to the Sudbury Basin, diamond drilling on sites in Falconbridge Township located by magnetic instruments. Detecting strong evidence of an ore body, Edison sunk one shaft but was stopped when he encountered quicksand. In time the American inventor allowed the claims to revert to the Crown.

In 1915 the area was restaked for the Minneapolis and Michigan Development Company and turned over to the E.J. Longyear Company of Minneapolis, Minnesota, for development. During 1916-1917 the E.J. Longyear Company was able to outline an ore body of some five million tons of nickel ore.

Thayer Lindsley, as a geologist for McIntyre, became interested in the area as early as 1924, and later, as president of Ventures Limited, he purchased the property. On August 28, 1928, Falconbridge Nickel Mines Limited was incorporated in order to develop the ore body.

Immediately the site experienced a flurry of activity with the sinking of a shaft and the construction of a 300-ton-per-day smelter. By February 1930 Shaft No. 1 was hoisting ore and the new smelter had been blown in. To secure territorial rights to a refining process, Falconbridge purchased a refinery in Norway in 1928. Two years later the first matte was shipped to the upgraded refinery, with refined Falconbridge nickel ready for the European markets by July 1930.

During the period prior to World War II, extensive development of the Falconbridge properties took place. Soon the Falconbridge concentrator (mill) was constructed to process the ore before smelting, beginning production in 1933 with a capacity to treat 153 tons of low-grade ore per day. Falconbridge Mine continued to

A noon hour in 1935 at Shaft No. 1 in Falconbridge. Falconbridge Nickel Mines Limited, until the 1970s, had two company towns—Falconbridge and the Onaping Townsite.

The first crew at Shaft No. 1 in September 1928.

112

The $83-million smelter complex is an important addition to Falconbridge Limited's Sudbury operations.

produce ore until 1984, when it was shut down following fifty-four years of operation. East Mine, adjacent to Falconbridge Mine, continues operations today—as does the original Falconbridge Mill.

World War II saw the Germans seize Falconbridge's Norwegian refinery on April 9, 1940. For the duration of the war Inco would refine Falconbridge smelter matte.

During the 1950s Falconbridge made a significant move to develop its properties northwest of Sudbury, moving from the continued dependence on the single ore body around Falconbridge Mine. By 1950 the first ore was received from McKim Mine and the development was under way at East Mine and Hardy Mine.

Though diamond drilling had indicated a significant ore body in Levack Township, serious work only began with the construction of the Hardy Mill and Mine in 1951. Soon Hardy would be followed by Fecunis Lake, Longvac, Boundary, Onaping Mine, and the Fecunis Lake Mill. Since 1960 the company's Onaping area mines have supplied the bulk of the ores. In 1968 the large Strathcona Mine and Mill began operations, Lockerby Mine in 1977, and the firm's first metric site, Fraser Mine, in 1981.

Not surprisingly, considerable changes have occurred in the mining industry. From 1974 to 1978 the energies and capital at Falconbridge Limited were concentrated on the construction of a new smelter at Falconbridge Township. Code-named SEIP (Smelter Environmental Improvement Project), the new smelter was designed to meet guidelines established by the Ontario government. In contrast to the 1950s, when 85 percent of the sulphur in the ore was released to the atmosphere during smelting, today about 88 percent is contained. Together with an associated sulphuric acid plant, the price tag was near $84 million. The new smelter, which provides an improved work environment, meets the regulations of the Ontario Ministry of the Environment.

Also, there has been an expansion of the use of labour-saving machinery. One development—a remote-control scoop tram—provides a way for ore to be recovered from difficult underground areas. An experimental hydraulic hoisting project, successfully tested at Onaping Mine, is a new technique of hoisting crushed ore to the surface in a stream of water.

In 1978 Falconbridge completed a $3-million tailings disposal and water-treatment facility where the water used in the various processing operations undergoes a purification process and is released to a pond. This area has since been declared a wildlife sanctuary.

Although once controlled by offshore interests, since 1983 Falconbridge Limited has been owned by Canadians with the head office in Toronto. William James is the president of Falconbridge Limited and George Reed is the Sudbury general manager.

Falconbridge Limited is a significant producer of not only nickel but also copper, cobalt, silver, and platinum with operations in Ontario, Quebec, Yukon Territory, the Northwest Territories, Norway, the United States, the Dominican Republic, Namibia, and Zimbabwe. The firm, whose Sudbury operation alone in 1985 produced seventy million pounds of nickel, is one of the largest nickel producers in the Free World. In the Sudbury Basin, with around 2,600 employees, Falconbridge Limited continues as one of the region's major employers.

The scoop tram exemplifies the use of the latest in technology at Falconbridge Limited.

THE SUDBURY REGION

TAMROCK CANADA INC.

Tamrock is a multinational company focussing on the development and manufacturing of percussive rock-drilling equipment. Tamrock Canada Inc. is the Canadian subsidiary of Tamrock Inc. of Finland.

Before the advent of hydraulic jumbos, Tamrock was at the forefront of production for pneumatic rigs. Such is the case today for hydraulics. The introduction of the hydraulic rock drill helped to establish Tamrock—a Canadian company that would be both a manufacturer and distributor of equipment for the mining and construction industries.

In 1978 Tamrock was established in Walden—a community just west of Sudbury that was selected as the location for the corporate headquarters. Considering the importance of Sudbury to the mining industry, the site selection was not surprising. Design and manufacturing is a key component of the Sudbury Basin operation. Vancouver has a marketing, parts distribution, and service facility to aid Tamrock in meeting the market demands of Western Canada.

Tamrock products are for both surface and underground drilling. Underground mining products include hydraulic jumbos, longhole drills, roofbolters, scalers, secondary drill units, and hand-held tools. Along with a range of equipment, Tamrock offers its clients a choice of hydraulic or pneumatic systems. Surface equipment production provides hydraulic track drills including the "Herbert" model—the world's largest percussion tophammer for open-pit operations. Indicative of the emphasis on versatility, Tamrock is manufacturing a rubber-tired unit specifically for road building. For the construction industry, equipment is designed for quarrying, road building, civil engineering construction, and tunnelling. To quote the firm's president, "Tamrock has been the forerunner in the design and application of large gantry jumbos." One current project of significance involves a large Canadian Pacific Railway tunnelling project through the Rockies near Revelstoke, British Columbia.

Design and development is an important aspect of Tamrock, and engineers work closely with the firm's clients to identify their specific needs. Most of what Tamrock manufactures is based on a modular concept; hence, existing and custom-made components combine to provide customers with a unit designed

Drilling jumbos being manufactured in Tamrock Canada's Sudbury operations, 1984.

Tamrock Canada Inc.'s corporate headquarters and manufacturing plant in Sudbury.

PARTNERS IN PROGRESS

A Tamrock solo drill used for sub-level cave mining at Inco's Stobie Mine in 1985.

to meet particular specifications. What results is a unit developed that will maximize performance.

Tamrock currently has a work force of over sixty people. As much as possible, local personnel have been hired, with the work force containing skilled mechanics, electricians, welders, and engineers.

Terry E. Sirois, president of Tamrock, came to Tamrock in 1983. He states, "... to our customers and to ourselves, Tamrock is a way of life." The corporate philosophy he expresses is one that embodies a commitment to excellence. Fundamental values emphasized include "quality, product integrity, performance, after-sales support, and trust." It is evident that there is considerably more to Tamrock Canada Inc. than just productivity and a balance sheet.

Tamrock is national in scope, serving the mining industry across Canada. Clients geographically range from New Brunswick Mining and Smelting in the East to Westmin Resources on Vancouver Island on the West Coast. Tamrock products are used in the North at the Polaris property on Cornwall Island in the Arctic. Customers include Inco, Falconbridge Limited, Lac Minerals (Hemlo), Noranda, Pamour in Timmins, Sherritt Gordon in Manitoba, and Echo Bay (forty miles south of the Arctic Circle).

First and foremost, Tamrock is committed to serving the domestic market. After national needs have been met, the firm helps to meet international needs. Tamrock often supplies the export market when Canadian-sponsored projects are undertaken. One example is the Chamera hydropower project in India, where the company provided twenty-seven large hydraulic jumbos and six pneumatic air tracks.

Tamrock provides a wide range of services with an emphasis on after-sales support. Customers are encouraged to utilize the training facilities at the Walden base in order to become familiar with their equipment. The firm also offers a field service staff to provide mechanical service on site. An extensive inventory of millions of dollars in spare parts is kept to service the domestic market.

Tamrock stands as an example of a progressive company in the area that has a conservative yet steady growth rate. Sirois notes, "... growth is pegged with the production improvements we can provide to the mining and construction industries in Canada." As a local manufacturer, Tamrock has had a significant impact on the Sudbury Basin in terms of local employment and dollars invested. In the truest sense, Tamrock Canada Inc. is an excellent example of local economic diversification.

A DHH track drill, manufactured by Tamrock, in operation at the Falconbridge Nickel Mine's No. 1 open pit mine.

115

THE SUDBURY REGION

INCO LIMITED

The year 1986 signifies 100 years of mining activity in the Sudbury Basin. Closely identified with this colourful saga of the area's history has been Inco Limited and her predecessors, dating back to 1886.

The Sudbury Basin was unwilling to yield its precious ore without some persuasion. In 1848, and again in 1856, the presence of nickel was identified in the area. However, because of limited uses for the metal and the problems associated with its extraction, the discoveries were ignored.

In 1883 the Canadian Pacific Railway was being pushed across Canada. One cutting through an outcrop yielded copper sulphide on the right of way. Almost immediately, there was a flurry of interest by surveyors and prospectors. Rinaldo McConnell, Francis Crean, Thomas Frood, James Stobie, F.J. Eyre, Henry Ranger, Robert Tough, John Cryderman, Thomas Baycroft, and William Mcvittie would all be identified with subsequent mineral discoveries.

Once located, the major task was to recover the ores. It is here that entrepreneur Samuel J. Ritchie of Ohio enters the Sudbury scene. On January 6, 1886, with capital of two million dollars, the Canadian Copper Company was incorporated and Ritchie became president. Mining would begin on May 1, 1886, at the Copper Cliff mine and later in the same year at the Evans and Stobie mines. Then the primary metal sought was copper; there was limited demand for nickel. In that year prominent visitors to the Canadian Copper Company mines included Prime Minister Sir John A. Macdonald and Lady Macdonald.

As well as acquiring properties for the Canadian Copper Company, Ritchie had two other tasks—to find a way by which nickel could be separated from copper ore and to secure markets for the products. R.M. Thompson and the Orford Copper Company of New Jersey had the technique for separation. As for the market, continued lobbying in the United States resulted in a U.S. government contract in 1890 for use of the alloy in connection with naval armaments.

In April 1902 the International Nickel Company was formed, resulting from the mergers of a number of firms, including the Canadian Copper Company and the Orford Copper Company. The corporate headquarters remained in Copper Cliff. Now most of the principal concerns involved in mining, smelting, and refining nickel were together.

During the next few years the International Nickel Company was closely associated with developments to increase the uses of nickel. In 1905 Monel metal—a new alloy noted for strength and resistance to acidity—was perfected. As well, other uses for nickel were found in the automotive and bridge construction industries.

During the war years Inco's energies were channelled toward the war effort. However, with the return to peace, research and development concentrated on identifying and promoting new uses for the product. A few areas of increased usage included appliances and the automotive industry, where materials that were both light and strong were sought.

For the first quarter of the twentieth century, International Nickel and the Mond Nickel Company controlled most of the nickel market, with the Sudbury Basin as their main supply source. International Nickel was concentrated west of Sudbury, with milling, smelting, and the administrative centre at Copper Cliff, and Mond east of Sudbury with its smelter at Coniston. In 1929 International Nickel and Mond merged to mine their adjacent Frood properties. Consolidation of numerous facilities

Copper Cliff miners around the turn of the century. Note the candle lamps on the miners' hats.

The continuous loader, built by Inco's Continuous Mining Systems, features an oscillating lip and steel flytes. Ore is continuously removed from a production stope and loaded onto conveyor belts or into haulage vehicles.

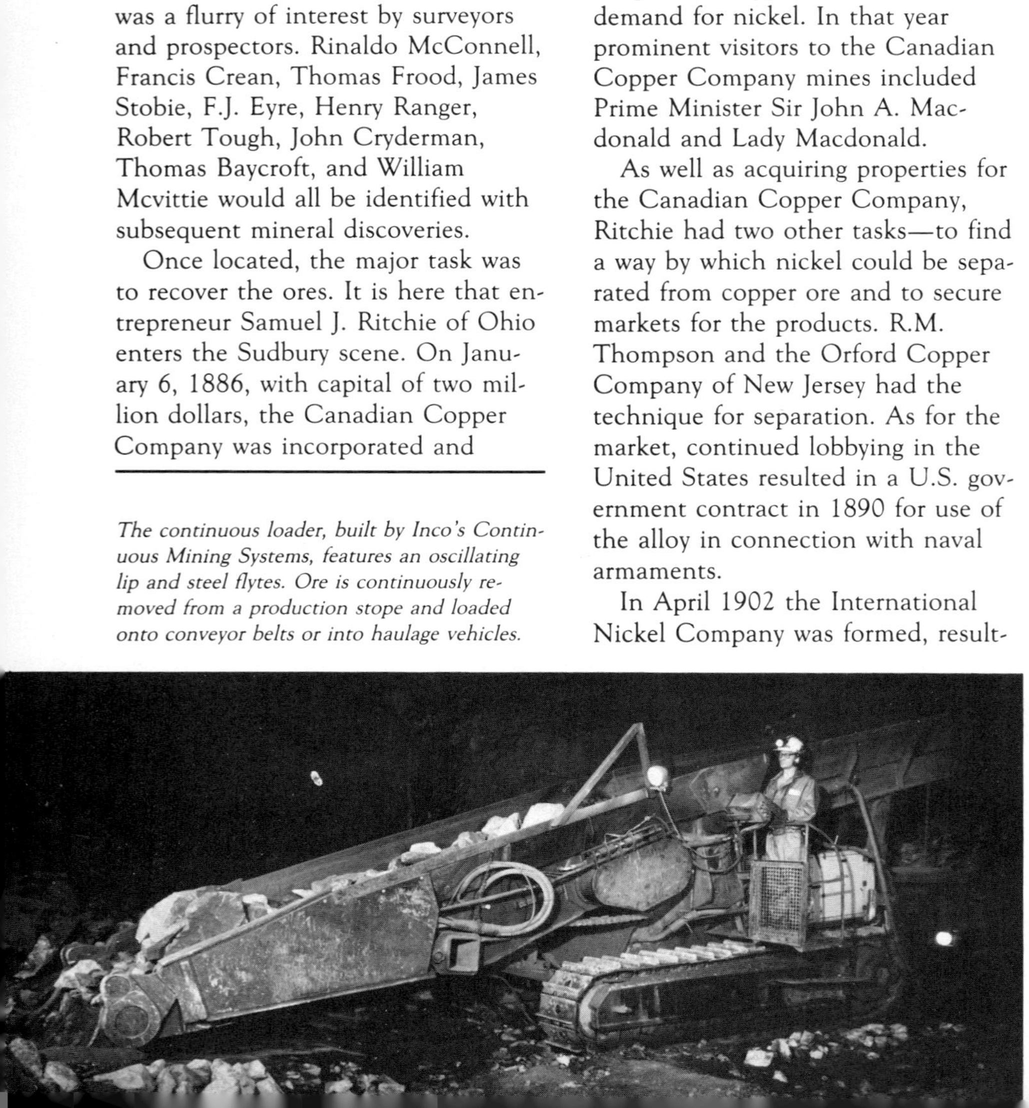

made the merger eminently practical. The following year the Copper Cliff smelter and the Copper Cliff copper refinery were built.

International Nickel, not surprisingly, was adversely affected by the Depression with production and wage reductions occurring from 1931 to 1933. Expansions followed the economic upswing and would mark the company's activities until World War II, when again the war would be a priority.

Inco Limited, so named since 1976, in recent years has had two main goals. One has been to increase corporate profitability, by achieving gains in productivity, while lowering costs. With nearly half of Inco's Canadian production costs being employment costs, there has been an emphasis on converting to bulk mining, which is less labour intensive, safer, and less costly. As well, new mining methods are being complemented by new Inco-developed mining machinery equipment which assists employees in improving safety and productivity.

Another main direction has been

An aerial view of the Copper Cliff smelter, one of the largest integrated mining, milling, smelting, and refining complexes in the world.

New types of equipment, such as these CD 90 drills, were developed by Inco to meet the needs of large diameter drilling for bulk mining. They are productive, compact, and easily moved to new locations.

to work toward controlling environmental pollution. In 1970 construction began on the Super Stack—a 1,250-foot-high cement chimney at the smelter—to disperse sulphur dioxide emissions high into the atmosphere. It commenced operation in 1972. The company continues its research and development of technology to reduce its sulphur dioxide emissions while operating within government regulations and controls. This is an ongoing objective since the sulphur-rich Sudbury ore contains approximately eight pounds of sulphur for every pound of nickel recovered.

Today Inco operates the following underground mines: Frood, Stobie, Little Stobie, Creighton, Levack, McCreedy West, Garson, Copper Cliff North, and Copper Cliff South. The company's processing operation includes three mills, the Copper Cliff smelter, and the Copper Cliff nickel and copper refineries.

Inco Limited has had a major impact on the well-being of Sudburians and their neighbours going back 100 years. The company continues its long-standing financial support and involvement in the community including assistance to educational, cultural, health, and civic organizations. In 1979 Inco initiated the feasibility study which led to the creation of Science North. The firm then contributed five million dollars toward the capital costs of the Science Centre—the single largest corporate donation in Canadian history—because of the centre's significant potential for the economic diversification and tourism development in Sudbury.

Inco and its 8,500 employees at Sudbury enter this second century of mining, benefitting from the increased knowledge and skills of dedicated employees and continually advancing technology—all of which contribute to the safe, productive, and cost-effective recovery of nickel, copper, and other products for world markets now and in the years ahead.

THE SUDBURY REGION

SUDBURY STEAM LAUNDRY AND DRY CLEANERS LTD.

In business since 1901, Sudbury Steam Laundry and Dry Cleaners Ltd., directed by three generations of the Bisset family, serves as an example of a successful family operation.

The enterprise began in a 28- by 52-foot building, two stories high, with John Ritchie Bisset as the founder. By 1903 he had a staff of fifteen serving a number of communities in the Sudbury area. Delivery wagons travelled to Copper Cliff twice weekly.

Ella (Eplett) and J.R. Bisset, married in 1903, would raise four children—Grace, Flora, Herb, and Gord—at their residences at the corner of Larch and Lisgar and later at 161 Larch. Their former home still stands—a visible reminder of that era when Sudbury was but a town and J.R. Bisset a beginning entrepreneur.

In 1935 Herbert Bisset became president of Sudbury Steam. Dorothy (Inkster) and Herb Bisset, married in 1941, would have three children—James, David, and Allan. With the help of their sons, the Bissets significantly expanded the business.

During the forty-year span that Herb Bisset was president, one major change was the relocation of Sudbury Steam to 208 Walnut. Previously it had been at downtown locations—first at 65 Larch and later at 171 Larch. Today, as a result of that 1970 decision to move to expanded quarters, Sudbury Steam utilizes 18,000 square feet with two divisions—dry cleaning and laundry. Under Herb Bisset, Sudbury Steam placed a major emphasis on automation, with the president keeping abreast of the latest technological innovations. Also very involved with Sudbury Steam during this period was Gord Bisset, who looked after the books, trained the staff, and kept the machinery running.

Sudbury Steam has now entered phase three with the purchasing of the business in 1975 by Dave Bisset. When he bought the company, there were two depots—one at Larch and another at Walnut. Under his leadership sales have more than doubled, and there are now six depots in the area: one each in Lively and Elliot Lake, and four in Sudbury.

In recent years the dry cleaning section has expanded significantly to where it now constitutes about 66 percent of sales. Much of the business in the laundry section is of a commercial nature involving hotels and restaurants. As well, rental services are available—such as professional garments, restaurant linens, kitchen supplies, and special occasion items.

President Dave Bisset notes that there is a low staff turnover rate, with some of the current staff having worked there for more than thirty-five years. The work force, including those in the depots, numbers fifty-eight with the majority being women. Since 1981 Scott Darling has been the manager at Sudbury Steam.

As was the case with his father, Dave Bisset has emphasized the utilizing of the latest technology. For the past three years an office computer system has been in place, providing inventory control and streamlining of the books and accounts. As well, lights and temperature are controlled by computer.

Concern for cost and energy efficiency as well as increasing service resulted in the installation of new tumble dryers. Sudbury Steam was the first company in northern Ontario to implement this type of dryer. In keeping with this trend, in 1986 the firm installed a new dry cleaning machine that is recognized as being the latest in technology.

For Sudbury Steam Laundry and Dry Cleaners Ltd., growth has been steady since its beginning in 1901. With J.R. Bisset, Herb Bisset, and now Dave Bisset, it is evident that the organization has successfully adapted to changing times in order to better serve its customers.

John Ritchie Bisset, founder of Sudbury Steam Laundry and Dry Cleaners Ltd.

An early view of the Sudbury Steam Laundry, and Larch Street.

PARTNERS IN PROGRESS

NORTHERN UNIFORM SERVICE CORP.

In Sudbury's annals, the Bisset family is featured prominently in connection with the laundry and dry cleaning trade. Jim Bisset—grandson of John Ritchie Bisset, who founded Sudbury Steam Laundry in 1901—is having an impact in a similar vein—that of a northern uniform rental business.

Northern Uniform Service Corp. began in 1970 at 208 Walnut Street as a small division of Sudbury Steam. By 1972 Jim Bisset would be operating the uniform service known as Northern Industrial Uniform Service as a separate entity.

Jim, one of Herb and Dorothy Bisset's three sons, was not unfamiliar with the trade. In a real sense, Sudbury Steam had been a second home, serving as a source of casual and later permanent employment. Sudbury Steam proved to be an excellent training ground for Jim prior to the establishment of the firm known today as Northern Uniform Service Corp.

In 1970, when Northern Uniform was still a small division of Sudbury Steam, there was a skeletal staff with Jim Bisset, aided by his wife and Chris Nowak, "... doing everything from cleaning and delivering to running the office." Today the operation employs thirty-eight people, with the management team comprising Dan Boyd, general manager; Al Morris, service and distribution manager; Mark Ferrier, shop foreman; and Jim Bisset, president.

Northern Uniform rents coveralls, shopcoats, shirts, and pants for industrial and commercial use. As well, a dust control service is provided with the rental of doormats and mops to help businesses maintain a clean environment. Fourteen vehicles help ensure extensive penetration of the northern Ontario markets for Northern Uniform.

From the onset, an emphasis has been placed on the marketing of these services to prospective customers. Sales personnel are on the road with territorial parameters bounded by Blind River to the west, Timmins to the north, and Mattawa to the east. The Nipissing-Timiskaming area is served by Northern Uniform from a North Bay Depot.

At Northern Uniform, Jim Bisset has placed a major emphasis on incorporating the latest technological advancements. For example, the installation of a computer system in 1982 has enabled the firm to grow by increasing efficiencies in the areas of inventory and billing, thus also benefitting the customers of Northern Uniform. Also, Northern Uniform became the first laundry in Canada to install a 99-percent thermally efficient submerged flame hot water system. New 450-pound washer-extractors and dryers enable Northern Uniform to wash and dry garments in a more cost-effective manner.

In 1981 an innovative locker control system was introduced. This modern garment service results in employees having personalized lockers accessible only to them. The supplier has access to the entire section for the quick retrieval of soiled articles and the delivery of clean replacements. In 1981 a trial program with Inco, involving the Coleman Mine workers, demonstrated the feasibility of the program to management, the workers, and Northern

Fourteen vehicles help Northern Uniform Service Corp. provide a full range of industrial uniform rental to Northern Ontario.

Uniform. Northern Uniform, the first business to link a computer with the locker system, has introduced the program extensively at RIO ALGOM in Elliot Lake and Inco in Sudbury.

For Jim Bisset, Northern Uniform is a company with an exciting future. He believes, "Sudbury is the hub of

James R. Bisset, president.

the North and Northern Uniform is an integral part of that network." With the continued emphasis on utilizing the latest laundry innovations, the promoting of the service through on-the-road salesmen, and the willingness to be innovative by introducing new concepts and products, Northern Uniform Service Corp. will continue to successfully provide a service to many Sudburians and their northern neighbours.

THE SUDBURY REGION

NORTHERN CABLE SERVICES LIMITED

In 1969 Baxter Ricard and Norman Bradley, both of Sudbury, formed a partnership with a Toronto-based cable communications company to make an application for a cable television licence for the community of Sudbury. This partnership subsequently developed into a company that would have the majority of its shares held by residents of northern Ontario.

Northern Cable Services Limited is a holding company with principal investments in cable television systems, radio and television stations, and an extensive multichannel microwave network. With more than 400 employees, Northern Cable Services is working toward the creation of a unified communications delivery system for northern Ontario that embraces cable communications, broadcasting, and telecommunications. The system is based on a microwave network that spans 1,100 miles and stretches from Ottawa to Hearst.

In all, the network involves 41 tower sites and more than 8,000 channel miles of microwave.

The entire network interconnects a complex multiple-community cable system involving a total of 1,200 miles of cable plant that provides cable communication services to the following communities: the Regional Municipality of Sudbury, Timmins, Elliot Lake, Blind River, Espanola, Sturgeon Falls, Cochrane, Smooth Rock Falls, Iroquois Falls, Kapuskasing, and Hearst.

The basic corporate objective has been to deliver the same quantity of broadcast services that are available in southern Ontario to the residents of northeastern Ontario with the same signal quality and at moderate cost, and to endeavour to provide the same service at the same cost to all communities—large or small—and regardless of where located—Sudbury or Hearst. In all, some 76,400 households can be potentially brought under service.

The implementation of the Canadian satellite service, Cancom, and the licencing of satellite-delivered pay-television networks have created opportunities for cable development of remote and sparsely populated communities previously underserved. During 1984 and 1985 Northern had constructed new satellite-fed cable systems in fifteen northern communities ranging in size from 150 to 800 potential homes.

The development of cable communications interest has been the key to the creation of a solid foundation for corporate expansion.

A wholly owned subsidiary of Northern Cable, Mid-Canada Communications (Canada) Corp., operates seven television stations and two radio stations in northern and central Ontario. It serves some 500,000 potential viewers across a service area larger than New Brunswick, Nova Scotia, and Prince Edward Island combined. The limited population density of the North, in combination with inevitable audience fragmentation arising from the introduction of new services, had created economic hardship for the area's existing broadcast operators, Cambrian Broadcasting and J. Conrad Lavigne Limited. Northern Cable's solution in acquiring these companies in 1980 was to combine the CBC and CTV network stations in Sudbury, Timmins, and North Bay, creating "twin stick" operations in these cities. The company also acquired the CBC-TV

The Northern management team includes (seated) F. Baxter Ricard, chairman of the board; Norman Bradley, vice-president and general manager/microwave and cable division; (standing, left to right) Eric Kanne, president/telecommunications division; Gaston Germain, vice-president/finance; George Lund, vice-president and general manager, broadcasting division; Paul C. Marleau, senior vice-president/finance and executive vice-president/broadcasting division; and Irv Whipple, assistant manager, microwave and cable divisions.

120

Peter Mallette hosts the popular program "Midday."

affiliate in Pembroke, serving most of the Ottawa Valley with a potential viewing audience of well over 500,000 people.

The Mid-Canada broadcast delivery system involves sixteen transmitters linked together by thirty-five hops and more than 1,300 channel miles of microwave. The nerve centre of the system is located at a technical facility in Sudbury, where traffic functions for the seven television stations are computer controlled, with all information lines, technical lines, and teletype facilities being routed via the micowave network.

Extensive local program production is undertaken by the various stations, the company having met or exceeded all CRTC conditions of licence. Programs originate from five different studio centres located throughout northern Ontario and the Ottawa Valley. Some twenty programs of local interest are produced each week, in addition to news, weather, and sports programs and a variety of television specials. Programs are specifically designed for northern audiences and are well received in the various communities under service.

Through the application of acquired operating and management experience to a new opportunity, the company was able to rationalize the private television broadcasting industry in northern Ontario and create a solid foundation for further expansion.

In 1985 Mid-Canada acquired six radio stations in Blind River, Elliot Lake, Espanola, and Sudbury. Also that year Mid-Canada acquired a minority interest in a new AM radio station in North Bay, which it continues to manage as part of its expanding radio broadcasting network in northern Ontario.

Consistent with its objective of becoming the principal provider of communication services in northern Ontario, Northern Cable is progressively moving into new business ventures in the area. Recent expansion into the sales and installation of private telephones has rapidly proven successful. The firm has acquired a 50-percent interest in a business providing this private telephone installation service as well as mobile radio and paging services in the market, and is actively engaged in exploring the potential for other telecommunications services.

In September 1954 Sudbury's first telephone answering service was registered as a business by Fred Somers and was called "Telephone Answering Service." It continued through successive proprietors until it was finally purchased by Eric and Christina Kannen on June 15, 1975.

The company was incorporated as Northern Communication Services Ltd. on October 2, 1975, and has grown steadily. Radio pocket pagers were the first electronic communications product, thus beginning a transition to high-technology products and professional marketing. Soon after, two-way radio sales and service, and burglar alarm systems were added to the list of products.

In March 1981 telephone interconnect became a reality, and a partnership was formed with Northern Cable Services Ltd. to create a wholly owned subsidiary, Mid-Canada Phonesystems Ltd. Mid-Canada Phonesystems offers business clients everything from electronic office telephone systems to high-speed digital facsimile transmission products.

With new markets developing in industrial equipment monitoring, long-distance video surveillance, and cellular mobile telephone service, the direction of Northern Communication Services Ltd. has been clearly established. A dedication to excellence by staff and continually expanding

The complex headend tower at Sudbury supports off-air reception equipment as well as long-haul microwave and VHCM facilities.

product lines ensures that Northern Communication Services Ltd. and Mid-Canada Phonesystems Ltd. will continue to grow and prosper throughout northeastern Ontario.

The company's ability to implement an effective long-term plan is rooted in the strength of its management team and board of directors. Many of its managers have been with the company during its formative period, creating a repository of skills and experience. Moreover, Northern Cable Services Limited is characterized by a low staff turnover and high job satisfaction at all levels.

The company is now well positioned for further growth in the communications field, particularly in northern Ontario. Future plans call for the continued application of experience in engineering, marketing, programming, financial administration, and customer service across the broad spectrum of communications services.

121

THE SUDBURY REGION

RELIABLE WINDOW CLEANERS (SUDBURY) LIMITED

The Bertuzzi family home at 323 Regent Street South, circa 1955. Today, after renovations, the former home serves as the main office for Reliable Window Cleaners (Sudbury) Ltd.

In 1951, with a pail and squeegee in hand, Leo Bertuzzi began a business that would later be incorporated as Reliable Window Cleaners (Sudbury) Limited. As very little equipment was required and numerous customers were located in the downtown core, operating out of a garage in the Larch Street laneway proved ideal.

Initially, Reliable was strictly a window-cleaning operation. It quickly expanded into janitorial cleaning with the attainment of a janitorial contract with the City of Sudbury. Through mutual respect and trust, the relationship with the city has continued to grow through the years.

In 1956 a partnership was formed between Leo and Noah Bertuzzi. Under the direction of both brothers the business continued to grow; this necessitated a move to the family home at 323 Regent Street South. It is with fondness that Noah recalls his youth at this location.

As Reliable continued to expand, Leo and Noah realized that diversification into the selling of cleaning supplies and equipment would be a natural addition to the company. This addition included a 4,000-square-foot warehouse and Noah's inclusion of family members among the work force. In fact, it was with good business judgment that Noah and Cecile chose to have a family of seven: Albert, Gail, Linda, Nora, Robert, Anne-Marie, and Joey.

The year 1972 saw the entrepreneurs purchasing the Woodland Hotel in Hanmer. Following the acquisition, Leo and Noah divided their energies. Leo concentrated on the hotel, and Noah, along with his son Albert, managed Reliable. By then the work force at Reliable consisted of twenty employees, up considerably from a staff of five in 1952. In 1979 Noah became the sole owner-operator of Reliable.

In 1980 a major step was implemented by the company when it entered the manufacturing field. This shift resulted in Reliable becoming the first such operation in northern Ontario to manufacture cleaning chemicals and waxes. Again the need for expansion arose, which resulted in the purchase of a 7,000-square-foot building at 351 Regent Street South. Employing a chemist consultant, Reliable now has the most recent information available on cleaning chemicals. President Noah Bertuzzi states, "We are in an excellent position to provide complete service to our customers."

Reliable has integrated all sectors of the cleaning industry in order to offer its customers complete service. By means of high standards, Reliable has maintained a regular clientele to which it provides such services as janitorial contract cleaning, window cleaning, and carpet cleaning. As well, Reliable distributes a complete line of janitorial equipment and cleaning supplies to all types of customers: residential, commercial, and industrial.

Expansion was again required in order to provide customers with complete janitorial services. Reliable enlarged its facilities through the construction of a new building on Regent Street, resulting in a 15,000-square-foot warehouse and office. The added facility will enable the firm to more efficiently and effectively serve its customers. This includes local clientele and northern customers, who range demographically from Sault Ste. Marie in the West, Hearst in the North, and North Bay in the East.

Over the years Reliable Window Cleaners (Sudbury) Limited and the Bertuzzi family have exhibited a commitment to the community. Noah has always stressed that with each other's support, the city will continue to grow and diversify.

At Reliable, one senses a consistent emphasis on customer satisfaction, which is a key to understanding the corporation's success.

The main office and retail outlet of Reliable Window Cleaners (Sudbury) Ltd.

PARTNERS IN PROGRESS

MASLACK SUPPLY LTD.

A good idea and determination often prove to be the key to success. For John Maslack, founder and owner of Maslack Supply Ltd., a combination of these factors has resulted in the firm becoming the fastest-growing industrial-products distributor in northern Ontario.

Raised and educated in Dryden, Maslack came to Sudbury in 1943, where he began work as a timekeeper for Nordal Construction. From 1945 to 1959 John Maslack worked for an industrial supply house beginning as a counterman and ultimately becoming general manager.

In 1959, sensing a market opportunity, Maslack, along with two partners who remained involved until 1964, established his own business.

For the new enterprise, a 960-square-foot building was constructed at 818 Barrydowne Road in 1960. Before long it was expanded to 6,000 and then to 15,000 square feet.

Soon the need for more space necessitated a move from the Barrydowne location. As a result, eleven acres of land were purchased at 488 Falconbridge Road, and a new 29,000-square-foot warehouse was constructed. From this new location a wide range of items that includes industrial tools and equipment, automotive parts, and body shop supplies are stocked and serviced.

Nordic Engine & Machine Ltd., 1355 Kingsway East.

Maslack Supply Ltd. supplies industrial products to northern Ontario mines, mills, and forestry sites covering, among others, the communities of Sudbury, Elliot Lake, Timmins, and North Bay. For customer convenience, an inventory of 40,000 items is computer controlled.

Recognizing a demand for rebuilt engines and drive line service in northern Ontario, in 1972 John Maslack established Nordic Engine & Machine Ltd. at 1355 Kingsway East in a 6,000-square-foot building. Immediate success required expansion to its present size of 18,000 square feet. In the words of the owner, "We have the most modern equipment available," in what is classified as one of the finest machine shops in Canada.

Maslack, noting the industry trend toward hydraulics and the need for a hydraulic equipment distributor in Sudbury, opened Nordic Fluid Power Inc. at 3175 Kingsway East in 1983. Available at Nordic Fluid Power are pumps, motors, industrial and mobile

Maslack Supply Ltd.'s 29,000-square-foot warehouse facility at 488 Falconbridge Road.

hydraulic valves, filters, sealing devices, steering units, and an array of accessories. Nordic Fluid Power opened a Timmins branch in 1985.

Both daughters of John and Leona Maslack, raised in an automotive- and mine-related environment, have opened their own businesses. In 1977 Betty Jane Marks opened Maslack Supply Northern Ltd. in Elliot Lake, to carry a wide range of mine supplies. Her husband, Stephen Marks, opened Valley East Auto Parts in the town of Valley East in 1985. Nordic Bearings Inc. was opened in 1979 by the Maslacks' other daughter, Judy Roy. Located at 488 Falconbridge Road, it specializes in power transmissions products.

At present the Maslack family businesses employ ninety-three people. The various enterprises speak well of the success of Maslack Supply Ltd. and the diverse business acumen of Sudbury's John Maslack.

THE SUDBURY REGION

BRISTOL MACHINE WORKS LIMITED

Canada's 1967 Centennial Parade, Sudbury. Note the 1890s L.D. Sawyer-Massey portable steam engine previously used for sawing lumber in Britt, Ontario.

The mention of Bristol immediately suggests the English community of that name noted for its precision work. In Sudbury, quality precision work is associated with the Sudbury firm of Bristol Machine Works Limited.

In 1965 Roy Gogolinski endeavoured to meet what he recognized as a demand for a quality custom production and general machining company in the Sudbury Basin. Hence, the machinist from International Nickel formed Bristol Machine Works.

Starting in a rented building on Armstrong Street in Sudbury, the company commenced serving the needs of the area. By 1967 business requirements resulted in the erection of a plant at the firm's current Sudbury location—2040 Algonquin Road. At that site Bristol Machine Works has undergone four expansions—in 1969, 1971, 1973, and 1976—with further expansion slated for the near future.

Today Ernie Weaver and Jim Eddy are the owner-operators of Bristol Machine Works. In the fall of 1968, following the untimely death of Roy Gogolinski, Ernie Weaver and Jim Eddy became sole owners of Bristol Machine Works. However, the involvement of both men predates 1968.

Jim Eddy hails from Saskatchewan, having arrived in Sudbury in 1942. In 1964 Jim Eddy joined Roy Gogolinski and Bristol Machine Works. However, prior to that year, experience in the trade had been gained from employment with the diamond drilling firm of Smith & Travers from 1949 to 1957, and from two years as a machinist with Dennison Mines in Elliot Lake. As well, there were a few years as a private entrepreneur in the contracting and trucking businesses.

As for Ernie Weaver, Sudbury has always been home. Experience that has served Weaver well was garnered at International Nickel, where he was a machinist starting in 1959. Weaver joined Bristol Machine Works in 1966. Today Weaver would be the first to state that his seven years' experience at International Nickel was "instrumental in supplying [him] with a valuable training as a machinist."

Bristol Machine Works has carved out a niche in the business sector by serving the mining, forestry, steelmaking, and construction industries. The firm provides general machining services for the maintenance of heavy equipment and the manufacture of custom-machined products for industry.

A well-established reputation for quality and reliability is maintained as Bristol Machine Works continues to expand its product line and services. Operating from "the most modern and versatile industrial machine shop in northern Ontario," the firm meets the needs of its customers across the province.

Today Bristol Machine Works Limited has a work force of thirty-three. With Ernie Weaver and Jim Eddy at the helm, the future continues to look positive.

A general view of the machine shop area in the early 1980s.

TRI-CARE GROUP OF COMPANIES

Sudbury serves as head office location for the Tri-Care Group of Companies—Tri-Care Services Limited, Multi-Care Systems Limited, Rx Plus, and Morcare Insurance Agency Limited. President and chief executive officer since inception is Bob Morel.

Born and raised in Sudbury, Morel received his education there, including a post-secondary education at Laurentian University. While at Laurentian, he worked at *The Sudbury Star*. After a one-year stint with *The Hamilton Spectator* as branch manager, Morel returned to work in the circulation department of the *Star*. Involvement with insurance began in 1967 when he was a group trainee with Confederation Life, and by 1970 he was associated with Dinan Insurance.

Recognizing a need in the marketplace, Morel founded Tri-Care Services Limited in October 1974. Today Tri-Care Services is Canada's largest independent employee benefits administrator. When Morel began the company with a sixty-dollar investment in 1974, all of the files could be found "in the bottom right-hand drawer of the desk." Employed were two persons—Morel himself and a secretary. Today, after just over a decade in the industry, Tri-Care administers benefits for more than 1,000 corporations across Canada. Tri-Care's premium portfolio is larger than that of half of the insurance companies operating in Canada.

Multi-Care Systems Limited is the computer division, responsible for all computer programming and operations required by the group of companies. Formed in 1980, Multi-Care has equipment valued at more than $.5 million and supports facilities for all company offices across Canada. Significantly, the staff includes programmers, operators, and analysts. All mainframe operations are located in Sudbury.

Rx Plus was formed in 1982 with

George Watson (left), group vice-president of the Crown Life Insurance Company, with Bob Morel, president and chief executive officer of Tri-Care, at the opening of their new head office at 50 Lisgar Street, Sudbury.

the consolidation of the pharmacy network system already established within Tri-Care. Customers include most Canadian and American insurance companies and a number of large corporations and labour unions. Rx Plus is the only Canadian firm operating in Canada to provide Canada-wide pay-direct drug card facilities. Contracts are held with over 6,500 pharmacies across the country. Today, after just a few years in operation, Rx Plus processes one million dollars of drug claims per month—up considerably from an initial $150,000 per month.

May 1983 saw the formation of Morcare Insurance Agency Limited to provide consulting services to such groups as school boards, corporations, chambers of commerce, and labour unions. As has been the case with the other companies, Morcare has experienced marked growth with staff and volume of business growing by over 100 percent in the past year. Today Morcare provides services to more than 200 corporations and associations collectively having over 13,000 employees.

The Tri-Care Group of Companies is an important component of the Sudbury business community. In sum, the firms maintain a budget of four million dollars with three-quarters of that spent in Sudbury. Headquartered at 50 Lisgar, the companies lease more than 15,000 square feet of office space. They employ over fifty persons in Sudbury and an additional thirty across Canada. Decentralized offices are located in Vancouver, Edmonton, Toronto, Windsor, Montreal, and Dartmouth.

Bob Morel and the Tri-Care Group of Companies have chosen Sudbury as their home base. As a Sudbury operation supportive of its community, the firm purchases 80 percent of its furniture, equipment, and supplies from local retailers. Pleased with the consistent support shown by the entire Sudbury community, Bob Morel states, though it is "nice to visit other areas, I always appreciate coming home."

Bob Morel (left) receiving a plaque from Tom Davies, chairman of the Regional Municipality of Sudbury. The plaque was presented to the Tri-Care Group of Companies in recognition of their contribution to the Sudbury area's economic development and expansion.

THE SUDBURY REGION

COLLÈGE CAMBRIAN COLLEGE

Cambrian College opened its doors in 1967. Much has changed since those early days when the College and the college system were virtually unknown.

Initial planning for the development of Cambrian College began in September 1966, with the appointment of its first board of governors and its first chairman, Dr. Walter Curlook of Sudbury. Designated to serve the districts of Algoma, Manitoulin, Sudbury, and Nipissing, Cambrian evolved into three widely separated campuses (Sault Ste. Marie, North Bay, and Sudbury), with administrative headquarters in Sudbury. Dr. John T. Koski, former principal of the Northern Ontario Institute of Technology in Kirkland Lake, was appointed president in February 1967. He was succeeded by Glenn N. Crombie, former president of Olds College, Olds, Alberta, in September 1982.

In 1972, following five years of rapid growth and expansion, the campuses became separate, independent colleges with Sudbury serving the districts of Sudbury and Manitoulin and retaining the original name. The name "Cambrian" was adopted to recognize the Pre-Cambrian Shield, the geological formation extending across northern Ontario where the College is located.

Cambrian College has two major locations within the city of Sudbury, the main campus on Barrydowne Road and the Regent Street campus, and accesses numerous facilities throughout the districts of Sudbury and Manitoulin including Noelville, Little Current, Onaping Falls, Espanola, and West Bay. The Barrydowne campus is situated on a 150-acre site in New Sudbury. Business and applied arts students have been located here since 1971. The Technology Division, formerly located in rented facilities on Notre Dame Avenue, moved to the main campus in September 1977, where it occupies a four-story wing completed during that year. Students in dental auxiliary programs also occupy this wing of the main campus.

Athletic facilities, consisting of a playing field, a softball diamond, a field house, and outdoor tennis courts, were opened at the main campus in 1978. The following year a 30,000-square-foot industrial training centre was constructed to meet an increased demand for skilled trades people.

The fourth stage of the College's multi-phase complex officially opened in 1981. It contains a double gymnasium, squash and racquetball courts, a weight room, saunas, classrooms, seminar/meeting rooms, lecture theatres, and the John T. Koski Conference Centre.

The College's second campus is located at 885 Regent Street South. Formerly the Northern Ontario Regional Health Science School, the Regent Street location houses the College's health science programs as well as a 203-bedroom student residence.

As Cambrian's physical plant has grown, so has its student population and range of program offerings. Compared to an enrolment of 184 full-time students in about 7 programs in the early days, Cambrian now offers approximately 70 diploma programs to some 3,000 post-secondary students. About a third of these programs are offered in a bilingual format, and this number is increasing steadily to serve the needs of the francophone population. In addition, about 1,500 students are enrolled in trades, skills, and apprenticeship programs and, over a period of three semesters, about 20,000 registrations are accepted for continuing education courses. Today Cambrian is one of the largest bilingual, post-secondary institutions in northern Ontario.

Cambrian is continually evaluating the economic climate and assessing and responding to the changing needs of business and industry as well as of individuals within the community. Advisory committees, consisting of representatives from the business, industrial, and professional communities, help Cambrian monitor the relevance and value of each program it offers.

Cambrian College, like Sudbury, is proud of its past and optimistic of its future.

Cambrian's Barrydowne campus. Le campus Barrydowne du collège Cambrian.

PARTNERS IN PROGRESS

COLLÈGE CAMBRIAN COLLEGE

Le collège Cambrian a ouvert ses portes en 1967. Depuis lors, le Collège et tout le système collégial ont connu beaucoup de changements.

Le collège Cambrian a connu ses débuts au mois de septembre 1966 avec la nomination de son premier Conseil des Gouverneurs et de son premier président du Conseil, M. Walter Curlook de Sudbury. Le Collège devait desservir les districts d'Algoma, de Manitoulin, de Sudbury et de Nipissing. Le collège Cambrian avait trois campus (Sault Ste. Marie, North Bay et Sudbury), les services administratifs étant à Sudbury. Au mois de février 1967, M. John T. Koski, ancien directeur du Northern Ontario Institute of Technology à Kirkland Lake, fut nommé président du Collège. M. Glenn Crombie, ancien président du collège Olds (Olds, Alberta), lui succéda en septembre 1982.

Au cours des cinq prochaines années, le Collège a connu un épanouissement rapide. Puis en 1972, les campus devinrent des collèges indépendants. Le campus de Sudbury a conservé le nom de "Cambrian", lequel a été choisi en raison du bouclier précambrien, formation géologique du nord de l'Ontario, qui caractérise la région où se situe le collège.

Le collège Cambrian a deux campus dans la ville de Sudbury, soit le campus principal situé dans le chemin Barrydowne, soit le campus de la rue Régent. En outre, il loue de nombreuses autres installations situées dans diverses communautés des districts de Sudbury et de Manitoulin, telles que Noelville, Little Current, Onaping Falls, Espanola et West Bay. Le campus Barrydowne occupe un terrain de 150 acres situé au Nouveau Sudbury. Les étudiant(e)s en commerce et en arts appliqués fréquentent ce campus depuis 1971. Au mois de septembre 1977, la Division polytechnique quitta les installations louées qu'elle occupait sur l'avenue Notre Dame et s'emménagea dans la nouvelle aile polytechnique de quatre étages au campus principal. Les étudiant(e)s des programmes dentaires occupent aussi cette nouvelle aile.

L'année 1978 a marqué l'ouverture d'installations sportives au Collège. Celles-ci comprennent un terrain de jeux, un centre sportifs, des courts de tennis à l'extérieur et un terrain de base-ball. L'année suivante, le Collège a construit un centre de formation industrielle de 30 000 pieds carrés en vue de répondre à la demande croissante de personnes qualifées dans le domaine des métiers.

L'ouverture de la quatrième aile du Collège a eu lieu en 1981. Cette nouvelle aile comprend un gymnase double, des courts de squash et de racquetball, une salle d'haltérophilie, des saunas, des salles de classe, des salles de séminaire/réunion, des amphithéâtres, et le Centre de congrès J.T. Koski.

Le deuxième campus du collège Cambrian est l'ancien Northern Ontario Regional Health Science School situé au 885 de la rue Régent sud. Ce campus dessert les programmes en sciences de la santé offerts par le Collège et renferme une résidence étudiante de 203 lits.

Au fur et à mesure que le collège Cambrian s'agrandissait, le nombre d'étudiants et de cours offerts augmentait. A ses débuts, le collège Cambrian ne comptait que 184 étudiants inscrits à temps plein dans près de sept programmes. Aujourd'hui, on y offre près de 70 programmes menant à un diplôme à quelques 3000 étudiants postsecondaires. Environ un tiers de ces programmes sont bilingues. Ce nombre augmente rapidement afin de répondre aux besoins de la population francophone. En outre, près de 1500 étudiants sont inscrits dans les programmes de métier, de formation professionnelle et d'apprentissage. Les inscriptions aux cours d'éducation permanente pour une période de trois semestres se chiffrent à environ 20 000. Le collège Cambrian est aujourd'hui le plus grand établissement postsecondaire bilingue du nord de l'Ontario.

Le Collège évalue constamment la situation économique afin de répondre aux besoins changeants tant du monde des affaires et de l'undustrie que des individus de la communauté. En vue d'assurer la pertinence et la valeur de tous les programmes, le Collège a mis sur pied des comités consultatifs composés de représentants du monde des affaires, de l'undustrie et des professions.

Le collège Cambrian, tout comme la ville de Sudbury, est fier de son passé et envisage l'avenir avec optimisme.

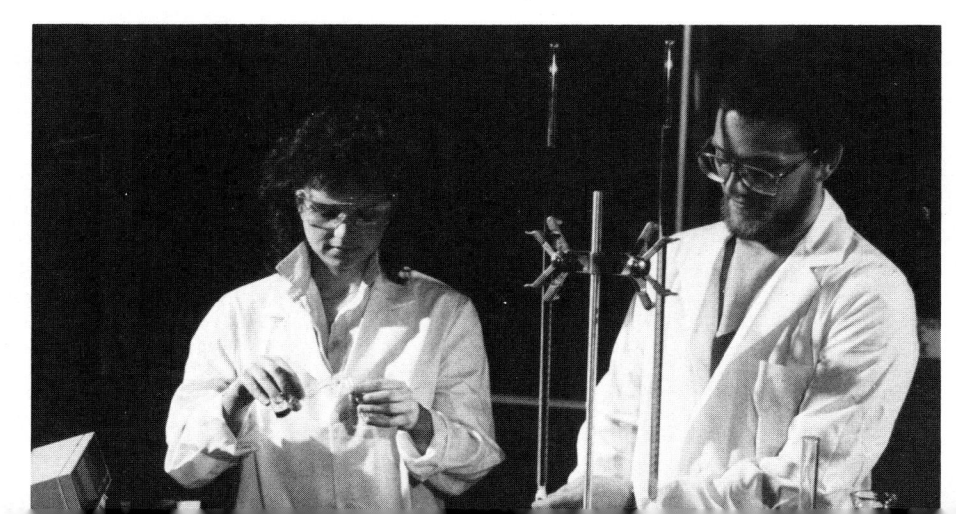

Des installations modernes sont à la portée des étudiants tant dans les salle de classes que dans les laboratoires. Students have access to modern equipment in classrooms and laboratories.

THE SUDBURY REGION

LOEB INC., SUDBURY DIVISION

From the establishing of a small wholesale operation in Ottawa in 1912, Moses Loeb began an operation that in 1983-1984 would have sales exceeding one billion dollars. Over the years numerous expansions and amalgamations have dramatically changed the scope and direction of Loeb Inc.

Since 1979 Loeb has been a wholly owned subsidiary of Provigo Inc., a Montreal-based company that—like Loeb—was largely involved in the wholesale distribution of grocery and dairy products, frozen foods, meats, fresh produce, and nonfood articles to retailers and institutions.

In Canada, as is the case with the U.S. operation known as Loeb Corporation, there are a number of territorial divisions, with the head office located in Ottawa. The Sudbury Division serves northern Ontario with a work force of 169 full-time employees and a fleet of twelve tractors, two straight trucks, and twenty-two trailers.

The year 1959 saw Loeb acquire J.A. Lapalme Ltd., a major area wholesaler that supplied Cloverfarm stores. As a result of this acquisition, a number of stores were converted to I.G.A. (Independent Grocer Alliance), starting the I.G.A. penetration into northern Ontario. That same year the Sudbury Division became the centre for Loeb distribution to the northern parts of Ontario, stretching from Sault Ste. Marie in the West to Mattawa in the East.

Until 1967 a warehouse at 560 Notre Dame was the centre for the Sudbury Division. However, in that year the Sudbury operation moved to a new 96,941-square-foot building located at 1010 Lorne Street. In November 1979 the produce and institutional food-service operations began transferring the grocery warehouse back to Notre Dame. This location serves as a produce and dairy warehouse.

The Sudbury Division of Loeb serves two Cash & Carry, one Orange store, thirty I.G.A. stores, over thirty Pinto stores, plus a number of other accounts. The various outlets cover an extensive territory approximating 60,000 square miles from Hornepayne in the North, Sault Ste. Marie in the West, North Bay and Mattawa in the East, and Parry Sound in the South. With the two warehouses combined, over 70,000 pieces of merchandise are distributed weekly with drivers covering 30,000 miles per week.

For the staff, a major emphasis has been placed on first-aid training and a safety-awareness program. Community involvement for Loeb has included support for such local ventures as Science North, the Heart Fund Program, and the CT Scan Program. Loeb's involvement with community ventures aptly demonstrates a commitment to the area and an appreciation for continued local support.

Loeb Inc. is a food distributor specialist that has significantly increased its presence since 1959. The I.G.A. area market share is currently 32 percent with stores in Valley East, Capreol, Rayside, Balfour, and Sudbury.

The front view of the Loeb Inc., Sudbury Division, site at 560 Notre Dame Avenue prior to 1967. Today this location serves as a produce and dairy warehouse.

Loeb Inc., Sudbury Division, 1010 Lorne Street, in 1984.

PARTNERS IN PROGRESS

FRONTENAC HOTEL

Over the years Sudbury has had its share of hotels. From an early era there were the Sudbury Hotel, Russell House, King Edward, Revere House, The American Hotel, Canadian Hotel, Balmoral Hotel, National Hotel, Queen's, Nickel Range Hotel, New American Hotel, and the Montreal House. Soon the Frontenac Hotel may join the above in the category of former businesses, for the Frontenac may well close its doors.

The story of the Frontenac goes back to Charles Davis, the original owner of the establishment at 14 Durham Street North. Records tell us that Charles Davis was a jeweller who came to Sudbury in 1909 upon the suggestion of Jim Mulligan, a Sudbury barrister, and formed a jewellery- and watch-repair business in the town when already seven such businesses were operating.

Quickly establishing a presence, Davis, using a stencil and white paint, quickly painted "C. Davis, Jewellery and Watch Repairing, Corner Elm and Lisgar Street, Sudbury, Ontario," on the flat rocks, barns, and fences on all highways leading to and from Sudbury. Soon his venture prospered to the point where he was employing five watch-repair men.

By 1918 Charles Davis' interests turned to real estate, resulting in the jewellery business being sold to his brothers, Sam and Peter. One of his purchases, with Alex Turpin, was the block at the corner of Elgin and Beech known as the Grand Opera House. Soon thereafter both Alex Turpin and Charles Davis would sell their shares to W.E. Mason, owner and publisher of *The Sudbury Star*.

In 1938 Turpin and Davis considered the construction of a theatre on the present site of the Frontenac. However, by 1940 plans called for a hotel at the corner of Beech and Durham, with the hotel completed at a cost of $100,000 and ready for patrons on New Year's Day of that year. To facilitate co-ordination of his business activities, the hotel became headquarters for Davis' real estate business. Upon the death of Alex Turpin in the early 1940s, Charles Davis purchased the remaining shares and became sole owner of the Frontenac.

In 1962 Michael Michael became the manager of the Frontenac, succeeding Simon Kingsley. Employed at the hotel since 1956, Michael remains as its manager. To Michael, Charles Davis was a natural businessman who gained his experience firsthand. He is remembered as being quite approachable and well known by his many patrons. In later years Davis was involved in community work and served on the board of regents of the University of Sudbury.

The Frontenac's Durham Street entrance, circa 1940. Note that the rooms were $3.50 and up.

A major development at the Frontenac occurred on September 12, 1964, with the opening of The Door. Cassidys Ltd. of Montreal, in business since 1801, completed what the *Toronto Daily Star* described as one of its "most elegant and striking" design jobs in the Frontenac. Featuring velvet-faced scroll wallpapers, elaborate stonework, and subdued lighting, the lounge has been called the finest in northern Ontario.

By 1964 amenities at the Frontenac included a formal dining room, as well as a banquet-style dining room, a ladies' and escorts' room, a banquet hall, and rooms priced from $3.50 per day. Advertised conveniences included elevator service, room service, a radio in each room, and free overnight parking.

Today the Frontenac stands more as a testimony to the past as opposed to a fixture for the future. According to Michael Michael, the year 1986 should see the Frontenac closing its doors as a hotel. This may well result in the demolition or conversion of the Frontenac and the adjacent former Jubilee Hall, built in 1904.

The main lobby of the Frontenac Hotel (Durham Street entrance) in 1958. Seated is owner Charles Davis.

THE SUDBURY REGION

BARNÉ BUILDERS

Sixty-nine Elm Street West is the new location for Barné Builders—a company that in the truest sense of the word is a family venture.

Romeo Diotte, born in Grande River, Gaspé, Quebec, came to Ontario in 1949. Sudbury became home, with Romeo Diotte working for the Foundation Company of Canada Ltd. from 1951 until 1964.

In 1968 Romeo Diotte ventured on his own with the formation of Barné, as general contractors, located at 68 Xavier Street, Sudbury. His brothers, Rod, Raynald, and Yvon, initially worked for the firm. Experience gained with Foundation Company proved ideal for the general contractor, who soon specialized in the supply and erection of pre-engineered steel buildings.

Initially the bulk of the work for Barné involved renovations, design, and supply to mining companies' and different institutions' pre-engineered buildings. At Barné Builders the work force varies from fifteen to thirty-five depending on the workload.

For a construction company, the buildings it erects serves as a visual record of its craft. Major ventures of Barné have included renovations and construction work for Mid Canada Communications, miscellaneous projects for the Sisters of Charity of Ottawa, and projects for the City of Sudbury. A 1985 contract saw the erection of a new pre-engineered steel building in the Walden Industrial Park for Fagersta Secoroc Ltd. As well, Barné Builders has maintenance contracts for a number of local clients, including K mart, Kresge, and the Department of National Defence.

In 1982, when there was a downturn in the construction industry, the Champlain Building at the corner of Ignatius and Ste. Anne's Road was purchased. Following extensive renovations by Barné Builders, Champlain Grandecare Lodge will open in 1986. Billed as a retirement home for gracious living, it will offer full care for senior citizens and is conveniently within walking distance to Sudbury's downtown.

Diversifying his interests, in 1982 Romeo Diotte formed Citadel Enterprises—a company separate from Barné Builders concentrating on the development aspect of the industry. At 69 and 73 Elm Street West, Barné Builders undertook extensive renovations for Citadel, with the two properties now at full occupancy.

Frontier Development, formed in 1983, concentrates on the acquisition of apartment blocks and renovates and subsequently rents apartments. Some properties held by the company are 89 Pine Street, 230 Elm Street West, 357-359 Frood Road, and St. George Street.

Barné, and its associated companies, definitely is a family operation: Romeo Diotte's wife, Carmel, is involved with the office administration and bookkeeping aspect of the business. Five sons—Richard, now president of Barné Builders, Jim and Daniel, field supervisors, and Patrick and Michel, share different responsibilities and functions. As for the Diotte daughters, Marie Claire, Diane, Lise, and Anne Marie have worked in the office at one time or another. Jacqueline, Carole, and Nicole currently help on weekends and after school.

For Romeo Diotte, Sudbury has proved to be ideal for raising his family where " . . . the opportunities are here if you go after them . . . " With his sons now earning a living from the company, Romeo Diotte has found more time to concentrate on his ventures associated with Frontier Development, Citadel Enterprises, and holdings.

Champlain Grandcare Lodge—a retirement home owned by Barné Builders.

PARTNERS IN PROGRESS

DEWIT + CASTELLAN ARCHITECTS

Dewit + Castellan of Sudbury is having a significant impact on the local scene. Sudbury's youngest architectural firm was established on May 1, 1984, at 289 Cedar Street with two partners, one secretary, and one technical person.

It is more than a casual comment when reference is made to Dewit + Castellan being a northern Ontario architectural practice. In fact, both Peter Dewit and Dennis Castellan had been involved in the Sudbury architectural community prior to the firm's founding. Dewit is an active member of the Parks and Recreation Committee in the Town of Valley East. Castellan is the past chairman of the City of Sudbury Local Architectural Conservation Advisory Committee.

A vast and varied range of services is provided by Dewit + Castellan, including interior, building, environmental, and urban design. Throughout the process there is an emphasis on the critical relationship so necessary with organizations and government authorities directly associated with a project.

Not surprisingly, the firm is being recognized for its design excellence both by the community and by its peers in the profession. Dewit and Castellan were the designers for the celebrated Valley East Recreation Complex. The prestigious Award of Merit for outstanding design and masonry workmanship for the Ontario Masons' Relations Council was received. A most recent Dewit + Castellan venture was praised in the November 1985 issue of *The Canadian Architect*.

Without hesitation it can be stated that Dewit + Castellan is a hands-on project architect, and the firm exudes a degree of professional commitment that involves it in undertakings from infancy to completion.

Current projects include the new Capreol Via Rail Station, the Ramsey Lake Waterfront Pre-Feasibility Study, and the recently commenced City of Sudbury Interdenominational Cemetery. Sudbury's newest architectural firm continues to demonstrate an uncompromising commitment to excellence. The legacy of Dewit + Castellan will be its direct involvement in helping to mould the site lines of the area. It will prove an enduring contribution to Sudbury's quality of life.

Right
The Via Rail Canada, Inc., passenger station in Capreol.

Below
The Valley East Recreation Complex in the town of Valley East. Duda & Dewit Architects

Above
A Dewit + Castellan-designed hairstylist's salon.

Left
The Sudbury Regional Credit Union, Copper Cliff Branch.

EVANS LUMBER AND BUILDERS SUPPLY LTD.

"Everything for Builders" has become a time-honoured slogan with Evans Lumber and Builders Supply Ltd. striving to meet the total needs of the builder.

In business since 1896, Evans Lumber began as a way for Thomas Evans to sell surplus material following the completion of a Copper Cliff job. However, the business continued with W.A. Evans, a son of Thomas Evans, becoming president in 1901 of the reorganized firm—then known as The Sudbury Building Supply Company.

For W.A. Evans, there was one primary intent—to assemble all building materials at one site. That site has been at the current location of 128 Pine since 1908. Previous locations at the foot of Cedar and on Xavier both succumbed to fire.

W.A. Evans, an astute, hard-working businessman in every way, believed in the principle of putting back into the community something of himself. In this regard, he was one of the principals to bring Bell Telephone to the city. He was an early promoter of and participant in rehabilitation programs and was actively involved in local sports programs. The Evans Cup for city soccer was a prize first presented by his widow to honour this interest.

Evans Lumber continues to be a family business. Presidents have included Thomas Evans, W. Arthur Evans (1901-1931), Del H. Andress (1932-1943), Henry M. Claridge (1944-1962), Ambrose C. Mantle (1962-1974), and E.D. "Ted" Evans (since 1974).

Community involvement and service within the management of Evans Lumber is almost a tradition. Principals have served as city alderman and have been members of the Sudbury and District Chamber of Commerce, the Planning Board, Lion's Club, Rotary Club, Thorneloe University, Salvation Army, Children's Aid, and the Church of the Epiphany. Three of the firm's presidents have been president of the Ontario Lumber and Building Material Dealers' Association.

Today Evans Lumber and Builders Supply Ltd. shares a nine-acre site with an A&P store and the Claridge Centre Office Tower, both built by the family. At Evans Lumber, customers will note that the policy is still "Everything for Builders," with construction needs from the foundation to the roof available at the firm's updated 13,000-square-foot showroom. A few of the services include the manufacture and sale of trusses, the installation of floors, and the supply of prefabricated kitchens. Unique to the area, Evans Lumber continues to operate a custom carpentry shop.

Thomas Evans founded the firm in 1896.

The firm recognizes that times change and businesses must adapt. However, one practice remains unaltered—W.A. Evans' notion to supply all the building materials for the builder. Today Ted Evans and the staff at Evans Lumber and Builders Supply Ltd. proudly carry on the company's long tradition of service—one that can be traced back to W.A. Evans and Thomas Evans.

The Sudbury Building Supply Company, predecessor to today's Evans Lumber and Builders Supply Ltd., circa 1906. This building was soon to become the CNR station.

Evans Lumber has been at 128 Pine since 1908.

RAINBOW CONCRETE INDUSTRIES LIMITED

HISTORICAL PROGRESSION OF RAINBOW CONCRETE INDUSTRIES LIMITED

1953 Two-man block operation.
1954 Built block plant to produce 6,000 blocks per day.
1961 Ready-mix plant on LaSalle Boulevard.
1963 Built Dowling plant.
1965 Built Espanola plant.
1968 Modernized block plant and expanded precast plant.
1971 Gravel pit, adjacent to airport.
1974 Block and precast plant in North Bay.
1976 Crushed slag work in Falconbridge, purchased ready-mix plant in Elliot Lake.
1977 Gravel pit in Elliot Lake.
1978 Ready-mix plant in Blind River.
1982 Concrete pipe plant in Sudbury, ready-mix plant in North Bay.
1984 Computerized ready-mix plant, Maley Drive.
1985 Kwik-mix manufacturing plant.
1986 Quarry in North Bay.

Nick Naneff was born and raised in Bulgaria and graduated with a degree in civil engineering from the University of Karlsruhe in Germany. At the end of World War II Bulgaria became a Communist country and Naneff's father's industry was nationalized; it was at this point that Nick Naneff chose to immigrate to Canada. In 1951 he arrived with no money and a very limited knowledge of the English language.

Settling in Sudbury, Naneff worked as an employee of one of the local mining companies for a short time. Recognizing the opportunities in the construction industry in northern Ontario, he started a small block plant with one employee in 1953.

In 1957 Naneff was joined by his wife, Gina, from Germany, and they built their home on the North Shore of Lake Ramsey. Mr. and Mrs. Naneff have two sons, both of whom are associated with the firm—Alexander, educated at Laurentian University, and Boris, a recent graduate of Carleton University with a degree in civil engineering.

Active in community affairs, Nick Naneff is a past president of the Rotary Club of Sudbury, past president of the Ready-Mix Concrete Association of Ontario, past president of the Sudbury Regional Development Corporation, a past director of the Sudbury Theatre Centre, and presently he is the chairman of the Joint Assessment and Planning Committee.

Through hard work, dedication to the needs of customers, imagination, and foresight, Nick Naneff has expanded his operations until today Rainbow Concrete Industries Limited is the largest, most modern firm of its kind in northern Ontario. He is most proud of the fact that during all his expansion programs he has never had to request financial assistance from the government. A man of vision and optimism, Naneff has the greatest faith in the continued expansion and business opportunities in Sudbury and northern Ontario.

Rainbow Concrete Industries Limited has supplied its fine concrete products to many projects in the Sudbury area, most notably Laurentian University, Sudbury's City Centre, Sudbury's Civic Square, the Provincial Building, the Taxation Data Centre, Cambrian College, the New Sudbury Shopping Centre, and the headframes of Falconbridge Nickel Mines' operations in Lockerby and Strathcona.

Nick Naneff, president.

Alexander Naneff

Boris Naneff

THE SUDBURY REGION

SII MINING EQUIPMENT COMPANIES CANADA

Located on a choice parcel of land in the Walden Industrial Park, SII Mining Equipment Companies Canada dominates the landscape on a ten-acre site. Today, with a work force of seventy and a payroll in 1985 exceeding two million dollars, the Sudbury Division of Smith International Canada Ltd. is a major economic presence in the Sudbury Basin. Yet the story of the Sudbury operation has a very local history that dates back to 1929.

That year John Edward "Jack" Rumball started the General Welding Company located at 10 Larch Street in Sudbury. During the next few years the firm would be located at a number of sites before moving to 34 Lorne Street in 1934, where it would have about twenty employees. One 1961 ad promoted the slogan, "If it's metal, we weld it." Jack Rumball, a welder by trade, operated a general repair shop where the emphasis was more on welding than machine work.

In 1950 J.E. Rumball was located at 26 Lorne Street. With Elliot Lake booming and production flourishing at Inco and the neighbouring sawmills, the firm's work force fluctuated between thirty and fifty. In 1957 J.E. Rumball was located at 433 McKim. Jack Rumball died in 1955 and there were five remaining partners: Reg Rumball, Stella Crawford, John Stanley, Alfred Cecil Smith, and Pryce Moorehouse. About twenty welders and fifteen machinists were employed.

Again, increased business necessitated a move, this time to expanded quarters at 1020 Elisabella Street. The partnership now consisted of John Stanley and Reg Rumball, brother of the founder. The work force expanded to about fifty, with the firm, now known as J.E. Rumball Ltd., having contracts with Cochranes, CIL, and EMCO. The securing in 1965 of a contract to lay pipeline from the Inco Oxygen Plant to the smelter swelled the work force to 70.

On November 1, 1971, the history of J.E. Rumball Ltd. entered a new phase following its sale by John Stanley to Drilco Industrial, a division of Smith International Inc. The local business that had offered the slogan, "If it's metal, we weld it," was now part of a large international corporation. Many of the employees, numbering sixty at the welding and machine shop and the retail business, were retained by Drilco.

A major decision for Smith International Inc. was the decision in 1977 to construct a million-dollar plant to replace the existing Elisabella Street site. With a grant of about $275,000, the Walden Industrial Park had its first tenant. Significantly, the emphasis would be on the

The J.E. Rumball shop at 34 Lorne Street, circa 1950. Gerry Edwards, with SII Mining Equipment Companies Canada, is shown in the back row, fourth from right. Stella Crawford and Reg Rumball are first and second from the right, respectively, in the same row.

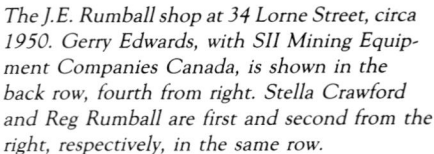

The ten-acre Walden plant site of SII Mining Equipment Companies Canada.

PARTNERS IN PROGRESS

Below
The shop at 1020 Elisabella Street in 1974. Enea Pividor, with SII Mining Equipment Companies Canada, is standing beside a blind-shaft drilling tool made for a West German client. The total weight of the drilling tool is 100,000 pounds with a capability of drilling up to a 108-inch-diameter hole.

Above
Raise drill rods are inspected at the Walden plant.

manufacturing of fabricated products for the mining industry. S.H. Hartley, president of Smith International Canada Ltd., commented at the sod-turning ceremony that with the larger facilities the company would be "more capable of serving our customers and the community."

The genesis of Smith International Inc. can be traced back to 1902, when the twenty-year-old H.C. Smith opened a blacksmith shop in Southern California. Soon Smith's blacksmith shop would be sharpening fishtail bits for oil drillers, beginning a business career that would parent a billion-dollar, international corporation. Today, with almost 7,000 employees around the world, Smith International Inc. earns 30 percent of its revenues from drill bits. In fact, the firm is the leader in American domestic sales of drill bits and is gaining steadily on the international market.

Drilco Industrial Canada, a division of Smith International Inc., was created in June 1972 with the mandate to specialize in the manufacturing of drilling tools for the mining, blind-shaft drilling, construction, water well, and mineral exploration industries. In 1972 J.E. Rumball Ltd. changed its name to Drilco Industrial Canada and commenced the manufacturing of drilling tools with the standard products of the Drilco line manufactured in Sudbury.

Since then, the Sudbury operation has been fabricating all items that relate to the drilling industry. Sudbury, the only such Drilco Industrial operation in Canada, has as its mandate the serving of the Canadian and Alaskan markets. Here products used in the mining of coal, base metals of lead, copper, zinc, precious metals, iron, and asbestos are manufactured.

At the Walden site, Smith International Inc. has managed successfully to blend experience from J.E. Rumball Ltd. with those relatively new to Smith International. Gerry Edwards, administration manager, came to J.E. Rumball in 1948; Enea Pividor, plant manager, in 1956; and Colleen Fenton, administrative assistant, in 1962. Robert Lipic, general manager, joined Smith International Canada Ltd. in 1974.

Smith International Inc. has facilities throughout the world, with manufacturing centres in Mexico, Italy, Germany, Scotland, South America, Australia, Canada, the United States, and a head office at Newport Beach, California. Smith International Inc. is affecting the international market more and more as the company serves the needs of the industry throughout the world.

In the case of the Sudbury operation, work has been shipped to Korea, Europe, the United Kingdom, Russia, South America, Australia, and Scandinavia. Manufactured in Sudbury are drill rods and stabilizers for underground and open-pit mining and exploration. As well, custom work for a wide range of clients is undertaken at the Sudbury plant. In 1985 some 2.8 million pounds of finished goods were shipped from the Walden plant. For Bob Lipic, "Canada's mining industry presents a challenge for mining companies to provide new technology and improved methods of metal recovery." In Sudbury, one senses these challenges are being met directly.

THE SUDBURY REGION

BRUNTON, BROWNING, DAY & PARTNERS

The firm of Brunton, Browning, Day & Partners, chartered accountants, has been part of Sudbury's business community since 1938, although not always under the same name.

On March 7, 1938, Stanley Brunton opened a small one-room office above the Grand Theatre on Elgin Street North and commenced to practise as a public accountant. Later that year he moved his office to the Northern Ontario Building on Durham Street and again in 1941 to the Balmoral Hotel on Elm Street. As the practice continued to flourish, larger offices were acquired in the Regent Theatre Building in 1942.

In 1945 Gordon Browning, a recent graduate, entered into partnership with Stanley Brunton, and the firm then became known as Stanley R. Brunton & Company. Edward "Ned" Brunton, a younger brother of Stanley, was admitted to the partnership in 1947, and over the ensuing five years the office staff expanded to ten people. This necessitated a relocation of the offices in 1952 to a new building that housed the Local Lines bus depot on Durham Street.

Partners, employees, and former employees gather to celebrate forty years of service of the late Aune Alho Maki. Mrs. Maki was employed as a bookkeeper in 1942 and served in that capacity until her retirement in 1984.

In December 1955 Frank Day joined the firm and was admitted to partnership on June 1, 1957. Expansion of the firm's business continued with clientele in Espanola, Blind River, Thessalon, Sault Ste. Marie, Chapleau, White River, and North Bay. On March 15, 1963, the name of the firm was changed to Brunton, Browning, Brunton & Day in recognition of the contributions made by the partners in these cities and towns.

On September 1, 1963, Ronald Heale and Edward Coe were admitted to the partnership. As a result of their contributions, over the next few years the firm's name was finally changed to Brunton, Browning, Day & Partners on September 30, 1970. Shortly thereafter, Ronald Heale became the resident partner of the office opened by the firm in Espanola. This office continues to flourish with Ronald Heale still at the helm. Edward Coe retired on March 1, 1986.

On December 1, 1972, John Ranger and Norman Yurich were admitted to the partnership, with James Corless following on June 1, 1976. Deborah Kuehnbaum was admitted on June 1, 1981, and Guy Forget on June 1, 1982.

Then, in October 1983, the firm moved its Sudbury offices to the sixth floor of the City Centre office building at 200 Elm Street East, and on December 1, 1983, Campbell & Babij, a Sudbury firm of chartered accountants, merged its practice with that of Brunton, Browning, Day & Partners, with John Campbell and Gregory Babij joining the partnership.

Back in 1942, Stanley Brunton employed a young woman as a bookkeeper. Her name was Aune Alho Maki. As the firm grew and partners were added, Mrs. Maki continued to manage the accounts and funds of the firm for forty-two years until her retirement in June 1984. With great sadness to the partners and staff, she passed away in November 1984.

Today a staff of thirty-six to thirty-eight is headquartered in the Sudbury office and seven in the Espanola office, including nine active partners, seven staff chartered accountants, three with other professional degrees, ten secretaries and computer operators, eight audit and computer technicians, and six to eight university students enrolled in co-operative courses leading to degrees such as bachelor of mathematics, bachelor of arts, and chartered accountants. Stanley Brunton continues to be professionally active with some estates of old clients. Deceased partners are Edward Brunton (April 14, 1973) and Gordon Browning (March 3, 1985).

Companies that have long been part of the business communities of Sudbury, Chapleau, Espanola, White River, and Sault Ste. Marie remain an integral part of Brunton, Browning,

Brunton, Browning, Day & Partners moved into the present offices in Sudbury's City Centre building in October 1983.

The firm's Durham Street office in 1938.

Day & Partners' clientele. Small family concerns are still using the firm's services, some now into the second generation of ownership.

The partners have contributed much to the growth and development of Sudbury and Espanola, some having served on boards of chambers of commerce, schools, hospitals, universities, golf clubs, and other nonprofit agency boards.

Brunton, Browning, Day & Partners has developed into one of the largest independent public accounting firms north of Toronto, servicing a clientele ranging in size from small businesses to branches of large public companies. The firm provides a full range of advisory services geared to the continued success of its clients in today's competitive and complex business environment. In addition to providing accounting and auditing services, Brunton, Browning, Day & Partners assists clients in developing cost-effective business plans, identifying sources of financing, and formulating personal and corporate tax planning strategies. Computer services with in-house and on-line capabilities are provided to many of the organization's clients. These services include the production of personal income tax returns. The Sudbury office also provides insolvency and receivership services.

The partners and staff of Brunton, Browning, Day & Partners are very proud to have been an integral part of the growth of Sudbury, Espanola, and Chapleau and confidently look forward to sharing the challenges ahead and to celebrating the firm's fiftieth anniversary in 1988.

137

THE SUDBURY REGION

MANITOULIN TRANSPORT INC.

Manitoulin Transport, headed by president D.A. Smith and vice-president W. Cumming, has established a solid reputation in the business of hauling freight based on the time-tested slogan, "The fastest service to and from the North."

In 1960 Manitoulin Transport began hauling between Manitoulin Island and southern Ontario. At the onset, the fleet was comprised of two trucks, three tractors, and four trailers.

The Sudbury Terminal for Manitoulin Transport dates from 1968 when the facility was first shared with its sister company, Roy E. Cooper Ltd., at 63C Elm Street West, behind the President Hotel. Opening a Sudbury terminal coincided with the firm's first direct Toronto to Sudbury service. This was a turning point for Manitoulin Transport. The Sudbury facilities have since served as the hub of all Manitoulin's services.

The Walden Industrial Park, just west of Sudbury, has been the location of the Manitoulin terminal and garage facilities since 1978. Located on a ten-acre site, the Sudbury Division has the latest in facilities. As well as being a major transfer point, it also houses the central repair facilities.

Located on ten acres in the Walden Industrial Park, just west of Sudbury, the Manitoulin Transport terminal is a major transfer point that serves most of northern Ontario.

Manitoulin developed the Super Truck especially for northern Ontario transport service.

Since its construction in 1978, the Sudbury site has undergone two expansions. In 1980 the garage was doubled in size. In 1985 further expansion occurred to both freight and garage facilities.

In 1980 Manitoulin Transport created and tested the first Super Truck. It was developed by the firm especially for northern Ontario freight needs. The vehicle is unique in that it consists of a modified conventional tractor equipped with a dromedary box behind the cab. Today, sporting eighteen-foot boxes, the Super Truck provides Manitoulin Transport with considerable flexibility in providing freight services.

Manitoulin Transport serves a significant percentage of northern Ontario from the Toronto-Hamilton and the greater Montreal areas. The company serves all points on Highway 17 from Sault Ste. Marie to Ottawa and on Highway 11 from Hearst to Barrie as well as the original Manitoulin points. In 1986 the firm commenced full-load service to and from the United States.

Hauling a wide range of commodities, Manitoulin Transport is a familiar sight on Ontario's highways. "Pulling for the North" has become a reality as Manitoulin Transport continues to reach destinations farther afield. The head office in Gore Bay houses all the corporate services, including financial, data-processing, central dispatch, and administrative services.

PARTNERS IN PROGRESS

TEAK FURNITURE CENTRE LTD.

In 1971 Tom Sorenson and Chris Jensen perceived a need for a new and different Sudbury furniture store—one specializing in quality European furnishings. Today Teak Furniture Centre Ltd. is one of the city's success stories.

Against advice to the contrary, Teak Furniture Centre was opened in October 1972 in the Edwards Building at 66 Elm Street. With an inventory totalling less than $10,000, Teak Furniture Centre entered a highly competitive market. Today Teak Furniture Centre Ltd. has stores in Sudbury, Sault Ste. Marie, Thunder Bay, North Bay, and Winnipeg.

Expansion of the Sudbury operation has been both steady and dramatic. Additional stores were opened in Sault Ste. Marie in 1973, Thunder Bay in 1976, North Bay in 1980, and Winnipeg in 1985. Today the total work force is about twenty-two.

The managers of the neighbouring stores have a one-third interest in their respective units while Chris Jensen and Tom Sorenson each retain equal interest. Thus, there is a linkage with the Sudbury operation and also a marked community presence. Managing the stores are Larry Ferguson in Sault Ste. Marie, Collins Springgay in Thunder Bay, Charlie Vlach in North Bay, and Leo Marsh in Winnipeg. In 1981 Sorenson, wishing to devote his energies more to his family, divested himself directly from the Sudbury operation. Jensen is now the sole owner-operator of the Sudbury store.

One important facet of the entire operation is the wholesale/importing unit of Teak Furniture Centre. All imports of teak furniture come from Denmark in forty-foot containers, each having one item in K.D. (knocked down) form for easier transporting. The various stores then draw from the warehouse. Sorenson and Jensen are joint owners of the division, which commenced in 1982.

Chris Jensen

Tom Sorenson

In 1953 Jensen came to Canada from Denmark, via Iceland. Following work in the oil fields of Alberta and stints in the mining communities of Uranium City, Elliot Lake, and Manitouwadge, he came to Sudbury. From 1966 until April 15, 1972, he was employed by McIsaac Mining and Tunnelling. Sudbury continues to be home for Jensen, his wife, Ruby, and their two children, Gitte and Erik.

Denmark was also home for Tom Sorenson. In 1961, responding to an exchange opportunity requiring farm hands, he ventured to Canada. After eight months working on farms, he decided to try mining and went to Manitouwadge—where he and his future partner met. After working in Manitouwadge and in the Maritimes, Sorenson migrated to Sudbury in 1968. There he was employed by McIsaac & Dravo and later Joy Manufacturing before Teak Furniture Centre was opened. Today Sudbury is home for Sorenson, his wife, Karen, and their two children, Kristee and Kory.

Teak Furniture Centre specializes in teak furniture, carrying about the same percentage of domestic and imported ware. Noted for a design that is "simple, practical, and timeless," Scandinavian teak furniture has enjoyed a steady increase in popularity since its introduction to the world market in 1930.

The firm's success can be attributed to a number of factors: the business acumen of Tom Sorenson and Chris Jensen, the quality of their wares with a full guarantee for life, and the emphasis on local ownership. It has proven a most appropriate combination for Teak Furniture Centre Ltd.

139

THE SUDBURY REGION

CARRINGTON'S BEAVER LUMBER

In 1944 two individuals very much identified with the building trade pooled their resources and bought the assets of Standard Planing Mills and Lumber Co. Ltd. With this, George C. Tate and Charles Carrington laid the base for one of Sudbury's continuing successes in the building supply industry.

For the two partners, the decision was not unusual in that both were well known to the construction trade. Charles Carrington, president of Carrington Construction, remained a partner until the late 1950s, when his interests were purchased by George Tate.

George C. Tate, born in Paris, Ontario, became familiar with northern Ontario as a sales representative for Gypsum Lime and Alabastine (which is now known as Domtar). To George Tate, who was then residing in New Liskard, Sudbury was "the growth area of northern Ontario," and hence a city of business opportunity. For the Tate family, Sudbury was soon home, and for many years George Tate contributed to the shaping of the community. A good example of his commitment to the area is that he was one of the founding governors of Laurentian University.

When Carrington Lumber and Builders Supply Ltd. opened on May 1, 1944, the site at 82 Lorne Street consisted of a small insul-brick building with a showroom of only 400 square feet. Over the years the building expanded into a modern facility of over 12,000 square feet. At first, the lumberyard consisted of only two storage sheds "behind the tracks";

"Everything for the Home Builder" was the motto of Carrington Lumber and Builders Supply Ltd. Shown is Sam Prince, formerly with Standard Planing Mills and Lumber Co. Ltd., who remained with Carrington's as the yard supervisor. Photo circa 1944

however, the actual site increased over the years to more than three acres as a result of the purchasing of adjacent businesses.

Today Carrington's Beaver Lumber remains in the Tate family, with two sons of George and Ruth Tate as joint owners and operators—Bob as president and Russ as secretary. In fact, a third generation of Tates is presently employed on both a full- and part-time basis.

From a skeleton staff of four in 1944, Carrington's continues to grow with Sudbury to the point where the firm's specialists are ready to help customers with a wide variety of products to suit their needs. With staff members having an average of thirteen years' service with the company, and five having over twenty-five years', experience continues to be a priority requirement for continued customer patronage. Whether it be paint, hardware, lighting, flooring, kitchen cupboards, plumbing, electrical, or, of course, lumber supplies, all can be found at this one location.

For Bob and Russ Tate there is an emphasis on providing a broad base of products and services to their customers. As their father before, they have made a commitment to Sudbury and exhibit community confidence. To this end, Carrington's Building Centre Ltd. in January 1984 purchased a Beaver Lumber franchise. As a member of Beaver Lumber, a firm that directs more than 170 stores in Canada, Carrington's is now associated with a group having "strong merchandising capabilities and sophisticated management expertise." The benefits are quite evident with the partnership of a well-known national name and a local independent operation of proven success.

Helping people "build dream homes out of houses" is thus an on-going desire for the Tate family. With a blend of time-honoured family tradition and the recognized drawing power of Beaver Lumber, Carrington's Beaver Lumber is well positioned to continue serving its Sudbury and area customers for years to come.

Carrington's Beaver Lumber at 82 Lorne Street in 1984.

PARTNERS IN PROGRESS

SLING-CHOKER MANUFACTURING LIMITED

Sling-Choker Manufacturing Limited, producer of rigging supplies for the mining, construction, and forestry industries, is located at 2122 Algonquin Road.

A partial view of Sling-Choker's wire-rope slings inventory.

It requires perception to detect a marketing opportunity. Such was the case in 1975 when Sling-Choker Manufacturing Limited was established, initially to provide slings and logging chokers.

Paul Villgren, the firm's president, was born in Finland and came to Sudbury at the age of five. Educated at the Haileybury School of Mines, he worked locally for both Inco and Falconbridge Limited in their engineering offices. The next step was sales, where he directed his energies toward the selling of mining equipment and supplies. After working for five and one-half years at a local outlet of the Timmins-based Hugh J. O'Neill Company, Villgren established Sling-Choker Manufacturing Limited on January 1, 1975.

At that time no Sudbury businesses were manufacturing slings for overhead lifting or chokers for the logging industry. Considering the community's emphasis on both mining and logging, the demand was most evident.

Over the past decade a number of related items have been added—cable bolting for mine-roof support, tow chains, nylon slings, tire chains, and a number of other products. With four industrial sewing machines, there stands the potential to manufacture tarps and to undertake heavy-duty industrial sewing of fabric or leather. In essence, Sling-Choker Manufacturing Limited has become—in the words of its president—"... a specialty house for rigging supplies." From 2122 Algonquin Road, products are manufactured for the mining, construction, and forestry industries.

Not surprisingly, sales for Sling-Choker Manufacturing Limited have been quite strong in northern Ontario. In fact, the company has expanded with manufacturing locations in Elliot Lake, Timmins, Sault Ste. Marie, and Noranda (Quebec). In total, the firm employs thirty-five persons—a marked increase from the two who began on January 1, 1975. At the Sudbury operation, with 12,000 square feet of plant on a three-acre parcel, seventeen persons are employed.

Sling-Choker Manufacturing Limited is a progressive company with a definite emphasis on the safety of its products. Membership in the U.S.-based Associated Wire Rope Fabricators and the Web Sling Association helps to ensure adherence to quality products being manufactured. Customers of Sling-Choker are provided with safety and rigging seminars at their convenience. Products from Sudbury and the other manufacturing locations are regularly tested for uniform quality content. Being the only sling manufacturer in northern Ontario to have a 250,000-pound pull-testing machine helps to ensure testing and quality control.

A combination of factors account for the organization's success—a close relationship with a relatively young and conscientious work force, that has an emphasis on quality control. With a growing demand for its products, Sling-Choker Manufacturing Limited has just begun its impact upon the market. The future appears bright for the young Sudbury-based firm.

BELANGER LINCOLN MERCURY SALES LTD.

To visit the only Lincoln Mercury dealer in the Sudbury region, one has to travel just a few minutes north of Sudbury to Chelmsford. There you will find what owner Gabe Belanger calls "the largest Mercury dealership in northern Ontario."

Belanger Lincoln Mercury Sales Ltd. began in 1971 with a staff of fifteen and sales of approximately two million dollars. By 1985 the staff complement had increased to over fifty, with sales near eighteen million dollars. Without hesitation, Gabe Belanger predicts that sales in 1986 will be the greatest yet, for "the market is there."

The official opening of the enlarged facilities occurred in April 1986. What is often referred to as the biggest Mercury showroom in Ontario has been expanded from 1,900 to 6,500 square feet and is located on seventy-seven acres. Other plans for growth are under way, including construction of a private landing strip for customers to be opened in 1986.

Though Belanger Lincoln Mercury is owned and operated by Gabe Belanger, the owner is quick to praise his staff for helping to bring success and recognition to the dealership. Included as part of the team are his wife, Laura, as vice-president and daughters Lynne and Louise as business manager and fleet and rental manager, respectively. In addition, he has hopes that daughters Frances and Josee will join the business in the future.

Belanger Lincoln Mercury carries a full line of Mercury cars and Ford trucks and has a complete parts department. As well, leases and rentals are an important facet of the dealership with the dealership being one of the larger lessors in the area. All customers are served in either the French or English languages.

If Belanger is not extolling the virtues of his models, he is praising the Sudbury area. The son of Adrien and Evelyn (Seguin), Belanger hails from the area, having been raised on the family farm with six sisters and four brothers. Gabe Belanger's involvement with sales began after World War II, when he helped his father sell meat at the Borgia Farmer's Market in Sudbury.

For Belanger Lincoln Mercury the direct emphasis on sales and follow-up service has resulted in repeat customers over the years. It has proven a winning combination for all associated with Belanger Lincoln Mercury Sales Ltd. of Chelmsford.

L'unique concessionnaire Lincoln Mercury de la région de Sudbury a pignon sur rue à Chelmsford, une quinzaine de kilométres au nord de la ville. Selon le propriétaire de l'entreprise, Gabriel Bélanger, il s'agit du "plus gros concessionnaire Mercury du nord de l'Ontario."

A ses débuts en 1971, Bélanger Lincoln Mercury avait un personnel de quinze personnes et un chiffre d'affaires de deux millions de dollars. Quatorze ans plus tard, l'équipe de Bélanger Mercury compte quarante-cinq personnes et les ventes s'élèvent à près de dix-huit millions. Les prédictions pour 1986? "Sans doute une année qui battra tous les records!"

L'inauguration des locaux agrandis et rénovés a eu lieu en avril 1986. La nouvelle salle de montre qui s'etend sur 6,500 pieds carrés est la plus grande des concessionnaires Mercury en Ontario. D'autres projets de développement, tel que la construction d'une piste d'atterissage pour accueillir les clients, sont déjà prévus pour 1986-1987.

Bien que Gabriel Bélanger soit le président et directeur général de Bélanger Lincoln Mercury, il est le premier à faire l'éloge de son personnel dynamique qui est certainement une des principales causes du succès de l'entreprise. L'équipe de Bélanger Lincoln Mercury comprend également l'épouse de Gabriel, Laura, qui est vice-présidente de la compagnie ainsi que ses filles Lynne et Louise qui détiennent respectivement les postes de gérante d'affaires et gérante de location. Le président de Bélanger Mercury espère bien que ses deux autres filles, France et Josée, se joindront également à l'équipe dans un avenir rapproché pour en faire une véritable entreprise familiale.

Bélanger Mercury offre toute la gamme de produits Mercury et camions Ford et possède un excellent département de pièces d'automobile pour desservir sa clientèle. On y retrouve également un département de location qui est d'autant plus important puisque le concessionnaire possède une gross part du marché des locations à court et à long terme. Signalons que tous les services sont disponibles en francais et en anglais.

Monsieur Bélanger s'enorgueillit d'avoir bâti une entreprise aussi prospère dans une région qu'il tient à coeur, puisqu'il y prend ses racines. Fils d'Adrien et Evelyne Bélanger (Séguin), Gabriel fut élevé sur la terre paternelle avec ses six soeurs et quatre frères, non loin de son actuel lieu de travail. Il se remémore ses débuts en affaires lorsqu'il accompagnait son père au Marché Borgia de Sudbury pour y vendre les produits de la ferme.

Si Bélanger Lincoln Mercury a connu une croissance aussi prospère dans le passé, c'est sans doute à cause de l'attention particulière que l'on porte aux clients et l'importance que l'on attribue aux ventes et aux services d'après vente. Pour Gabriel Bélanger et ses collègues, voilà la clè du succès.

IMPERIAL AUTO BODY

Unibody cars, paint booths, MIG welders, and plasma cutting systems all epitomize the changes associated with the auto body trade. Times have changed with Imperial Auto Body, a business that has worked to keep abreast of the latest technological innovations.

In May 1964 a partnership formed between Tarcisio "Tarcy" Stradiotto and Romano Pierobon resulted in Imperial Auto Body's opening on July 2. The enterprise was located at 51 Elm Street West on land leased from the Canadian Pacific Railway. Three structures—measuring forty by ninety, forty by sixty, and forty by sixty—were rebuilt and used until the lease expired in 1968. Then the move would be to 1000 Kingsway—the current location of Imperial Auto Body.

For the partners, experience in the field had been gained prior to 1964. In 1955 Tarcisio Stradiotto came to Canada from Bologna, Italy; his brother Joe had preceded him to Sudbury and established Joe's Auto Body Shop. It was there that Tarcy Stradiotto learned the trade. After attending a trade school in Toronto, the brothers became partners for about five years. As for Romano Pierobon, a community near Venice, Italy, had been home prior to his immigration to Sudbury in 1958. After a brief stint in Blind River, he returned to Sudbury in 1959 and began working at Joe's Auto Body Shop.

In 1964, when Imperial Auto Body began at 51 Elm Street West, the work force consisted of the two partners plus two others. With the move in 1968 to a much larger building where Pioneer Construction formerly had been located, opportunities for expansion occurred. Today fifteen are on the payroll at Imperial Auto Body.

Talking with the partners, it is evident that two major developments have dramatically changed the nature of work in the trade. However, with the correct equipment and skilled labour, vehicles can be repaired back to factory specifications. One change relates to the way in which automobiles are constructed. In the past, they were built around heavy steel frames. Repairs would occur following stringent measuring and frame-straightening techniques. However, in the interest of making cars lighter and more fuel efficient, heavy steel frames have been replaced. Today vehicles are constructed in panels welded together, with the car design referred to as "unibody."

To repair unibody vehicles, a bench system is required. Imperial Auto Body was the first shop in Sudbury to install a bench system. At the present time Imperial Auto Body has a Globaljig Bench. With about 85 percent of North American cars and 99 percent of European cars using the unibody design, a bench repair system is essential.

Another major change relates to the refinishing of vehicles. Currently being installed at Imperial Auto Body is a DeVilbiss downdraft spray and bake booth. Spray booths, the latest advancement, are self-contained units for the painting of cars. A downdraft of heated air envelopes the car, eliminating the possibility of overspraying, creating virtually dust-free conditions. As well, the paint is baked in the booth—thus giving the perfect cure cycle. Considering paint changes, the need for a spray booth is becoming more and more recognized for the maintenance of the highest standards of refinishing excellence.

In the 120- by 70-foot building, Imperial Auto Body has three spray booths, four preparation bays, and two cleanup areas in the paint section. The body shop section can accommodate seventeen vehicles in nine bays and an area for smaller cars.

Throughout Imperial Auto Body, one will find the latest in equipment. MIG welders that weld at a lower temperature in order that unibody steel will not heat up are in use. Soon what is known in the trade as a plasma cutting system will be installed to ensure sharp, clean cuts.

For years Imperial Auto Body has been a preferred shop for a number of major insurance companies. Considering the emphasis on a trained work force and the latest in equipment, it is not surprising that Imperial Auto Body has been favoured with a share of the market. Tarcy Stradiotto explains, "Technology is changing and we have to keep up to date." This results in the commitment made to excellence in the auto body industry by Imperial Auto Body.

Tarcy Stradiotto checking the Globaljig Bench.

Romano Pierobon in the new spray booth.

THE SUDBURY REGION

SUDBURY BOAT AND CANOE COMPANY LTD.

For many years Lake Ramsey has served as a recreation focal point for Sudburians and tourists. Helping to this end has been one business of long standing—Sudbury Boat and Canoe Company Ltd.

In 1920 Sudbury Boat and Canoe was founded by Allan "Skip" Chalmers—a Sudburian since 1890 when he arrived with his family at the age of three.

When Chalmers began Sudbury Boat and Canoe, the outboard motor was still in its infancy. Many, perhaps resistant to change, still were content to row or paddle. However, in 1920, Chalmers secured a Johnson Outboard Motor dealership, making Sudbury Boat and Canoe the oldest such dealership in Canada. In 1923 an invoice records that a detachable rowboat motor could be purchased for $140.

W.C. "Bill" Scott, who joined the company in 1937 as a dock boy, recalled that during the early years there were 100 canoes for rent—with all usually rented by noon on Sundays. Using the basement of a private home in the winter, Sudbury Boat and Canoe built canoes both for itself and the market.

Bill Scott bought the company from Allan Chalmers in 1958. Considering Scott's long association with the business, his purchasing of the firm would ensure a continuing genuine enthusiasm for Sudbury Boat and Canoe.

Under Scott, Sudbury Boat and Canoe changed with the times. Beginning as a supplier of rowboats and canoes, the firm now sells chain saws, lawn mowers, outboard motors, snow blowers, and many marine supplies. No longer is there the essential need there once was for a ferry service to camps on the islands or to Coronation Beach—a popular recreation site.

Maintaining a tradition first involving Allan Chalmers, Bill Scott served as an honorary judge in the Annual Sudbury Star Ice Guessing Contest. Reaching back over forty years, the tradition has generated considerable interest as many try to guess when the ice will officially leave Lake Ramsey each spring.

Since 1985 Sudbury Boat and Canoe has had a new owner, Gary Hodgins. Like Scott, he began at a young age as a dock boy and initially learned the trade working at Sudbury Boat and Canoe. With Hodgins, changes have included the selling of larger boats, the adding of the Ski-doo line, and the carrying of the Canadian Doral line of boats. By late 1986 new docks will be in place. The emphasis is on keeping pace with the changing times, supporting long-standing customers, and growing with tourism.

Suffice it to say that Sudbury Boat and Canoe Company Ltd. has a rich history, with both Allan Chalmers and Bill Scott leaving their special marks. Now the responsibility of carrying on the tradition lies with Gary Hodgins.

Allan Chalmers (left) hands over the keys to Bill Scott, who purchased Sudbury Boat and Canoe Company Ltd. in 1958. Note the 1922 Johnson outboard motor.

A recent photograph of the Sudbury Boat and Canoe Company Ltd.'s facilities. It is the oldest Johnson Outboard Motor dealership in Canada.

144

PARTNERS IN PROGRESS

GROUND CONTROL (SUDBURY) LIMITED

In late 1977 Ground Control was incorporated as a company for the distribution of products specific to mine-roof support. The firm's president is Paul Villgren and the general manager is Stephen McMurray.

From 1150 Kelly Lake Road, Sudbury, a variety of products are marketed—including rock bolts, rebars, rock bolt plate washers, and cable bolting, to name but a few. A wide variety of underground supplies and equipment is stocked. In addition, at Ground Control there is a commitment to custom fabricate a wide gamut of products to meet the needs specific to the individual customer. Soon, to better serve its customers, the corporation will be manufacturing its own rock bolts, rebars, and mining hardware.

Ground Control also manufactures resin cartridges. The sausage-shaped cartridges, which contain a resin grout and a catalyst kept separate by a thin plastic film, are designed to be inserted into drill holes. When activated, they achieve a stronger compressive strength than the surrounding rock, bonding steel rods or bars to inside drilled holes in order to secure unstable ground. The resin cartridges have a number of applications to the mining and civil engineering industries.

For Ground Control's resin cartridges, there is national distribution as well as an international market—with exports to the United States, Saudi Arabia, and South America. The Sudbury operation is the only plant in Canada of this type.

Serving as a competitor to the resin cartridge has been a cement cartridge. The ultimate cement cartridge was manufactured in England. In the interest of diversification, Villgren and McMurray travelled to England in June 1985, intent upon purchasing the operation. Soon the only plant of this type in the world was dismantled, with the equipment shipped to Canada and installed at 1150 Kelly Lake Road.

With this transaction a number of plusses came to Ground Control. The international customers in such areas as Norway, Australia, and South America were added to the growing list of Ground Control patrons. As well, a 10,000-square-foot expansion was added to the base 8,000-square-foot plant in March 1986. The work force of fourteen will be increased by about 40 percent.

Paul Villgren has tried to establish an operation not already in the area. With an operation unique to Canada, Ground Control is well poised to serve the local, national, and international markets. A continued willingness to custom fabricate products and an insistence on quality-control testing has ensured repeat customers. Ground Control serves as an excellent example of the way in which economic diversification is occurring in the Sudbury Basin.

Paul Villgren, president, founded Ground Control (Sudbury) Limited in 1977.

Stephen McMurray, general manager, loading a chartered airplane to deliver emergency supplies during the blocking of the St. Lawrence Seaway at Welland in 1985.

145

THE SUDBURY REGION

A. LAFRANCE & SONS LTD.

Lafrance Furs of Sudbury and North Bay has a rich history that spans much of northern Ontario. The name has been identified with the industry for almost eight decades.

Adelard Lafrance, the founder, was born at Chapleau on December 5, 1887, and had his first association with the fur business when he bought raw hides as an independent trader at his general store in 1908. From 1910 to 1922 he was the fur buyer for Revillon Freres of Paris; and he was located in Missinabie, Chapleau, and finally in Sudbury. His territory encompassed most of northern Ontario, west from Fort Francis, north to James Bay, and over to Ungava. In 1925, when Revillon sold its Ontario interests, Lafrance once again purchased raw hides on his own behalf.

He quickly perceived the need for repair and storage facilities for fur garments and in 1927 opened such an operation, as well as a retail outlet, at 8 Durham Street North—where the firm is still located. Through business contacts in Montreal he brought in skilled fur craftsmen to do the repairs.

Also in 1927 his eldest son, Edouard, began learning the art of raw fur buying, as well as the repair and storage aspects of the industry. Within five years the repair shop became a full-scale manufacturing facility; in addition, a fur cold-storage plant was constructed, just five minutes from the city's core, with a capacity to store more than 10,000 fur garments.

Subsequently, other sons joined the business: Laurent, in 1932, who eventually became manager of manufacturing and raw fur buyer; Yvon, the youngest, in 1934, as accountant and later as manager of the Sault Ste. Marie store from 1951 to 1983; and Adelard Jr., in 1937, assuming management of the North Bay store from 1945 until 1972.

A. Lafrance & Sons Ltd. continues to offer complete professional fur services from both its Sudbury and North Bay locations. Third-generation furriers Marc, in North Bay, and Gerard, in Sudbury, learned the business from their father, Edouard, and their uncles.

The family environment of the company is reflected by employee service, which in some cases exceeds forty years. This is a source of pride and satisfaction to the firm, as is the large and loyal family clientele often extending through four generations.

Each fur garment is individually and painstakingly selected for quality and style; and when the label "A. Lafrance & Sons Ltd." is sewn into the finished garment, it guarantees a tradition of the finest quality and workmanship.

Adelard Lafrance, founder, 1887-1967. Courtesy, The Sudbury Star

Edouard Lafrance

Yvon Lafrance, 1916-1984.

Marc Lafrance

Gerard Lafrance

PARTNERS IN PROGRESS

MUIRHEAD STATIONERS INC.

With a pedigree that goes back to 1891, Muirhead Stationers Inc. proudly rates as one of Sudbury's long-standing businesses. Although the name, location, and owners have changed with the passing years, there has been one constant: The store has always had stationery and office supplies as part of its stock.

Muirheads can be traced back to 1891, when Dan Baikie opened what was referred to as "The Sudbury Bookstore." An 1891 advertisement announced the following: "700 novels just arrived and blank books and note books in great variety." As well, Baikie's store stocked paper bags, wrapping paper, newspapers, and fashion journals. In 1903 the firm moved to a new location, formerly the site of a drugstore. Dr. W.H. Mulligan, J.S. Gill, and D. Baikie gave a contract to J.G. Henry to construct a new block to cost in the neighbourhood of $10,000.

Working for Baikie for seventeen years was F.C. Muirhead, who started at the age of thirteen just prior to the dawn of this century. The young employee's tasks included sweeping the floor, washing the windows, and meeting the train every morning for the magazines and newspapers. In 1915 he purchased Baikie's Bookstore, in the Baikie-Gill Block, and soon under the business name of F.C. Muirhead sold books, stationery, and school supplies.

The company would remain in the Muirhead family until 1972, with F.C. Muirhead at the helm until his death in 1941. Aside from his association with the business, Muirhead is remembered as an accomplished curler, taking part in the McDonald Brier Championships on more than one occasion.

A contemporary view showing the enlarged Baikie-Gill Block as it looks today. With the extensive expansion, Muirheads now has about 6,000 square feet of retail space.

In 1938 Bill Muirhead entered his father's operation and directed the business from 1941 until 1972, at which time it was sold to Alan Querney. Under Bill Muirhead's direction the business expanded its divisions—adding office furniture in 1945, an office machines division in 1947, and in 1957 opening the Larch Street location for office furniture and machines. With the various expansions the staff also enlarged from what in 1945 had comprised three people—Bill Muirhead and two young women.

Alan A. Querney, a chartered accountant with experience in the lumber industry, has continued the firm's expansion. In 1976 Muirheads received the Office Supply Order System (O.S.O.S.) franchise for Sudbury and area, with computerized systems enabling larger customers to monitor and control office supply usage by department. In 1978 the Larch Street operation moved to 9 Elm Street. A consultant was commissioned to consolidate the various departments under one roof for customer convenience and to provide a "new look."

Today Muirheads has five divisions—Social Stationery, Commercial Stationery, Office Furniture, Office Machines, and Drafting Supplies. With an expanded staff and increased services offered to customers, the largest office supply dealer in northern Ontario serves the business communities of Sudbury, Espanola, Elliot Lake, and Blind River.

Muirhead Stationers Inc., the "Complete Office Outfitters," continues to have a marked presence in the business community as it nears its centennial.

An early view of the Baikie-Gill Block, built in 1903, on Elm Street. The middle door was the entrance to Dan Baikie's store. J.S. Gill's Jewellery Store was entered from the door on the right.

THE SUDBURY REGION

ALEXANDER CENTRE INDUSTRIES LIMITED

Loading Happy Med, *the first ship loaded at Fisher Harbour. The cargo is lumber for Lebanon.*

With $300 from his father and $500 from a friend (Bill O'Lakey), and two $2 bills in his pocket, Cliff Fielding bought one red truck. That purchase of a two-ton red dump truck in 1935 launched the firm of C.A. Fielding Limited.

A son of George Parker Fielding and Agnes Ceasar, Cliff Fielding was born in Waters Township and raised in the Copper Cliff area. The family homestead has since become the Fielding Memorial Park—a recreation site and bird sanctuary. Cliff Fielding was one of eight sons and one daughter of George and Agnes Fielding. On May 16, 1936, Cliff Fielding married Lily Kivi, and the couple raised two children, Malcolm James and Brenda Elaine Wallace.

When Cliff Fielding ventured into the construction industry, sole sales were of two basic ingredients—sand and gravel. The building in 1935, by August Cecchetto, of the Copper Cliff Community Hall marked the new company's first gravel order. Soon this would be followed by a 2,000-yard order from Inco and a 9,000-yard order from Levack Mine in 1937. The year 1936 saw the first contract for smelter clay using two teams of horses, one truck, and three men handling 8,000 tons of clay per year.

At the time of its fifteenth year in business, 1950, C.A. Fielding Limited had grown to include a fleet of forty trucks and a staff of fifty. As well, two subsidiaries had been formed—Wavy Industries Ltd. and Northern Ski Company. In 1950 the head office of C.A. Fielding Limited was at 140 Douglas Street West.

In 1943, during a period of growth for the parent company, Cliff Fielding began the Northern Ski Company

Ltd. Promoted as Canada's largest ski factory, Northern Ski operated from 581 Edna Street. There, one could purchase cross-country and Alpine skis, along with all the accoutrements. Specific models were for children, youths, and adults, with the materials being hickory, birch, and maple. Thousands of pairs of Northern-made skis were fabricated in Sudbury, with sales made locally, nationally, and internationally. The firm identified itself with the slogan, "It Pays to Play," helping to popularize the sport in Canada during the 1940s.

Wavy Industries Limited, closer related to the parent company, began in 1946 when Cliff Fielding expanded into the area of concrete ready mix. Today the firm is located at One Ceasar Road, with the main plant within a large granitic knoll. The first of its kind in the world, Wavy Industries' plant is entirely underground to eliminate dust and noise and to protect the aggregates from winter exposure.

Located 150 feet beneath Precambrian rock, the plant is designed to serve as both a ready-mix and bulk cement mixing plant. The plant has a 135-foot-deep shaft, 80 feet in diameter for storage of materials and truck access by way of a 600-foot-long tunnel. To service the fleet of 50 ready-mix and bulk cement plants is an 80,000-square-foot garage.

From the original construction company of 1935, Cliff Fielding diversified to include not only Northern Ski and Wavy Industries, but also Fisher Construction Limited, Fisher Block, and Pioneer Construction, Inc. All operate under the aegis of Alexander Centre Industries Limited.

In 1948 Fisher Construction Limited used its tractor equipment to break or rip the waste slag from Inco's smelting operation; this was eventually shipped by rail cars to the railway companies for ballast. Since that time the firm has used millions of tons of ballast slag, as it was found superior to gravel ballast. In 1959 Ernie Loney, manager of Fisher, developed a new product that was called "Dry-Pac," where the slag is crushed to five-eighths of an inch and mixed with sand to make a granular "A" material. This has been accepted as an ideal material for top-dressing roads and general surface maintenance. A new plant opened in 1961 on Highway 144 to consolidate all the slag operations at one convenient site.

Fisher Block, an ideal adjunct to the cement business, produces and markets cement blocks and paving stones. Pioneer Construction, Inc., is readily recognized as a road builder and paving contractor.

Today the main focus of Cliff Fielding's activities is the promoting of Fisher Harbour. Purchased by Cliff Fielding, LaCloche Island, to the west of Sudbury, has 30,000 acres of level land. The proposed fresh-water harbour, with a depth of thirty-six feet, can accommodate any ship that currently uses the St. Lawrence Seaway, which has a water depth of twenty-nine feet six inches. When linked by a four-mile rail link with C.P. Rail, Fisher Harbour will be but seventy miles from Sudbury. All bulk commodities, metallic concentrator liquids and gases, pulp and paper products, general cargoes, and roll-on, roll-off traffic can be accommodated from this fresh-water harbour.

Community involvement has characterized Cliff Fielding's activities when he is not operating his business ventures. From May 6, 1970, to September 14, 1971, he was a director of the Canadian Pacific Railway and was reappointed as a director in August 1984. He is a former governor of Memorial Hospital and was the Thornloe University representative on the board of governors of Laurentian University.

In recognition of his support for the Boy Scouts and Girl Guide movement, Cliff Fielding was distinguished by being named an honorary patron of the Boy Scouts of Canada. In 1971 the Sudbury and District Chamber of Commerce named him one of Sudbury's outstanding citizens. In recognition of his achievements as a boxer and his support for the profession, in 1974 he was made a member of the Canadian Boxing Hall of Fame.

Proud of the Copper Cliff-Kelly Lake area and his roots in the region, Cliff Fielding has never stopped short of promoting northern Ontario. Heading a management team consisting of his son, Jim Fielding, and sons-in-law, Jamie Wallace and Kenneth L. McNamara, Cliff Fielding has forged a business enterprise that stands in stark contrast to its beginning at the Fielding homestead in 1935 when that one red truck was purchased.

The first ready-mix truck (1946), owned by Wavy Industries Ltd., a division of Alexander Centre Industries Limited, is kept on display.

Cliff Fielding, founder and chief executive officer.

MacISAAC MINING & TUNNELLING COMPANY

One route to success involves continuous personal perseverance over the long haul. This characterizes the story of John Carl MacIsaac, who in 1986 marked sixty-one years of underground mining experience.

Born in Butte, Montana, in 1906, J.C. MacIsaac moved with his parents to the silver-mining camp of Cobalt at the age of four. From there, they moved east to Cape Breton where his parents, as their parents before, tried mixed farming. At the age of eighteen J.C. MacIsaac left the farm to start on his own. The McIntyre Mines in Timmins proved to be the drawing card with work beginning on February 14, 1925, at fifty-three cents an hour.

Through the 1920s, 1930s, and 1940s, J.C. MacIsaac learned the mining operations first-hand while working as a miner at a number of sites in northern Ontario and northern Quebec. With this experience, MacIsaac soon learned what it cost to sink a shaft in the Precambrian Shield.

In 1947 MacIsaac had his first payroll and clerk as he secured a private contracting job—a shaft-sinking project at McKim, across from Murray Mine. From that start to 1985, MacIsaac Mining and Tunnelling has completed contracts for over twenty-five Canadian mining companies. Recent work has involved Inco, Falconbridge Limited, Noranda-Hemlo, Teck-Corona, Detour Lake, Rio Algom, and Science North.

Incorporation of the company occurred in 1953, and three years later the business address became 2070 Old Burwash Road. Prior to the move the firm had operated from the basement of the MacIsaac home at 160 Patterson Street with the office over the garage. At MacIsaac Mining and Tunnelling, virtually all aspects of mining operations are undertaken. Indicative of the scope of work, since 1947 MacIsaac has compiled the following statistics: shafts sunk in excess of twenty miles, over forty-six miles of track drifts completed, about thirty-two miles of raises undertaken, and close to seven million tons of ore removed. Shaft No. 77 was completed at Detour Lake in the latter part of 1985. Not surprisingly, at one time MacIsaac employed as many as 800 men in the Sudbury district.

In 1968 J.C. MacIsaac established Baycar Steel Fabricating Ltd. because the previous year the firm had eighteen jobs in the Sudbury area and the securing of mine hardware had proved to be a problem. Baycar Steel is a service-oriented steel fabricating company with the capacity to design and fabricate a wide range of mining equipment. A few of the main product lines at Baycar Steel include mine cars, ore chutes, mobile cranes, backhoes, and scoop-tram buckets. Contracts for custom work have been secured by Baycar Steel across the United States and Canada.

A third MacIsaac venture is Sudbury Downs Holdings, a wholly owned, totally integrated harness racing operation that opened on June 4, 1974. Situated on a 149-acre parcel of land just minutes from Sudbury in Rayside Balfour, Sudbury Downs has

J.C. MacIsaac, founder, learned the mining business first-hand during the decades of the 1920s, 1930s, and 1940s. He sank the first shaft for his own mining operation in 1947.

facilities for about 3,000 people, barns for 360 horses, and a half-mile track. According to J.C. MacIsaac, "I've been a horse-racing fan for years and there just wasn't a track in the area." Employed at Sudbury Downs are 12 permanent and about 200 part-time workers. For those who enjoy fine horse racing—pacers and trotters—the evenings are Wednesday and Saturday with ten to eleven races to the card.

J.C. MacIsaac would be the first to acknowledge that many changes have occurred in the mining industry since he went underground sixty-one years ago at Timmins. Since 1947 MacIsaac Mining and Tunnelling has ranged over North America and India, Baycar Steel has established itself as a custom fabricator, and Sudbury Downs has brought enjoyment to many. Recently, with his son, Pat, installed as vice-president, J.C. MacIsaac has had more time to enjoy other interests including horses and Sudbury Downs. It is a well-deserved respite.

PARTNERS IN PROGRESS

LAW OFFICES OF JOE ZITO

Old City Hall, at 83 Cedar Street in downtown Sudbury, houses the Law Offices of Joe Zito.

Called to the Bar on March 25, 1977, Joe Zito practises his profession in the community where he was born. A son of Gaetano and Rosina Zito, who emigrated from Calabria, Italy, with their infant daughter, Immacolata, born in Calabria, Italy, Joe Zito was educated at St. Charles College, the University of Western Ontario, and attended law school at the University of Ottawa. The aspiring lawyer articled in Sudbury from 1975 to 1976.

The Law Offices of Joe Zito is in general practice with work undertaken in criminal and civil work, family and municipal, real estate and commercial law.

Joe Zito serves as the lawyer for the Town of Rayside-Balfour, the Township of Spanish River, and Mine Mill Local 598. As well, he was appointed solicitor for northern Ontario, representing OMR Insurance Brokers Ltd.—a firm working in the area of municipality liability insurance. A particular interest of the lawyer relates to municipal litigation.

The renovation of the Old City Hall, a project with which Joe Zito has been actively involved, has served to rejuvenate a heritage landmark. Erected in 1914, the facility first served as the Bell Telephone Exchange Building until it became the location of Sudbury's Municipal Offices. Today, appropriately called Old City Hall, the four-storey building has 17,000 square feet of office space and there is full occupancy. The Old City Hall contains boutiques, the Casablanca Tavern, a branch of the Bank of Montreal, an office of the Canada Life Assurance Company, and the Law Offices of Joe Zito.

Renovated under the direction of Gaetano Zito, the structure has retained a traditional form, with the exterior lines virtually intact. The law offices have been altered to a style more reflective of an era earlier than that depicted on the other floors. Interspersed throughout are print images that quickly evoke a feeling of nostalgia.

A major emphasis for Joe Zito has been a continued effort to make his practice accessible. There are branch offices in Chelmsford and one at the New Sudbury Shopping Centre. Clients of Joe Zito are served in one of three languages—Italian, French, or English. Associated in the law practice are lawyers John Luczak, Carolyn Dawe, Frank Anzil, Louise Chevrier, and Elizabeth Cari.

Community involvement has been varied. Joe Zito has played an active role in the annual Easter telethons and the Montessori Club. As well, he has served on the board of directors of the Victoria Order of Nurses and St. Leonard's Sudbury House. Also, the firm's employees participate in local soccer, baseball, and bowling teams under the banner of Old City Hall.

Joe Zito and his wife, Sonja, believe that Sudbury is an ideal community for raising their two children, Rosalie and Guy. Considering his marked community involvement and the desire to retain a bit of the past, it is evident that Joe Zito has made a commitment to his hometown.

Fully renovated by Gaetano Zito, the Old City Hall at 83 Cedar Street houses the Law Offices of Joe Zito.

Joe Zito, shown here in his office in Old City Hall, whose general law practice serves the Sudbury community.

THE SUDBURY REGION

ATLAS ALLOYS

For more than fifty years Atlas Alloys and its founding companies have serviced the metal needs of Canadian industries. Atlas Alloys began in 1966 when the warehousing divisions of Atlas Steels Company amalgamated with Alloy Metal Sales Limited. Since then, it has operated as a division of Rio Algom Limited—a Canadian public company that is part of the Rio Tinto Zinc Corporation.

Atlas Steels opened a chain of warehouses in the 1930s to stock the products made at its Welland, Ontario, plant—principally alloy steel bars for tooling and machinery uses.

Alloy Metal Sales opened its doors in January 1941 as a wholly owned Inco subsidiary. Its initial function was to allocate the supply of primary nickel and wrought nickel alloys that were important to the war effort. After the war the firm became identified as a supplier of corrosion and heat-resistant alloys and aluminum.

Initially metal distribution was primarily a warehousing operation offering customers off-the-shelf availability

Atlas Alloys' Metal Service Centre in Sudbury's Walden Industrial Park. It serves as the first fully integrated centre of its kind to serve the mining and pulp and paper industries in northern Ontario.

The Etobicoke branch of Atlas Alloys serves as the firm's head office in Canada.

of standard mill items. Some warehouses became metal service centres where the basic inventory was converted into sizes or pieces close to the customer's actual needs, providing savings in processing and scrap costs.

Atlas Alloys has been a pioneer in the adoption of these first-step processing facilities, becoming the first Canadian metal centre to install a level-and-cut line to convert coils of stainless steel and aluminum to flat sheets for its customers. Also, it was the first in the field to use plasma arc technology to cut thick plates of stainless steel and nickel alloys to specific shapes. Now more than 75 percent of the orders filled are processed in one way or another before the materials are shipped.

As a result of the amalgamation and the emergence of new Canadian markets, the company now has a presence from coast to coast with twelve warehouse locations. In 1977 Atlas Alloys selected the Walden Industrial Park in Sudbury as the site for its first fully integrated Metal Service Centre serving the mining and pulp and paper industries in northern Ontario. A major expansion in 1982 resulted in a new 15,000-square-foot facility.

Today Atlas Alloys is one of Canada's premier distributor organizations of stainless steel, Inco high-nickel alloys, aluminum, tool steels, and machinery steels. The quality assurance of material is an important part of all operations.

The Sudbury Basin is a major supplier of many key alloying elements to the specialty steelmakers of the world. The companies of northeastern Ontario are major consumers of these materials through specialty steel service centres such as Atlas Alloys.

PARTNERS IN PROGRESS

TOWNEND, STEFURA, BALESHTA AND NICHOLLS, ARCHITECTS

The architectural firm of Townend, Stefura, Baleshta and Nicholls has added much to the skyline of Sudbury with (clockwise) St. Andrew's Place; General Leasehold Towers; Christ the King Senior Citizens Building; City Centre Tower; the Government of Ontario Building; Bell Canada; Civic Regional Building; and Sudbury Theatre Centre.

Historically, the architectural profession in the Sudbury area is not very old. P.J. O'Gorman is recognized as the pioneer architect of northeastern Ontario (1919 to 1959). He designed many of the local schools, hospitals, churches, and commercial buildings, among them the Lansdowne School, St. Elizabeth School of Nursing, Christ the King Church, and the Mackey Block. Readily recognized as the second generation of architects are John Bernard Sutton and Louis N. Fabbro. Their individual work includes the Sudbury Arena, and the former Canadian Legion Hall and Sudbury General Hospital, respectively.

In 1964 Arthur Townend and John Stefura established their original partnership, and they were joined by John Baleshta a year later. Several changes in the organization occurred between 1965 and 1973. Blaine Nicholls joined the firm in 1977 and it has been known as Townend, Stefura, Baleshta and Nicholls since then.

Through its design talents, the firm has contributed to many major changes in the skyline of Sudbury and its neighbouring communities. It has been associated with many projects that have improved Sudbury's living, working, and learning environment. The high quality of the design work of Townend, Stefura, Baleshta and Nicholls has been recognized with three national design awards—

St. Mary's Ukrainian Catholic Church, Sudbury. Townend, Stefura, Baleshta and Nicholls, Architects.

for the Northern Ontario Health Sciences School, the Thorneloe University Chapel, and the Information Centre at Fielding Park in Walden.

Whether as volunteers of community organizations, or as architects, the partners have exhibited unwavering support for the region and dedication toward the enrichment of the quality of life of its citizens.

A small but representative sample would include Teachers' College at Laurentian University, 1965; Northern Ontario Health Sciences School, 1966; Thorneloe University Chapel, Laurentian University Campus, 1967; Rayside Composite School, 1969; Laurentian Hospital, 1969-1974; Cambrian College, 1969-1980; Walden Community Centre and St. Mary's Ukrainian Catholic Church, 1970; St. Andrew's Place, 1971; Mail Processing Building, 1972; Civic Square, 1973-1976; Bell Canada and Peter Piper Hotel, 1975; Ontario Government Building, 1978-1980; Taxation Centre (joint venture with Page and Steele) and Southridge Shopping Mall, 1979; Northern Telephone's headquarters, 1980; City Centre Tower, 1981; Sudbury Science Centre, 1981-1982 (joint venture with R. Moriyama); Christ the King Senior Citizens Building and Fielding Memorial Park, 1982; Parry Sound Coast Guard Base, 1983-1986; Smooth Rock Falls General Hospital, 1985-1986; and Northeastern Ontario Cancer Treatment Centre at Laurentian Hospital, 1986—.

Before the introduction of railroads, freight was transported by canoes. This circa 1909 view is of Elm Street, looking west. Courtesy, Michael J. Mulloy

PATRONS

The following individuals, companies, and organizations have made a valuable commitment to the quality of this publication. Windsor Publications and the Sudbury & District Chamber of Commerce gratefully acknowledge their participation in *The Sudbury Region: An Illustrated History.*

Air Canada
Alexander Centre Industries Limited*
Atlas Alloys*
Barné Builders*
Belanger Lincoln Mercury Sales Ltd.*
Bristol Machine Works Limited*
Brunton, Browning, Day & Partners*
Robert G. Bryson Limited
Cambrian Insurance Brokers Limited
Campeau Corporation*
Carrington's Beaver Lumber*
Collège Cambrian College*
Dewit + Castellan Architects*
D.S. Dorland Limited
Evans Lumber and Builders Supply Limited*
Falconbridge Limited*
Frontenac Hotel*
Ground Control (Sudbury) Limited*
Henninger's Diesel Limited
Imperial Auto Body*
Inco Limited*
Lacroix, Forest & Del Frate
A. Lafrance & Sons Ltd.*
L'Université Laurentienne*
Laurentian University*
Law Offices of Joe Zito*
Loeb Inc., Sudbury Division*
MacIsaac Mining & Tunnelling Company*
Manitoulin Transport Inc.*
Marcotte Mining Machinery Services Inc.*
Maslack Supply Ltd.*
Mid North Motors and Sudbury Auto Body Supply*
Muirhead Stationers Inc.*
National Bank of Canada
Northern Cable Services Limited*
Northern Uniform Service Corp.*

Ontario Centre for Resource Machinery Technology
H.A. Perigord Co. Ltd.
W.B. Plaunt & Son Limited
Rainbow Concrete Industries Ltd.*
Reliable Window Cleaners (Sudbury) Limited*
Voitto and Esme Rintala
Sheraton Caswell Inn
SII Mining Equipment Companies Canada*
Sling-Choker Manufacturing Limited*
Sudbury & District Medical Society, Dr. J.B. Mulloy, President
Sudbury Boat and Canoe Company Ltd.*
Sudbury Steam Laundry and Dry Cleaners Ltd.*
Sudbury Welding Limited
Tamrock Canada Inc.*
Teak Furniture Centre Ltd.*
The Toronto Dominion Bank
Thorne Riddell
Townend, Stefura, Baleshta and Nicholls, Architects*
Tri-Care Group of Companies*
James Wendler Limited
Mayor Peter Wong and the City of Sudbury

*Partners in Progress of *The Sudbury Region: An Illustrated History.* The histories of these companies and organizations appear in Chapter VII, beginning on page 104.

BIBLIOGRAPHY

Abella, Irving Martin. *Nationalism, Communism, and Canadian Labour: The CIO, the Communist Party, and the Canadian Congress of Labour.* Toronto: University of Toronto Press, 1973.

Beach, Noel. "Nickel Capital: Sudbury and the Nickel Industry, 1905-1925." *Laurentian University Review* VI, no. 3 (June 1974).

Berton, Pierre. *The Last Spike: The Great Railway, 1881-1885.* Toronto: McClelland and Stewart, 1971.

Bray, Matt, and Ernie Epp. *A Vast and Magnificent Land.* Thunder Bay and Sudbury: Ministry of Northern Affairs, 1984.

Bray, R.M. "The Province of Ontario and the Problem of Sulphur Fumes Emissions in the Sudbury District—An Historical Perspective." *Laurentian University Review* XVI, no. 2 (February 1984): 81-90.

Cadieux, Lorenzo. *Frédéric Romanet du Caillaud: "Compte" de Sudbury.* Montreal: Editions Bellarmin, 1971.

Chrétien, Jean. *Straight From The Heart.* Toronto: Key Porter Books, 1985.

Croatians in the Sudbury Centennial. Sudbury: 1983.

Department of History, Laurentian University. *Biographies of the Sudbury Region.* Sudbury: 1980.

Devereaux, Helen. "The Last 8000 Years." *Polyphony* V, no. 1 (Spring 1983).

Deverell, John, and the Latin American Working Group. *Falconbridge: Portrait of a Canadian Mining Multinational.* Toronto: Lorimer and Company, 1975.

Dorian, Charles. *The First Seventy-Five Years: A Headline History of Sudbury.* Ilfracombe, Devon: Arthur H. Stockwell, Ltd., 1959.

Gervais, Gaetan. "Les Franco-Sudburois, 1883-1983." *Polyphony* V, no. 1 (Spring 1983).

_____. "Le Reseau Ferroviaire du Nord-Est de l'Ontario, 1851-1931." *Laurentian University Review* XIII, no. 2 (February 1981).

Hallsworth, Gwenda. *"A Venture into the Realm of Higher Education": A Brief History of Laurentian University.* Sudbury: Laurentian University Press, 1985.

Havel, Jean. *Politics in Sudbury.* Sudbury: Laurentian University Press, 1967.

Higgins, E.G. *Twelve O'clock and All's Well: A Pictorial History of Law Enforcement in the Sudbury District (1883-1978).* Sudbury: Journal Printing, 1978.

Higgins, Edwin G., and F.A. Peake. *Sudbury Then and Now: A Pictorial History of Sudbury and Area, 1883-1973.* Sudbury: Sudbury and District Chamber of Commerce, 1977.

Howey, Florence. *Pioneering on the CPR.* Privately printed, 1938.

Humphries, Charles W. *"Honest Enough to Be Bold": The Life and Times of Sir James Pliny Whitney.* Toronto: University of Toronto Press, 1985.

Ignatieff, George. *The Making of a Peacemonger: The Memoirs of George Ignatieff.* Toronto: University of Toronto Press, 1985.

Kealey, Gregory S. "1919: The Canadian Labour Revolt." *Labour Le Travail: Journal of Canadian Labour Studies,* XIII (Spring 1984).

Kelly, Michael C. "By Divine Right. Sudbury as a Regional Metropolis, 1900-1910." Unpublished research paper, University of Toronto, 1985.

Kelly, Michael C., et. al. *Inventory and Guide to Historic Buildings in Sudbury.* Sudbury: Young Canada Works, 1978.

Krasic, Ljubo. "Croatians of Sudbury: Mobility of the Immigrants, 1880s to 1940s." *Polyphony* V, no. 1 (Spring 1983).

Krats, Peter V. "Suomalaiset Nikkelialuella: Finns of the Sudbury Area, 1883-1983." *Polyphony* V, no. 1 (Spring 1983).

Lang, John B. "A Lion in a Den of Daniels. . ." M.A. thesis, University of Guelph, 1970.

Lautenbach, William. *Land Reclamation Program: Regional Municipality of Sudbury, Preliminary Report.* Sudbury: Vegetation Enhancement Technical Advisory Committee, 1985.

LeBourdais, D.M. *The Sudbury Basin: The Story of Nickel.* Toronto: Ryerson, 1953.

Lemieux, Germain. *De Sumer au Canada Francais: Sur les Ailes de la Tradition.* Sudbury: Société Historique du Nouvel-Ontario, 1968.

Lewis, Gertrud Jared. "German-Speaking Immigrants in the Sudbury Region." *Polyphony* V, no. 1 (Spring 1983).

_____. "Germans in Northern Ontario." *Laurentian University Review* XV, no. 1 (November 1982).

McClelland-Wierzbicki. *The Great Depression in Northern Ontario, 1929-1934.* Sudbury: Laurentian University Press, [1978].

Malcolm, Andrew H. *The Canadians.* Markham, Ontario: Fitzhenry and Whiteside, 1985.

Mount, Graeme S., and Michael J. Mulloy. *A History of St. Andrew's United Church, Sudbury.* Sudbury: Journal Printing, 1982.

Newman, Peter C. *The Canadian Establishment.* 2d ed. Vol. 1. Toronto: McClelland and Stewart-Bantam.

Pagnucco, Frank. *Homegrown Heroes.* Sudbury: Miller Publishing, 1982.

Peake, F.A. *The Church of the Epiphany, Sudbury, Ontario.* Sudbury: Journal Printing, 1982.

Peake, F.A., and R.P. Horne. *The Religious Tradition in Sudbury, 1883-1983.* Sudbury: Journal Printing, 1983.

Peters, T.H. "Inco Limited Tailings Revegetation Program, 1950-1980." Paper presented at the Tenth Annual Meeting of the Canadian Land Reclamation Association, Laval University, 1985.

_____. "Case 7-8. Rehabilitation of Mine Tailings. . ." In *Effect of Pollutants at the Ecosystem Level.* New York: John Wiley & Sons, 1984.

Pye, E.G., et. al. *The Geology and Ore Deposits of the Sudbury Structure.* Toronto: Ministry of Natural Resources, 1984.

Radecki, Henry. "Polish Immigrants in Sudbury, 1883-1980." *Polyphony* V, no. 1 (Spring 1983).

Roberts, Wayne, ed. *Miner's Life: Bob Miner and Union Organizing in Timmins, Kirkland Lake and Sudbury.* Hamilton: Labour Studies Programme, McMaster University.

Saarinen, O.W. "Finns in Northeastern Ontario with Special Reference to the Sudbury Area." *Laurentian University Review* XV, no. 1 (November 1982).

Schull, Joseph. *Ontario Since 1867.* Toronto: McClelland and Stewart, 1978.

Serbanescu, M.D., T.H. Peters, and J.D.

Shorthouse. "Environmental Conditions within a Northern Ontario Mine Converted for Vegetable Production." *Canadian Journal of Plant Science* (January 1982).

Simon, Victor. *Le Reglement XVII: Sa mise en vígeur à travers l'Ontario, 1912-1927.* Sudbury: Société Historique du Nouvel Ontario, 1983.

Solski, Mike, and John Smaller. *Mine-Mill: The History of the International Union of Mine, Mill and Smelter Workers in Canada Since 1895.* Ottawa: Steel Rail Publishing, 1984.

Southern, Frank. *The Sudbury Incident.* Toronto: York Publishing and Printing, 1982.

Stefura, Mary. "The Process of Identity: A Historical Look at Ukrainians in the Sudbury Area Community." *Laurentian University Review* XV, no. 1 (November 1982).

Stelter, Gilbert A. "Community Development in Toronto's Commercial Empire: The Industrial Towns of the Nickel Belt, 1883-1931." *Laurentian University Review* VI, no. 3 (June 1974).

_____. "The Origins of a Company Town: Sudbury in the Nineteenth Century." *Laurentian University Review* III, no. 3 (February 1971).

Sudbury and District Chamber of Commerce. *To Our City: Sudbury Centennial, 1883-1983.* Sudbury: 1983.

Tester, Jim. *The Shaping of Sudbury: A Labour View.* Address to a public meeting of the Sudbury and District Historical Society, April 18, 1979.

Thompson, John F., and Norman Beasley. *For The Years To Come.* Toronto: Longmans, Green and Company, 1960.

Visentin, Maurizio. "The Italians of Sudbury." *Polyphony* V, no. 1 (Spring 1983).

Young, Scott, and Astrid Young. *Silent Frank Cochrane: The North's First Great Politician.* Toronto: 1973.

ARCHIVES

Canadian Club Archives
Community Concert Archives
Croatian Archives of Sudbury
German Archives of Sudbury, Laurentian University
Huntington University Archives, Sudbury
Northern Life Archives
St. Andrew's United Church Archives, Sudbury
Sudbury Industrial Archives, Laurentian University
Sudbury Regional Archives, Civic Square

This circa 1940 view is of Elm Street, downtown Sudbury. Courtesy, Gary Peck

THE SUDBURY REGION

INDEX

PARTNERS IN PROGRESS INDEX

Alexander Centre Industries Limited, 148-149
Atlas Alloys, 152
Barné Builders, 130
Belanger Lincoln Mercury Sales Ltd., 142
Bristol Machine Works Limited, 124
Brunton, Browning, Day & Partners, 136-137
Campeau Corporation, 108
Carrington's Beaver Lumber, 140
Collège Cambrian College, 126-127
Dewit + Castellan Architects, 131
Evans Lumber and Builders Supply Limited, 132
Falconbridge Limited, 112-113
Frontenac Hotel, 129
Ground Control (Sudbury) Limited, 145
Imperial Auto Body, 143
Inco Limited, 116-117
Lafrance & Sons Ltd., A., 146
L'Université Laurentienne, 111
Laurentian University, 110
Law Offices of Joe Zito, 151
Loeb Inc., Sudbury Division, 128
MacIsaac Mining & Tunnelling Company, 150
Manitoulin Transport Inc., 138
Marcotte Mining Machinery Services Inc., 109
Maslack Supply Ltd., 123
Mid North Motors and Sudbury Auto Body Supply, 107
Muirhead Stationers Inc., 147
Northern Cable Services Limited, 120-121
Northern Uniform Service Corp., 119
Rainbow Concrete Industries Ltd., 133
Reliable Window Cleaners (Sudbury) Limited, 122
SII Mining Equipment Companies Canada, 134-135
Sling-Choker Manufacturing Limited, 141
Sudbury & District Chamber of Commerce, 106
Sudbury Boat and Canoe Company Ltd., 144
Sudbury Steam Laundry and Dry Cleaners Ltd., 118
Tamrock Canada Inc., 114-115
Teak Furniture Centre Ltd., 139
Townend, Stefura, Baleshta and Nicholls, Architects, 153
Tri-Care Group of Companies, 125

GENERAL INDEX
Italicized numbers indicate illustrations.

A
Abbott, Harry, 14
Apolloni, Gordon, *80*

Arthur, Mayor Robert, 26
Artists, 47, *81-83*
Asians, 24-25

B
Badminton, 79
Ballet, 44, 49
Baseball, 71
Basketball, 77
Basketball teams, 77, *80*
Baumann, Alex, 100-*101*
Beaton, Bill, 79
Bell Park, 15, *70, 85, 89*
Bell, William Joseph, 15, 57
Biscotasing, 13
Blakey, Thirston "Rusty," *60*
Borden, Robert, 35, *58,* 60
Boxing, 77-78, *80*
Bristol, Edmund, *58*

C
Caillaud, Frédéric Romanet du, 18
Canadian Club, 49-50
Canadian Copper Company, 14, 15, *16,* 18, 21, 36
Canadian Pacific Railway (CPR), 9, 10, 13, 20, 24, 39
Canadian Women's Army Corps (CWAC), *32, 39*
Canoeing, 79-80
Cape Breton, 12
Capreol, 9, 34, *82,* 83
Carlin, Robert H., 41-42, 65, 66, 69
Centre des Jeunes, 46, *65*
Chelmsford, 34, *81,* 83
Chew, Sam, 26-27
Chinese, 24, *27,* 28; treatment of, 25-27
Chorale des Benevoles, *46*
Chretién, Jean, *65*
Clark, Joe, 63
Cochrane, Frank, *58,* 59-60, 69
Collins, E.A., *42*
Communism, 41, 49, 65, 66
Conservatives, 36, 42, *58,* 60, 61, 65
Co-operative Commonwealth Federation (CCF), 50, 65
Co-operative Commonwealth Federation/ New Democratic Party (CCF/NDP), 61
Copper: development of, 15; discovery of, 14; origin of, 11; production during World War I, 34
Copper Cliff, 9, 10, 15, *16-17,* 18, *21, 34,* 35, *42,* 66, 68-69, *92*
Copper Cliff Highland Band, *31*
Copper Cliff Highlanders Cadet Corps, *22*
Copper Cliff Museum, 57
Copper industry, 34
Corringham, Robert, 67
Crean, Charles Francis, 14
Creighton, 21
Creighton Mine, 14, *68*

Croatians, 25, *28,* 29
Culture, 8, 9, *44*-57
Curling, 72
Cycling, 99-*100*

D
de la Riva, Paul, *97*
de la Riva, Ricardo, *62,* 72, *74*
de la Riva, Richard, *99*
Depression, the, 35
Desmarais, Paul, 66, 69
Devereaux, Helen, 12
Dixon, Dr. Thomas, 66

E
Erola, Judy, 31, 63-64, 69

F
Fabbro, Joe, 31
Falconbridge, 9, 18, 37, 40, 41, 51, 56, 61, 65, 66, 69, 102
Falconbridge Lecture Series, *50-51*
Falconbridge Nickel Mines, 18, 51
Field, Dr. Paul, 67
Figure skating, 76
Finns, 24, 27, 28, 29, 30, 31, 47, 57, 76, *78, 88,* 89
Flanagan, Tom, 14
Floods, 36
Flour Mill Heritage Museum, 57
Foligno, Mike, 75, *77*
Football, 71-*72*
Forster, Sid, 72
French Canadians, 18, 20, 23, 28, 35, 42, 43, 52
French language, 25, 45-46, 48, 51
Frith, Doug, 63, *64*-65
Frood Mine, 15, *37*
Frood, Thomas, *14*
Frost, Leslie M., 55, 61, 65

G
Gemmell, Welland, 61, 65, 69
Germans, 23, 24, 25, 28
Gordon, Jim, 61
Government, 63, 103

H
Hanmer, 9, 35, *91*
Hennessy, Thomas "Spike," *62,* 102
Highlanders, the, *22,* 30, 31
HMCS *Copper Cliff, 42*
Hockey, 72-73, 75-76, 77
Howey, William H., 20
Huntington College, 54, *55,* 56

I
Ida Sauvé Dance Company, 44
Immigrants, 24, 30, 72; treatment of, 25. See also Asians; Chinese; Croatians; Finns; Italians; Germans; Poles; Ukrainians
Inco, 9, 14, 35, 38, 40, 41, 56, 60, 61,

158

INDEX

63, 65, 66, *68,* 69, *92,* 102
Inco Loppet, *78*
Initial Woodland people, 12-13
International Nickel Company, 14, 18, 37. *See also* Inco
International Union of Mine, Mill and Smelter Workers. *See* Mine-Mill Union
Italians, 23, *24, 25,* 28, 30, 31, 42

J
Jerome, Jim, 61, 63, 69
Journal, the, 21

K
King, Mackenzie, 29, 42

L
Lake Nepahwin, 8, *92*
Lake Ramsey, 8, 13, 15, *70, 84,* 85, *86,* 87
Laurentian Hospital, 67, *92*
Laurentian University, 25, 36, 51, *54, 55, 68, 86,* 87; and the arts, 56; colleges of, 54, *55,* 56; history of, 54-56; sports at, *80,* 97, *98,* 102
Laurentian University Museum and Arts Centre, 56-57
Lautenslager, Reverend Earl, *55*
Liberals, 35, 43, 56, 60, 61, 63, 64, 65, 69
Loughrin, John, 14
Lumber industry, 15, 38

M
McConnell, Rinaldo, 14
McCrea, Charles, 60-61, 69
Macdonald, Sir John A., 13, 18
MacKinnon, Archie F., *30*
McNaughton, Andrew, 20
Martel, Eli, 61
Medical profession, 66-67, 69
Methodists, 20, 34-35, *47*
Mine-Mill camp, *49*
Mine-Mill Union, 30, 40-41, 42, 49, 57, 65-66
Mond Nickel Company, 16
Muredda, Battista, *100*
Murray Mine, 16
Murray, Alexander, 14
Murray, Thomas, 14
Murray, William, 14
Musical performances, *24, 28, 29, 46,* 52-53, 57. *See also* Sudbury Male Chorus; Sudbury Philharmonic Society; Sudbury Symphony Orchestra

N
National Curling Brier, 72, *76*
National Hockey League (NHL), 73, 75-76
New Democrats, 61
Nickel: development of, 15-16; discovery of, 14; markets of, 15, 16, 18, 33, 103; origin of, 11
Nickel Belt, 31, 56, 61, 63
Nickel industry, 9, *10,* 20, 21, 30, 31, 33, 36, 37, 57, 59, 60, 61-63, 65-66, 69, 102; during World War I, 34, 35; during World War II, 33, 37, 40; pollution from, 36-37, 65, 68-69; unionization of, 43; unions of, 30, 40-41, 42, 49, 57, 61, 65
North Bay, 11, 55, 56, 66
Northern Lights Festival Boreal, 52, *57*

P
Pan American Games, 79, 97, *98, 99,* 101
Patterson, Dave, 66
Poles, 23, 24
Presbyterians, 20, *47*
Progressive Conservatives, 55, 61, 63, 103

R
Ramsay, William A., 13
Reaume, Joseph Octave, *58*
Recreation, 8, *70, 73, 86, 87, 88, 90*
Regreening, 68-69, 102
Regulation 17, 35, 46
Reid, Weir, 49
Ritchie, Samuel J., *15*
Roberts, Dennis, 66
Robinson, Reid, 41
Rodriguez, John, 63, 64
Russo-Finnish War, 40

S
St. Andrew's Concert Series, 8-9
St. Andrew's United Church, 47, 51-52, 55, *103*
St. Joseph's Hospital, 66-*67*
Salter, A.P., 14
Science Centre North, 8, 57, *94, 95*
Shield Archaic people, 12
Shorthouse, Joseph, *68*
Skiing, 76-77, *78,* 79, *88,* 89
Soccer, 72, *74*
Solski, Mike, 66
Sopha, Elmer, 61, 103
Spanish-American War, 16
Sports, 71-80, 86, 88, 97-101
Steelworkers unions, 30, 61
Subterranean food production, *68,* 102
Sudbury Algoma Hospital, 67
Sudbury Canoe Club, 79-80
Sudbury City Council, *62*
Sudbury Community Concert Association, 51
Sudbury Cycling Club, *99-100*
Sudbury General Hospital, 66-67, *89*
Sudbury Junction, 13, *14,* 20
Sudbury Little Theatre Guild, 47-48
Sudbury Male Chorus, 52-53
Sudbury Methodist Church, *47*
Sudbury Philharmonic Society, 53
Sudbury Post Office, 38
Sudbury Region *81-96, 103;* communities of, *9,* 21, 34, *82-83;* economy of, 15, 21, 31, 34, 35, 37-38; elections of, 34-35, 42-43, 60-61, 63-65; environmental damage in, 8, 18, 36-37, 68-69, 102; ethnic population of, *22*-31; geology of, 11-*12;* minerals of, 11, 14, 15; naming of, 13; origin of, 11; politics of, 39, 59-61; population of, 23, 34, 35-36, 61; reputation of, 8; settlement of, 13-15, 18, 20-21; school system of, 25, *46,* 54, 59. *See also* Immigrants; Nickel; Nickel industry; Transportation
Sudbury Regional Development Corporation, *62*
Sudbury Regional Multi-Cultural Centre, 8
Sudbury Star, the, 25, 26, 28, 34, 38-39, 40, 43
Sudbury Symphony Orchestra, 9, *53,* 56
Sudbury Theatre Centre (STC), 8, *48-49, 52, 103*
Sudbury Town Council, 21, *26*
Swimming, 101

T
Taxation Data Centre, 63, 69
Terminal Woodland people, 13
Theatre, 47, 56
Théâtre du Nouvel Ontario (TNO), 8, 48
Thompson, R.M., 15
Thornloe College, 56
Thornloe Players, 56, *57*
Track and field, 80, 97-100
Transportation, *18, 19,* 20, 66. *See also* Canadian Pacific Railway
Trevisiol, Gary, *100*
Trudeau, Pierre, 31, 61, 63, 64
Turner, John, 31, *64*-65

U
Ukrainians, 23, 25, *29*-30, *90,* 91
United Copper Nickel Workers Union, 40, 41
United States Navy, 15
United Steelworkers of America (USW), 66, 74
University of Sudbury, 56

V
Valley East Recreation Centre, *73*
V-J Day, *43*

W
Weightlifting, 79
Whitney, James Pliny, 35, *58,* 60
Wong, Peter, 27, *62*
World War I, 16, 24, 25, 34, 35, 40
World War II, 25, 28, 30, *32,* 33, 37-40, 41, 43, 49-50
Worthington, James, 13
Wrestling, 78-79

159

THE SUDBURY REGION

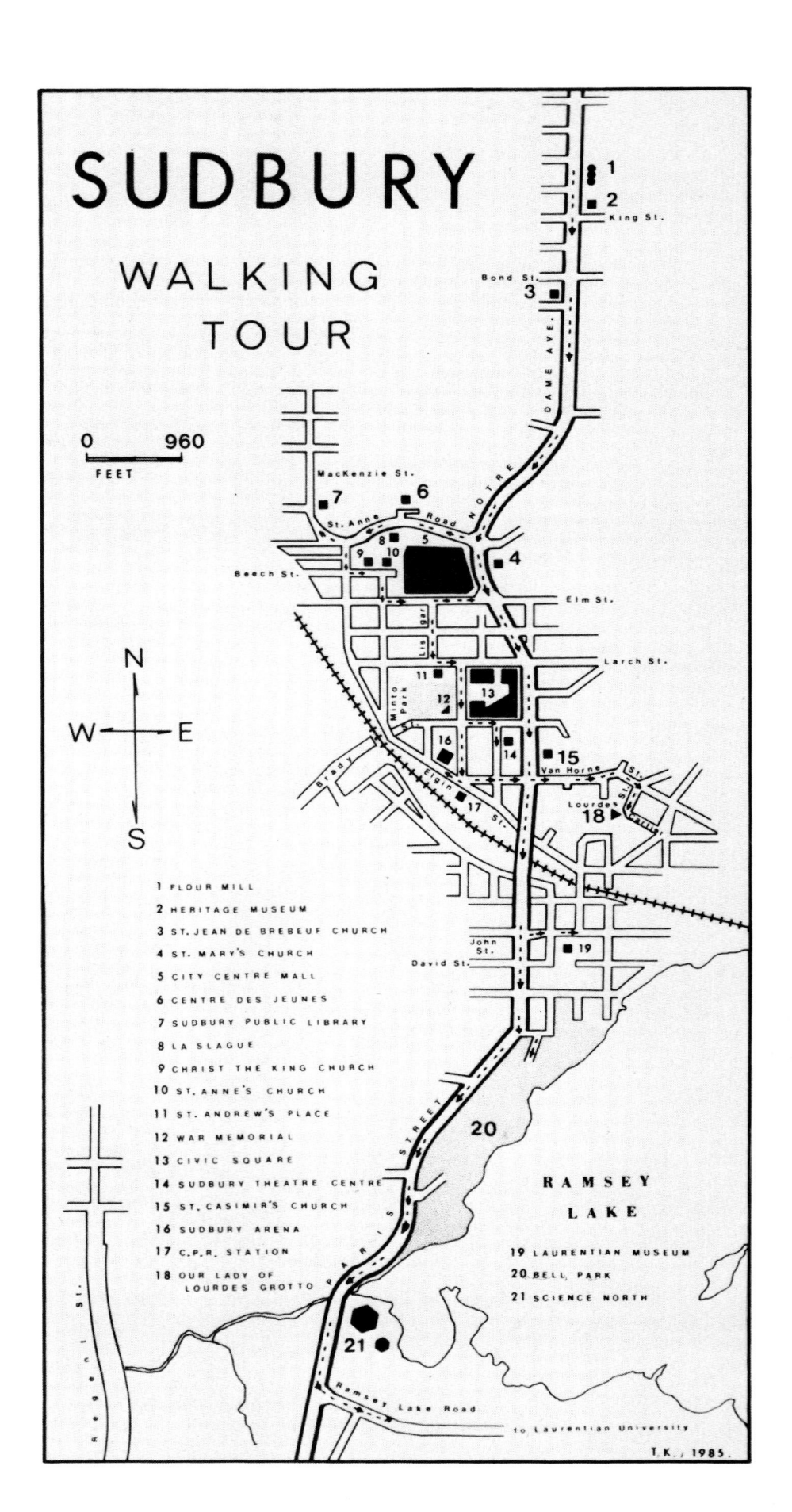

SUDBURY WALKING TOUR

1 FLOUR MILL
2 HERITAGE MUSEUM
3 ST. JEAN DE BREBEUF CHURCH
4 ST. MARY'S CHURCH
5 CITY CENTRE MALL
6 CENTRE DES JEUNES
7 SUDBURY PUBLIC LIBRARY
8 LA SLAGUE
9 CHRIST THE KING CHURCH
10 ST. ANNE'S CHURCH
11 ST. ANDREW'S PLACE
12 WAR MEMORIAL
13 CIVIC SQUARE
14 SUDBURY THEATRE CENTRE
15 ST. CASIMIR'S CHURCH
16 SUDBURY ARENA
17 C.P.R. STATION
18 OUR LADY OF LOURDES GROTTO
19 LAURENTIAN MUSEUM
20 BELL PARK
21 SCIENCE NORTH

This map covers the main attractions of Sudbury's downtown district. Courtesy, Graeme S. Mount

West Nipissing Public Library